Henry Cornelius Agrippa's Fourth book of occult philosophy, of geomancy.

Magical elements of Peter de Abano.
Astronomical geomancy. The nature of spirits,
arbatel of magic

Translator
Robert Turner

Alpha Editions

This edition published in 2019

ISBN : 9789353862381

Design and Setting By
Alpha Editions
email - alphaedis@gmail.com

Henry Cornelius Agrippa

HIS

Fourth BOOK

OF

Occult Philofophy.

Of GEOMANCY.

MAGICAL ELEMENTS of *Peter de Abano.*

ASTRONOMICAL GEOMANCY.

The NATURE OF SPIRITS.

Arbatel of MAGICK.

Tranflated into Englifh by *Robert Turner,*
φιλομαθἡς.

LONDON,
Printed by Afkin Publifhers, 16 Ennismore Ave
at the Eaft-end of Chyfwick. 1978

CONTENTS

The Preface to the unprejudiced Reader

Commendatory Poems

INTRODUCTION

It is amazing how often it is said that The Fourth Book of Occult Philosophy *is spurious. This is repeated by one 'authority' after another, obviously without any reference to the text itself. For this volume is not so much a single book as a collection of six treatises on various aspects of practical magic and divination. A glance at the table of contents will confirm that only the first two treatises actually claim to be by Henry Cornelius Agrippa.*

Agrippa (1486–1535) was in many ways an all round Renaissance man, being a writer, soldier, and physician. However, his main claim to an important place in the history of the thought of the period is as a magician, and this is by no means a belittlement of his other attainments for as Agrippa himself says:

'Some that are perverse.... may take the name of Magick in the worse sense and, though scarce having seen the title, cry out that I teach forbidden Arts, sow the seed of Heresies, offend pious ears, and scandalize excellent wits; that I am a sorcerer, and superstitious and divellish, who indeed am a Magician: to whom I answer, that a Magician doth not, amongst learned men signify a sorcerer, or one that is superstitious or divellish; but a wise man, a priest, a prophet.'

Turning to the contents of this volume let us examine each treatise in turn:

I. Of Geomancy — *Henry Cornelius Agrippa*

Probably it is this treatise which is mentioned by Agrippa in 1526 when he sent to Metz for his work on geomancy. Again Agrippa refers to a work on geomancy in his De Incertitudine *(Cap 13) where after listing earlier geomancies by Haly, Gerard of Cremona, Bartholomew of Parma, and Tundinus, he says of his own geomantic treatise "I too have written a geomancy quite different from the rest but no less superstitious and fallacious or if you wish I will even say 'mendacious'''* Agrippa was nothing if not frank about his own work!

Geomancy was from the 12th to the 17th Century one of the major forms of divination in Europe, taking second place to astrology but precedence over the tarot. The first part of this book is concerned with the mechanics of geomantic divination, the second part with their application in an astrological context, and the third, and by far the bulkiest part, is concerned with the meanings of each of the sixteen geomantic figures in each of the 12 Houses of heaven.

This text on geomancy is extremely interesting in that it provides much of the material for later derivative works on the subject. Interestingly, it expands greatly Agrippa's remarks on the subject in his Three Books of Occult Philosophy.

The actual practice of geomancy is set out in a rather compressed form. For example the table on page 6 is not very clear, and the diagram on the following page suffers severely from the deficiencies of the printer's art. So as to preserve the facsimile quality of the text these have not been altered. Reconstructions of these, together with complete instructions for geomantic practice appear in the present writer's The Oracle of Geomancy, *Warner Destiny, New York, 1977, and a history of the subject in* Divinatory Geomancy.

II. Of Occult Philosophy, or Of Magical Ceremonies:
   The Fourth Book — *Henry Cornelius Agrippa*

This treatise which appeared in Latin about 30 years after Agrippa's death, is effectively a self contained grimoire or grammar of sorcery which draws upon the Three Books of Occult Philosophy *for its theoretical background.*

Johannes Weir, who was for a while Agrippa's disciple and amanuensis, declared in one of his voluminous works that this treatise was not after the style of his master, but elsewhere admits that Agrippa was so prolific that it was impossible to be sure exactly what amongst posthumously published material was actually by him.

After an initial excursion into an astrological system

for generating the names of good and evil spirits, Agrippa goes on to discuss the magnitudes of the stars and their symbols. A set of characters for both good and evil spirits follows, according to their rank and dignity. The familiar shapes of the spirits of the various planets are delineated to identify a particular spirit with its planetary ruler. Agrippa then explains how to make pentacles and what signs are to be used in their preparation. The form of these pentacles is similar to some given in The Key of Solomon *where the picture is drawn representing a Biblical or Apocalyptic theme and then surrounded with the appropriate verse and Godname.*

The work then touches upon the details of consecration of the various instruments necessary for the art of magic, the types of conjurations, unctions, suffumigations, prayers and benedictions to be used. There is special emphasis on the consecration of water, fire, oils and perfumes. Details of the consecration of the circle, which is to be the sanctum sanctorum for the practice of magic and the use of the Liber Spirituum, *or Book of Spirits, is explained. This book must be inscribed with the image and sigil of the spirit together with the oath which it must take when it is conjured.*

Finally, Agrippa reaches the details of the actual invocation of spirits. He outlines the type of place in which the ceremony must take place, the preparation and condition of the Magus, the names to be worn and the days and times in which the operation is permissible. Further Agrippa explains dream oracles and the tablets and talismans requisite for this art, so covering the various forms of invocation not requiring a circle, and dealing with Nature spirits as well as the spirits of the grimoires.

III. Heptameron: or, Magical Elements — *Peter de Abano*

Peter of Abano (1250–1317) was one of the most influential men of learning of his time. Many of his writings on medicine, philosophy and astronomy are extent, together with works on geomancy and magic often attributed to him, the latter possibly spurious. However it is easier to consider the Heptameron or Magical Elements *and the* Geomantia *as by him: as he had quite a well paid practice as a physician*

*and a place in society to keep up, it is conceivable that the
above treatise remained in manuscript form till sometime
after his death, especially as he was in some trouble with the
Inquisition.*

*He studied medicine in Paris before returning to Padua to
practice as a physician. Towards the end of his life he was
actually accused of practicing sorcery by the Inquisition and
was imprisoned. He was later acquitted but then re-arrested
and died in prison in 1317 whilst awaiting trial.*

*Amongst the less salubrious works from his pen was a
work on poisons, commissioned by the then incumbent pope,
possibly Pope Honorius IV.*

Of the books of magic attributed to Peter, the Heptameron
*is the best known, but Naudé states that two other books of
his were banned after his death, the* Elucidarium Necroman-
ticum *and* Liber Experimentorum Mirabilium de Annulis
Secundum 28 Mansiones Lunae, *or 'Book of marvelous
experiments with rings according to the 28 mansions of the
moon'.*

The Heptameron, *which draws heavily on the* Picatrix, *a
magical text by the Arab pseudo—Maġrītī, may have first
appeared in Latin at Venice in 1496 before being bound with
Agrippa in 1565. The* Heptameron *has well earned its reputation as a key work on practical magic and it follows in the
tradition of Trithemius'* Steganographia *in as much as it
catalogues the names of many angels and the times of their
conjuration.*

*He commences his book on the magical elements by des-
cribing the composition of the circle which is described as a
certain fortress to defend the operator safe from the evil
spirits. The names of the hours and the angels ruling them
follows his succinct description of the circle, giving the names
for each season, its beginning and end.*

*Next follow the consecrations and benedictions to be per-
formed before the magical operation, the exorcism of the
fire, the manufacture of the garments to be worn and the
pantacle to be used as a lamen on the magician's breast.
Orations similar to those in the* Key *of Solomon are given for
the donning of robes before the ceremony.*

In many ways Abano's instructions for invocation are

*much more straightforward than most grimoires the empha-
sis being on the careful recitation of the conjurations in latin
to the spirits of the elements. These conjurations are primarily
qabalistic words of power, with the occasional word of Greek
or Gnostic derivation cropping up every so often. After these,
specific instructions are given for each day of the week beginning with the circle to be used, the name of the angel for
the day, his sigil, planet and sign of the zodiac, together with
his ministers and the names of power to be used at each
quarter, which precede a specific conjuration suitable for the
day in question. Peter also wrote a geomancy which is a
classic in its field, neatly complimenting the two studies of
the subject included in this collection.*

IV. Isagoge … Of the Nature of Spirits – *Georg Pictorius
Villinganus (c 1500–1569)*

*The fourth treatise is an introductory discourse on the
nature of such spirits as occur in the sublunary sphere; their
origin, names, offices, illusions, powers, prophecies, miracles,
and how they may be expelled.*

*Pictorius began his career as a schoolmaster at Freiburg-im-
Breisgau where he became an MD and professor of medicine,
before taking the position of physician at the archducal court
at Ensisheim in Alsace. His first publications (1530) were
medical works, commentaries, scholia, collections and tabula-
tions of mediaeval authors such as Macer on herbs and Marbod
on gems, or classical writers such as Hippocrates, Pliny,
Aristotle, Galen and Oppian. In 1563 Pictorius published the
work here translated.*

*Much of Pictorius' writing is a summary of earlier writers,
often unimaginative, but quite faithful to the originals and
conscientiously acknowledged. As such Pictorius' writings
are valuable in accurately indicating the longevity and survival
of the ideas on magic which he puts forth.*

In the Isagoge *Pictorius cites Apuleius, Augustina, Iamblichus, Pliny, Saxo Grammaticus, Psellus (whom he calls
a necromancer) Peter Lombard, Trithemius and Marcus
Cherrhonesus (whom he refers to as a 'distinguished devotee
of demons').*

The Isagoge *is set out as a conversation between the*

classical Greek twins Castor and Pollux. The argument attempts to prove that the word daemon "is not an horrible or odius name, but the name of one that doth administer, help or succor unto another, and whom Pliny calleth a god" This book is an important essay for the time because it seeks to differentiate between the evil spirits of Christian theology and Greek daemons, who were of three degrees, ranging from spirits of the air up to what Homer called gods. It was certainly important then, and of interest to practical magicians now, to distinguish the difference between these types of spirit. This book forms a bridge between the magical theory of Iamblicus of Chalcis and the grimoires such as Peter de Abano's Heptameron. *Using the form of dialogue Pictorius is able to set forth the objections of the church and counter each one by referring to various authorities including scripture, Peter of Lombard, Sappho and Diocletian concerning the position of spirits in the world, and the form and nature of their bodies.*

The doctrine that spirits are guardians of the treasures of the earth, gems and precious metals as well as buried treasure, is examined in detail, for the discovery of buried treasure by the use of spirits was an all absorbing pastime. In days before banks the burial of treasure was quite a common occurrence and its discovery by accident or magic almost as common. Various acts of the devil and his ministers on earth together with accounts of apparitions and the occurrence of spirits naturally are then invoked with long anecdotes from Pliny.

In many ways this book is an excellent summary of all of the diverse influences both Christian and pagan which came together during the late middle ages and early renaissance to form the magical tradition of the west. It in fact is almost a bibliography of source books on magic and stories about demons, as well as being an insight into the attitude of the period towards magic.

Pictorius dwells at some length upon the different types of divination, all of which he attributes to the agency of the devil, and goes into detail about the different demons, distinguishing between northern and southern sublunar demons, criminatores *and* exploratores, *and* tentatores *and* insidiatores *(who accompany each man as his evil genius). Pictorius' armory against spirits is very traditional and includes, the name of Jesus, fire, the sword, contumelies, suffumigations, the bell and even the shaking of keys and clash of arms!*

Unfortunately Pictorius took a very strong line against witches and would have them all put to death, not so much for their non-Christian or malefic activities, but for having carnal intercourse with spirits, which Pictorius thought were both fertile and potent!

Johannes Weir, Agrippa's pupil already mentioned above, spoke rather slightingly of Pictorius' 'jejune writing...concerning sublunar matters'. It may be that the publication of this work by Pictorius with the alleged Fourth Book *by his master prompted Weir to deny the authenticity of the latter.*

V. Of Astronomical Geomancy—*Gerard Cremonensis(1114-87)*

Gerard of Cremona was pehaps one of the greatest translators of the twelfth century having been responsible for translating into Latin the Almagest *of Ptolemy (the most influential book on astrology of the age) works by Aristotle, Euclid, Galen, Avicenna, and many more. Working at Toledo he is credited by his pupils with translating most of the Greek and Arabic texts available in the middle ages, a total of 71 different texts, some of immense size. Critics have suggested that our present text was translated by Gerard of Sabbionetta, a town near Cremona, but this seems unlikely.*

The Astronomical Geomancy *offers a different system of geomancy to that outlined by Agrippa in the first treatise in this volume. Although the points are generated in the same manner, the figures are immediately translated into their planetary or zodiacal equivalents and placed into a horoscope.*

The bulk of the treatise is devoted to questions of the different astrological Houses and their intepretation according to the geomantically generated planets and signs occupying that house.

VI. Of Magick — *Arbatel*

This small treatise on the magic of the ancients was issued at Basel in 1575 as Arbatel, De Magia Veterum. *Despite the fact that the word Arbatel is also printed in Hebrew, it is obvious that the author was a Christian, by the liberal sprinkling of pious sentiments and Biblical quotes. Because of* references in the 30th and 31st Aphorisms to obscure details of Italian history, the author may have been from that country, perhaps even a Neapolitan magistrate. The word 'Arbatel' however, is probably not an assumed name, but that of a revelatory angel of one of the four quarters.

This book supposedly contains nine 'tomes'. The first 'tome' containing 49 Aphorisms upon the general precepts of magic, forms the introduction or Isagoge, and is the only part included in the edition of 1575 or its present translation.

However the preface to the book claims eight more, of which none appear to be extant.

Although it is likely that the first 'tome' was the only one actually written it more than once overlaps with what should have followed.

For example the 16th Aphorism concerns itself with the 7 Olympic Spirits and their Provinces. (In the text the number of Provinces is put at 186 of which 32 are ruled by Bethor. This is probably a misprint for 196 and 42 respectively, for with the later arrangement each Olympic spirit rules 7 less Provinces than its predecessor). Each Olympic Spirit is said to govern an epoch of 490 years (of which the current governing spirit is Ophiel). Each is also attributed various planetary correspondences, a sigil, a list of powers, and an enumeration of the legions of spirits under their command.

It is interesting to note that a recently published grimoire called The Secret Grimoire of Turiel by Marius Malchus which was supposedly discovered in Las Palmas in 1927, as a latin manuscript dated 1518, appears to be derived from this Aphorism with additional details drawn from other parts of this volume.

Translation

This translation is the first English translation of this collection of six treatises. A. E. Waite (who was only too happy to criticize the scholarship of other translators) gave Robert Turner's work the highest accolade when he wrote: 'I shall depart from my usual custom of translating at first hand, and make use..of the version of Robert Turner, which is quite faithful and has, moreover, the pleasant flavour of antiquity'. The translation was published in 1655 just one year before

his translation of Paracelsus' work Of the Supreme Mysteries
of Nature *which is published as* The Archidoxes of Magic,
*Volume 2 of the Source Works of Mediaeval and Renaissance
Magic series.*

*Turner's contribution to the spread of magical knowledge
in the vernacular in the seventeenth century England is con-
siderable as he made some of the best occult writings of the
time generally available.*

Agrippa's Three Books of Occult Philosophy *were also
translated by Robert Turner, but to date have not been reprinted except for a 'modernised' version of the first volume
only, which was issued by Willis Whitehead in 1897, and has
been subsequently reprinted several times. It was erroneously
titled to give the impression that it contained all three books.
In fact it contains only the first book which is concerned
mainly with 'natural' or sympathetic magic. The two other
volumes which deal more closely with correspondences, the
Qabalah, invocation, and evocation have not in fact been
reprinted in English since Turner's original translation. It is
hoped to issue all three as Volume 3 in the present series.*

*Turner felt obliged to defend magic in terms of his own
period, using Biblical and Classical quotations, and to point
out the difference between* malefici *or* venefici *(the sorcerers
or poisoners who relied for the most part on low cunning,
fear and poison) and the committed student of 'natural
philosophy' for whom the gates of experimental science were
just beginning to open. The latter took all of nature, including
that which seemed beyond nature, or supernatural, as his
territory: he could be equally interested in spirits or in the
refractive and image projecting properties of glass lenses (as
was Dr. John Dee), and feel that both fields were equally
within his area of study, or if you prefer, equally outside his
range of scientific certainty: both were to him still miraculous.*

*Today, only spirits remain miraculous, the fabulous
'burning glas' long since having been accommodated within
the realms of the known. But today opinion is in a sense less
open to experiment, less honest, and less open minded than
in the late Renaissance. For the idea of spirits is no longer
open to dispute.it has simply been dumped on the scrap heap.
However, since the beginning of the last century an insidious*

phenomena has begun to grow up within magic itself, a phenomena roughly equivalent to Turner's seventeenth century attempts to make magic acceptable in the eyes of his religiously minded contemporaries. In some ways this modern growth is an extension of the religiously orientated defence of magic, except that it is in fact a scientifically orientated defence, as there has always been a compulsion by apologists to bend their argument into a contemporary mould.

Magic is basically the science and art of causing change to occur in conformity with Will, through spiritual agencies which have been evoked or invoked from either the microcosm (man's own normally subconscious wellsprings of power) or the macrocosm (the universe). This definition also includes the 'magical technologies' such as the various forms of divination which are necessary adjuncts to the above. It is the loss of the latter half (macrocosmic part) of the definition, which has allowed modern apologists for magic to hint that the changes are all internal and psychological, aimed at improving the interior man and enabling him to transcend his limitations of personality and achieve enlightenment. The early stages of this phenomena can easily be explained away in terms of Jungian psychology — the pursuit of integration; the latter stages can be explained by invoking religious and mystical precedents, thereby avoiding the essence of magic as it was worked prior to the nineteenth century.

This is not to say that there is not a great deal of value in a Jungian or Reichian approach to magic, just that it leaves a proportion of magic unaccounted for.

One might say that magic has developed over the last couple of centuries, but how can a subject develop which narrows its focus so far as to throw out the bulk of its theory (for the belief in external entities was a central belief) without actually improving on its techniques?

It is for this reason that this book and others in the same series are being republished, to bring forward some of the best thought in the field, before it is smothered by a mass of 'scientific' rationalisation, just as oppressive in its own way as religious bias.

— Stephen Skinner
London, March 1978

Henry Cornelius Agrippa
HIS
Fourth B O O K
OF
Occult Philosophy.

Of GEOMANCY.

MAGICAL ELEMENTS of *Peter de Abano.*

ASTRONOMICAL GEOMANCY.

The NATURE of SPIRITS.

Arbatel of MAGICK.

Tranflated into Englifh by *Robert Turner,*
Φιλομαθής.

LONDON.
Printed by *J. C.* for *John Harrifon*, at the Lamb
at the Eaft-end of *Pauls.* 1655.

The PREFACE
To the unprejudiced Reader.

AS the fall of man made himselfe and all other creatures subject to vanity; so, by reason thereof, the most noble and excellent Arts wherewith the Rational soul was indued, are by the rusty canker of Time brought unto Corruption. For Magick it selfe, which the ancients did so divinely contemplate, is scandalized with bearing the badg of all diabolical forceries: which Art (saith *Mirandula*) *Pauci intelligunt, multi reprehendunt, & sicut canes ignotos semper allatrant:* Few understand, many reprehend, and as dogges barke at those they know not: so doe many condemne and hate the things they understand not. Many men there are, that abhor the very name and word *Magus*, because of *Simon Magus*, who being indeed not *Magus*, but *Goes*, that is, familiar with evill Spirits, usurped that Title. But Magicke and Witchcraft are far differing Sciences; whereof *Pliny* being ignorant, scoffeth thereat: for *Nero* (saith *Pliny*) *Plin.lib.30.* who had the most excellent Magicians of the East *Nat.Hist.* sent him by *Tyridates* king of *Armenia*, who held that kingdome by him, found the Art after long study and labour altogether ridiculous. Now Witchcraft and Sorcery, are workes done meerely by the devill, which with respect unto some covenant made with man, he acteth by men his instruments, to accomplish his evill ends: of these, the histories of all ages, people and countries, as also the holy Scriptures, afford us sundry examples.

But *Magus* is a Persian word primitively, whereby

is expreſt ſuch a one as is altogether converſant in things divine ; and as *Plato* affirmeth , the art of Magick is the art of worſhipping God : and the Perſians called their gods Μαγᾶς˙ hence *Apollonius* ſaith, that *Magus* is either ὁ κατὰ φύσιν Θιὸς, or Θεραπευτὴς Θιῶν˙ that is, that *Magus* is a name ſometime of him that is a god by nature, & ſomtimes of him that is in the ſervice of God : in which latter ſence it is taken in *Matth.2.1,2.* when the wiſe men came to worſhip Jeſus, and this is the firſt and higheſt kinde, which is called divine Magick ; and theſe the Latines did intitle *ſapientes*, or wiſe men : for the feare and worſhip of God, is the beginning of knowledge. Theſe wiſemen the Greeks call *Philoſophers* ; and amongſt the Egyptians they were termed *Prieſts*: the Hebrews termed them *Cabaliſtos*, Prophets, Scribes and Phariſees ; and amongſt the Babylonians they were differenced by the name of *Caldeans*; & by the Perſians they were called *Magicians*: and one ſpeaking of *Soſthenes*, one of the ancient Magicians, uſeth theſe words : *Et verum Deum merita majeſtate proſequitur , & angelos miniſtros Dei, ſed veri ejus venerationi novit aſsiſtere; idem dæmonas prodit terrenos, Vagos, humanitatis inimicos* ; Soſthenes aſcribeth the due Majeſty to the true God, & acknowledgeth that his Angels are miniſters and meſſengers which attend the worſhip of the true God ; he alſo hath delivered, that there are devils earthly and wandring, and enemies to mankind.

So that the word *Magus* of it ſelf imports a Contemplator of divine & heavenly Sciences ; but under the name of *Magick*, are all unlawful Arts comprehended ; as Necromancy and Witchcraft, and ſuch Arts which are effected by combination with the devil, and whereof he is a party.   Theſe

Thefe Witches and Necromancers are alfo called *Malefici* or *venefici* ; forcerers or poifoners ; of which name witches are rightly called, who without the Art of Magicke do indeed ufe the helpe of the devill himfelfe to do mifchiefe ; practifing to mix the powder of dead bodies with other things by the help of the devill prepared ; and at other times to make pictures of wax, clay ; or otherwife (as it were *facramentaliter*) to effect thofe things which the devil by other means bringeth to pafs. Such were, and to this day partly, if not altogether, are the corruptions which have made odious the very name of Magick, having chiefly fought, as the maner of all impoftures is, to counterfeit the higheft and moft noble part of it.

A fecond kind of Magick is Aftrologie, which judgeth of the events of things to come, natural and humane, by the motions and influences of the ftars upon thefe lower elements, by them obferv'd & underftood.

Philo Judæus affirmeth, that by this part of Magick or Aftrologie, together with the motions of the Stars and other heavenly bodies, *Abraham* found out the knowledge of the true God while he lived in *Caldea, Qui Contemplatione Creaturarum, cognovit Creatorem* (faith *Damafcen*) who knew the Creator by the contemplation of the creature. *Jofephus* reporteth of *Abraham*, that he inftructed the Egyptians in Arithmetick and Aftronomy; who before *Abraham's* coming unto them, knew none of thefe Sciences.

Abraham fanctitate & fapientia omnium præftantiffimus, primum Caldæos , deinde Phœnices, demum Egyptios Sacerdotes, Aftrologia & Divina docuerit. *Abraham* the holieft and wifeft of men, did firft teach the Caldeans

ans,then the Phœnicians,laſtly the Egyptian Prieſts, Aſtrologie and Divine knowledge.

Without doubt, *Hermes Triſmegiſtus* , that divine Magician and Philoſopher, who (as ſome ſay) lived long before *Noah*,attained to much Divine knowledg of the Creator through the ſtudie of Magick and Aſtrologie ; as his Writings, to this day extant a-mong us, teſtifie.

The third kinde of Magick containeth the whole Philoſophy of Nature; which bringeth to light the inmoſt vertues, and extraɾteth them out of Natures hidden boſome to humane uſe:*Virtutes in centro centri latentes* ; Vertues hidden in the centre of the Centre, according to the Chymiſts: of this ſort were *Alber-tus, Arnoldus de villa nova,Raymond,Bacon,* and others, *&c.*

The Magick theſe men profeſs'd,is thus defined.*Ma-gia eſt connexio a viro ſapiente agentium per naturam cum patientibus,ſibi, congruenter reſpondentibus , ut inde opera prodeant, non ſine eorum admiratione qui cauſam ignorant.* Magick is the connexion of natural agents and pa-tients, anſwerable each to other, wrought by a wiſe man,to the bringing forth of ſuch effeɾts as are won-derful to thoſe that know not their cauſes.

In all theſe, *Zoroaſter* was well learned, eſpecially in the firſt and the higheſt : for in his Oracles he confeſſeth God to be the firſt and the higheſt; he believeth of the Trinity , which he would not inve-ſtigate by any natural knowledge : he ſpeaketh of Angels, and of Paradiſe ; approveth the immorta-lity of the ſoul ; teacheth Truth, Faith, Hope, and Love , diſcourſing of the abſtinence and charity of the *Magi.*

Of

The Preface.

Of this *Zoroaster*, *Eufebius* in the Theologie of the Phœnicians, ufing *Zoroaster's* own words: *Hæc ad verbum fcribit* (faith *Eufebius*) *Deus primus, incorruptibilium, fempiternus, ingenitus, expers partium, fibiipfi fimillimus, bonorum omnium auriga, munera non expectans, optimus, prudentifsimus, pater juris, fine doctrina juftitiam perdoctus, natura perfectus, fapiens, facræ naturæ unicus inventor*, &c. Thus faith *Zoroaster*, word for word: God the firft, incorruptible, everlafting, unbegotten, without parts, moft like himfelf, the guide of all good, expecting no reward, the beft, the wifeft, the father of right, having learned juftice without teaching, perfect, wife by nature, the onely inventor thereof.

So that a Magician is no other but *divinorum cultor & interpres*, a ftudious obferver and expounder of divine things; and the Art it felf is none other *quam Naturalis Philofophiæ abfoluta confummatio*, then the abfolute perfection of Natural Philofophy. Neverthelefs there is a mixture in all things, of good with evil, of falfhood with truth, of corruption with purity. The good, the truth, the purity, in every kinde, may well be embraced : As in the ancient worfhipping of God by Sacrifice, there was no man knowing God among the Elders, that did forbear to worfhip the God of all power, or condemn that kinde of Worfhip, becaufe the devil was fo adored in the Image of *Baal*, *Dagon*, *Aftaroth*, *Chemofh*, *Jupiter*, *Apollo*, and the like.

Neither did the abufe of Aftrology terrifie *Abraham*, (if we believe the moft ancient and religious Writers) from obferving the motions and natures of the heavenly bodies. Neither can it dehort wife and learned

men

men in thefe days from attributing thofe vertues, influences, and inclinations, to the Stars and other
Lights of heaven, which God hath given to thofe his
glorious creatures.

I muft expect fome calumnies and obtrectations againft this,
from the malicious prejudiced man, and the lazie affecters of Ignorance, of whom this age fwarms: but the voice and found of
the Snake and the Goofe is all one. But our ftomacks are not
now fo queazie and tender, after fo long time feeding upon folid
Divinity, nor we fo umbragious and ftartling, having been fo long
enlightned in Gods path, that we fhould relapfe into that childifh
Age, in which *Ariftotles* Metaphyficks, in a Councel in *France*,
was forbid to be read.

But I incite the Reader to a charitable opinion hereof, with a
Chriftian Proteftation of an innocent purpofe therein; and intreat
the Reader to follow this advice of *Tabæus, Qui litigant, fint
ambo in confpectu tuo mali & rei.* And if there be any fcandal
in this enterprife of mine, it is taken, not given. And this comfort
I have in that Axiome of *Trifmegiftus*, *Qui pius eft, fumme
philofophatur.* And therefore I prefent it without difguife, and
object it to all of candor and indifferencie: and of Readers, of
whom there be four forts, as one obferves: Spunges, which attract
all without diftinguifhing; Hour-glaffes, which receive, and pour
out as faft; Bags, which retain onely the dregs of Spices, and let
the Wine efcape; and Sieves, which retain the beft onely. Some
there are of the laft fort, and to them I prefent this *Occult Philofophy*, knowing that they may reap good thereby. And they who
are fevere againft it, they fhall pardon this my opinion, that fuch
their feverity proceeds from Self-guiltinefs; and give me leave to
apply that of *Ennodius* that it is the nature of Self-wickednefs, to
think that of others. which themfelves deferve. And it is all the
comfort which the guilty have, Not to find any innocent. But that
amongft others this may find fome acceptation, is the defire of

London, ult. *Aug.* 1654.   *R. Turner.*

To

To his special friend Mr. *R. Turner*, on his judicious Translation of *Corn. Agrippa*.

As one that just out of a Trance appears,
Amaz'd with stranger sights, whose secret fears
Are scarcely past, but doubtful whether he
May credit's eyes, remaineth stedfastly
Fix'd on those objects; just like him I stand,
Rapt in amazement to behold that can
By art come neer the gods, that far excel
The Angels that in those bright spheres do dwell.
Behold Agrippa *mounting th' lofty skies,*
Talking with gods; and then anon he pries
Int' earths deep cabinet, as t' Mercury,
All kindes of Spirits willing subjects be,
And more then this his book supplies: but we
Blinde mortals, no ways could be led to see
That light without a taper: then thou to us
Must be Agrippa *and an* Oedipus.
Agrippa *once again appears, by thee*
Pull'd out o' th' ashes of Antiquity.
Let squint-ey'd envie pine away, whilst thou
Wear'st crowns of Praise on thy deserving brow.

I.P.B. Cantabrigiæ.

To

To his ingenious friend Mr. *Turner,* upon his Tranſlation.

THrice-noble Soul! renown'd Epitome
    Of Learning and Occult Philoſophie ;
That unknown Geomancie doſt impart,
With profound Secrets of that abſtruſe Art !
T' expound Natural Magick is thy task ;
Not hell-born Necromancie to unmask ;
Expoſing Myſteries to publike view,
That heretofore were known to very few.
Thou doſt not keep thy Knowledge to thy ſelf,
(As baſe-covetous Miſers do their pelf ;
Whoſe numerous bags of ruſt-eaten gold,
Profits none, till themſelves are laid in mold)
But ſtudious of Publike good, doſt make
All of th' fruits of thy labours to partake.
  Therefore if ſome captious Critick blame
Thy Writings, ſurely then his judgement's lame.
Art hath no hater but an empty pate,
Which can far better carp, then imitate.
Nay Zoilus or Momus will not dare
Blame thy Tranſlation, without compare
Excellent. So that if an hundred tongues
Dame Nature had beſtow'd and brazen lungs ;
Yet rightly to chuccinate thy praiſes,
I ſhould want ſtrength, as well as polite phraſes.
But if the gods will grant what I do crave,
Then Enoch's Tranſlation ſhalt thou have.

W. P. S. John's *Cambr.*

To his friend the Author, on this his Translation.

WHat, not a Sibyl or Caffandra *left?*
    Apollo *ceas'd? Has sharp-fang'd Time bereft*
Us of the Oracles? Is Dodan's *grove*
Cut down? Does ne'er a word proceed from Jove
Into the ears of mortals that inherit
Tirefias *soul, or the great* Calcha's *spirit?*
What is become o' th' Augurs *that foretold*
Nature's intents? Are th' Magi *dead, that could*
Tell what was done in every Sphere? Shall we
Not know what's done in the remot'ft Country
Without great travel? Can't we belowe descry
The minde o' th' gods above? All's *done by thee,*
Agrippa; *all their Arts lie couch'd in thee.*
Th' Art that before in divers heads did lie,
Is now collect int' one Monopoly.
But all's in vain; we lack'd an Oedipus,
Who should interpret's meaning unto us :
This thou effect'ft with such dexterity,
Adding perhaps what th' Author ne'er did fee;
That we may fay, Thou doft the Art renew :
To thee the greater half of th' praife is due.

J. B. *Cantabrigiæ.*

To the Author, on his Translation of Cornelius Agrippa.

*P*Allas *of Learning th' art, if Goddeſs nam'd ;*
  Which Prototype thy knowledge hath explain'd ;
Which Nature alſo ſtriving to combine,
Science and Learning, in this Form of thine,
To us not darkly, but doth clearly ſhew
Knowledge of Myſteries as the ſhrine in you.
By thy permiſsion 'tis, we have acceſs
Into Geomancy ; which yet, unleſs
Thou hadſt unmask'd, a myſtery 't had lain,
A task too hard for mortals to explain.
Which ſince thou haſt from the Lethæan floods
Preſerv'd, we'll conſecrate the Lawrel buds
To thee : (Phœbus diſmiſſed) thine ſhall be
The Oracle, to which all men ſhall flee
In time of danger ; thy predictions ſhall,
To whatſoever thou command'ſt, inthral
Our willing hearts ; yea, thou ſhalt be
Sole Prophet, we obedient to thee.

J. R.

To

To the Author, on his Translation of Cornelius Agrippa.

DOth Phœbus *ceafe to anfwer t' our demands ?*
Or will he not accept at mortals hands
A *fad Bidental ? And is* Sibyls *cave*
Inhabitable ? Or may Tirefias *have*
No fucceffor nor rival ? How fhall we
Then Oedipus *to th' world direct ? If he*
Do Inceft adde to Parricide, th' are dumb,
That could predict what things fhould furely come :
And they are filent that knew when t' apply
T' *our body Politick Purge and Phlebotomy.*
How will bold thieves our treafures rob, who fhall
Loft goods regain , or by his Charms recal
The nocent ? Th' Art is by thee repriv'd :
In thee the Magi *feem to be reviv'd.*
Phœbus *is not brain-fick,* Joves *doves not dead,*
Th' *Oracles not ceas'd :* Agrippa's *bed*
(*Like the Arabian birds felf builded neft,*
Which firft her Urn proves, then her quickning reft
Hath thee produc'd more then his equal fure,
Elfe had this Art as yet remain'd obfcure,
A *miracle to vulgars, well known to none,*
Scarce read by deepeft apprehenfion.
Then I'll conclude Since thou doft him explain,
That th' younger brother hath the better brain.

John Tomlinfon,
of St. John's *in* Cambridge.

To his good friend the Author, on his Tranflation of Occult Philofophy and Geomancie.

MOſt noble undertakings! as if Art
And Prudence ſhould a bargain make, t' impart
Refulgent luſtres: you ſend forth a ray
Which nobleſt Patrons never could diſplay.
Well may Diana love you and inſpire
Your nobleſt Genius with cœleſtial fire,
Whoſe ſparkling Fancie with more power can quell,
And ſooner conquer, then a Magick Spell.
The Author thought not, (when he pen'd the Book)
To be ſurmounted by a higher look,
Or be o'ertopt b' a more triumphant ſtrein,
Which ſhould exalt his then-moſt pleaſant vein.
But ſeeing that a later progeny
Hath ſnatch'd his honour from obſcurity,
Both ſhall revive, and make Spectators know
The beſt deſervers of the Lawrel bow.
Nature and Art here ſtrive, the victory
To get: and though to yeeld he doth deny,
Th' haſt got the ſtart: though he triumph in praiſe,
Yet may his Ivie wait upon your Bays.

M. S.
Cantabrigiæ.

To the Author, on this his ingenious Translation of Cornelius Agrippa.

WHat is 't I view? Agrippa *made to wear*
  An English habit? Sure 'tis something rare.
Or are his Romane garments, by thy Wit,
Translated to an English garb so fit
T' illustrate him? for that thou hast, we see,
Enlightned his obscure Philosophie ;
And that which did so intricate remain,
Thou hast expos'd to ev'ry vulgar brain.
If then thy beams through such dark works shine clear,
How splendent will they in thine own appear !
Then go thou on, brave soul, to spread such rays
Of Learning through the world, may speak thy praise.
And fear no Criticks : for thou, by a Spell,
Canst force their tongues within their teeth to dwell.

Jo. Tabor,
of St.John's *in* Cambridge.

Henry Cornelius Agrippa, *of Geomancy.*

 EOMANCY is an Art of Divination, wherby the judgement may be rendred by lot, or deftiny , to every queftion of every thing whatfoever, but the Art hereof confifteth efpecially in certain points whereof certain figures are deducted according to the reafon or rule of equality or inequality, likeneffe or unlikeneffe; which Figures are alfo reduced to the Cœleftiall Figures, affuming their natures and proprieties, according to the courfe and forms of the Signes and Planets ; notwithftanding this in the firft place we are to confider, that whereas this kinde of Art can declare or fhew forth nothing of verity , unlefs it fhall be radicall in fome fublime vertue , and this the Authours of this Science have demonftrated to be two-fold : the one whereof confifts in Religion and Ceremonies ; and therefore they will have the Projectings of the points of this Art to bee made with figures in the Earth, wherefore this Art is appropriated to this Element of Earth , even as Pyromancy to the fire , and Hydromancy to the Element of Water : Then whereas they judged the hand of the Projector or Worker to be moft powerfully moved , and directed to the terreftriall fpirits ; and therefore they firft ufed certaine holy incantations and

B   deprecations,

deprecations, with other rites and obfervations, provoking and alluring fpirits of this nature hereunto.

Another power there is that doth direct and rule this Lot or Fortune, which is in the very foule it felfe of the Projector, when he is
carried to this work with fome great egreffe of his owne defire, for
this Art hath a naturall obedience to the foule it felfe, and of necef-
fity hath efficacy and is moved to that which the foule it felf defires,
and this way is by far more true and pure ; neither matters it where
or how thefe points are projected ; therefore this Art hath the fame
Radix with the Art of Aftrologicall Queftions : which alfo can
no otherwife bee verified, unleffe with a conftant and exceffive
affection of the Querent himfelfe : Now then that wee may
proceed to the Praxis of this Art; firft it is to be knowne, that all
Figures upon which this whole Art is founded are onely fixteen, as
in this following Table you fhall fee noted, with their names.

The

The greater Fortune.	The lesser Fortune.	
* * * * * *	* * * * * *	*Solis.* ☉
Via. * * * *	*Populus.* * * * * * * * *	*Lunæ.* ☽
Acquisitio. * * * * * *	*Lætitia.* * * * * * * *	*Jovis.* ♃
Puella. * * * * *	*Amissio.* * * * * * *	*Veneris.* ♀
Conjunctio. * * * * *	*Albus.* * * * * * *	*Mercurii.* ☿
Puer. * * * *	*Rubeus.* * * * * * *	*Martis.* ♂
Carcer. * * * *	*Tristitia.* * * * * *	*Saturni.* ♄
☊ *Dragons head.* * * * * *	☋ *Dragons taile.* * * * * *	

Now

Now we proceed to declare with what Planets thefe Figures are diftributed ; for hereupon all the propriety and nature of Figures and the judgement of the whole Art dependeth : Therefore the greater and leffer Fortune are afcribed to the Sun ; but the firft or greater Fortune is when the Sun is diurnall, and pofited in his dignities ; the other , or leffer Fortune is when the Sun is nocturnall, or placed in leffe dignities : *Via*, and *Populus* (that is, the Way, and People) are referred to the Moone ; the firft from her beginning and encreafing, the fecond from her full light and quarter decreafing ; *Acquifitio*, and *Lætitia* (which is Gaine, Profit ; Joy and Gladnefs) are of *Jupiter* : But the firft hath *Jupiter* the greater Fortune . the fecond the leffe, but without detriment; *Puella*, and *Amiffio* are of *Venus* ; the firft fortunate, the other (as it were) retrograde, or combuft : *Conjunctio* and *Albus* are both Figures of *Mercury*, and are both good ; but the firft the more Fortunate : *Puer*, and *Rubeus* are Figures afcribed to *Mars* ; the firft whereof hath *Mars* benevolent , the fecond malevolent : *Carcer*, and *Triftitia* are both Figures of *Saturn* and both evill ; but the firft of the greater detriment : the Dragons head, and Dragons tayle doe follow their owne natures.

And thefe are the infallible comparifons of the Figures , and from thefe wee may eafily difcerne the equality of their fignes ; therefore the greater and leffer Fortunes have the fignes of *Leo*, which is the Houfe of the Sun : *Via* and *Populus* have the figne of *Cancer*, which is the Houfe of the Moone : *Acquifitio* hath for his figne *Pifces* ; and *Lætitia Sagitary*, which are both the Houfes of *Jupiter* : *Puella* hath the figne of *Taurus* , and *Amiffio* of *Libra*, which are the Houfes of *Venus* : *Conjunctio* hath for its figne *Virgo*, and *Albus* the figne *Gemini*, the Houfes of *Mercury* : *Puella* and *Rubeus* have for their figne *Scorpio* , the Houfe of *Mars* : *Carcer* hath the figne *Capricorne* , and *Triftitia Aquary* , the Houfes of *Saturne* : The Dragons head and taile are thus divided , the head to *Capricorne* , and the Dragons taile adhereth to *Scorpio* ; and from hence you may eafily obtaine the triplicities of thefe figns after the manner of the triplicities of the fignes of the Zodiack : *Puer* therefore, both Fortunes, and *Lætitia* do govern the fiery triplicity ; *Puella* , *Conjunctio*, *Carcer*, and the Dragons head the
earthly

earthly triplicity : *Albus, Amitia,* and *Triſtitia,* doe make the
Airy triplicity : and *Via, Populus,* and *Rubeus,* with the Dragons
taile, and *Acquiſitio* do rule the watry triplicity, and this order is
taken according to the courſe or manner of the ſignes.

But if any one will conſtitute theſe triplicities according to the
natures of the Planets, and Figures themſelves, let him obſerve this
Rule, that *Fortuna major, Rubeus, Puer,* and *Amiſſio* doe make
the fiery triplicity : *Fortuna minor, Puella, Lætitia,* and *Conjunctio*
triplicity of the Ayre : *Acquiſitio,* the Dragons taile, *Via,* and
Populus doe governe the watry triplicity ; and the earthly triplicity is ruled by *Carcer, Triſtitia, Albus,* and the Dragons head.
And this way is rather to be obſerved then the firſt which we have
ſet forth ; becauſe it is conſtituted according to the Rule and manner of the ſignes.

This order is alſo far more true and rationall then that which vulgarly is uſed, which is deſcribed after this manner : of the Fiery
triplicity are, *Cauda, Fortuna minor, Amiſſio,* and *Rubeus :* of the
Airy triplicity are, *Acquiſitio, Lætitia, Puer,* and *Conjunctio :* of
the watry triplicity are, *Populus, Via, Albus,* and *Puella :* And
Caput, Fortuna major, Carcer, and *Triſtitia* are of the earthly triplicity.

They doe likewiſe diſtribute theſe Figures to the twelve ſignes
of the Zodiack, after this manner, *Acquiſitio* is given to *Aries;*
Fortuna, both *major* and *minor* to *Taurus ; Lætitia* to the ſigne
Gemini ; Puella and *Rubeus* to *Cancer ; Albus* is aſſigned to *Leo,*
Via to *Virgo;* the Dragons head, and *Conjunctio* to *Libra ; Puer*
is ſubmitted to *Scorpio ; Triſtitia* and *Amiſſio* are aſſigned to *Sa-*
gitary ; the Dragons taile to *Capricorne ; Populus* to *Aquarius ;*
and *Carcer* is aſſigned the ſigne *Piſces.*

And now we come to ſpeake of the manner of projecting or ſet-
ting downe theſe Figures, which is thus ; that we ſet downe the
points according to their courſe in four lines, from the right hand
towards the left, and this in foure courſes : There will therefore
reſult unto us foure Figures made in foure ſeverall lines, according
to the even or uneven marking every ſeverall line ; which foure Figures are wont to be called *Matres :* which doe bring forth the
reſt, filling up and compleating the whole Figure of Judgement,

an

an example whereof you may fee heere following.

```
  *    *  | HHHHHHHH
    *   * |   HHHHH
      *   | IHHHHHH
    *   * |   HHHHH
  _____|_____
     *·   | I HHHHH
  *  *  * | I  HHHH
     *    |  HHHHH
         | I  HHHH
  _____|_____
  *    *  | HHHHHH
  *    *  | HH HHHH
  *    *  | HHHHHH
     *    | I HHHHH
  _____|_____
     *    | I HHHHH
  *       | I HHHH
     *    | I HHHH
  *       |
```

Of thefe foure *Matres* are alfo produced foure other fecondary Figures, which they call *Filia,* or Succedents, which are gathered together after this manner; that is to fay, by making the foure *Matres* according to their order, placing them by courfe one after another * * ; then that which fhall refult out of every line, maketh the Figure of *Filiæ*, the order whereof is by difcending from the fuperior points through both *mediums* to the loweft: as in this example.

Matres. / Filiæ produced.

And thefe 8 Figures do make 8 Houfes of Heaven, after this manner, by placing the Figures from the left hand towards the right:
as the foure *Matres* do make the foure firft Houfes, fo the foure
Filia doe make the foure following Houfes, which are the fift,
fixt, feaventh, and eighth: and the reft of the Houfes are found after this manner; that is to fay, out of the firft and fecond is derived
the ninth; out of the third and fourth the tenth; out of the fifth and
fixth the eleventh;and out of the feventh and eighth the twelfth: By
the combination or joyning together of two Figures according to
the rule of the even or uneven number in the remaining points of
each Figure. After the fame manner there are produced out of the
laft foure Figures; that is to fay, of the ninth, tenth, eleventh, and
twelfth, two Figures which they call *Coadjutrices*, or *Teftes*; out
of which two is alfo one conftituted, which is called the Index of
the whole Figure, or thing Quefited: as appeareth in this example following.

A Theme of Geomancy.

Filiæ.   Matres.

And this which we have declared is the common manner obferved by Geomancers, which we do not altogether reject neither extoll; therefore this is alfo to be confidered in our judgements : Now therefore I fhall give unto you the true Figure of Geomancy, according to the right conftitution of Aftrologicall reafon, which is thus.

As the former *Matres* doe make the foure Angles of an Houfe, the firft maketh the firft Angle, the fecond the fecond Angle, the third maketh the third Angle, and the fourth the fourth Angle; fo the foure *Filiæ* arifing from the *Matres*, doe conftitute the foure fuccedent Houfes; the firft maketh the fecond Houfe, the fecond the eleventh, the third the eighth, and the fourth maketh the firft Houfe ; the reft of the Houfes, which are Cadents are to be calculated according to the Rule of their triplicity ; that is to fay, by making the ninth out of the fourth and fifth, and the fixth out of the tenth and fecond, of the feventh, and eleventh the third, and of the fourth and eighth the twelfth.

And now you have the whole Figure of true judgement conftituted according to true and efficatious reafons, whereby I fhal fhew how you fhall compleat it : the Figure which fhall bee in the firft Houfe fhall give you the figne afcending, which the firft Figure fheweth ; which being done, you fhall attribute their fignes to the reft of their Houfes, according to the order of the fignes : then in every Houfe you fhall note the Planets according to the nature of the Figure : then from all thefe you fhall build your judgement according to the fignification of the Planets in the fignes and Houfes wherein they fhall be found, and according to their afpects among themfelves, and to the place of the querent and thing quofited ; and you fhall judge according to the natures of the fignes afcending in their Houfes, and according to the natures and proprieties of the Figures which they have placed in the feverall Houfes, and according to the commifture of other Figures afpecting them: The Index of the Figure which the Geomancers for the moft part have made, how it is found in the former Figure.

But here we fhal give you the fecret of the whole Art, to find out the Index in the fubfequent Figure, which is thus : that you number all the points which are contained in the lines of the projections,
and

and this you ſhall divide by twelve: and that which remaineth projeƈt from the Aſcendent by the ſeveral Houſes, and upon which Houſe there falleth a final unity, that Figure giveth you a competent Judgement of the thing queſited; and this together with the ſignifications of the Judgements aforeſaid. But if on either part they ſhall be equal, or ambiguous, then the Index alone ſhall certifie you of the thing queſited. The Example of this Figure is here placed.

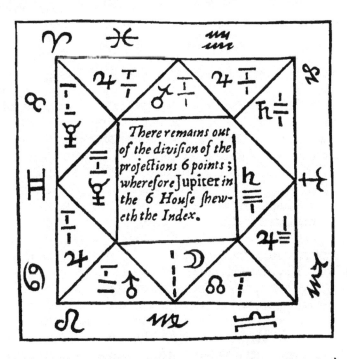

It remaineth now, that we declare, of what thing and to what Houſe a Queſtion doth appertain. Then, what every Figure doth ſhew or ſignifie concerning all Queſtions in every Houſe.

Firſt therefore we ſhall handle the ſignifications of the Houſes; which are theſe.

The firſt Houſe ſheweth the perſon of the Querent, as
often

C

often as a Queſtion ſhall be propoſed concerning himſelf of his own matters, or any thing appertaining to him. And this Houſe declareth the Judgement of the life, form, ſtate, condition, habit, diſpoſition, form and figure, and of the colour of men. The ſecond Houſe containeth the Judgement of ſubſtance, riches, poverty, gain and loſs, good fortune and evil fortune: and of accidents in ſubſtance; as theft, loſs or negligence. The third Houſe ſignifieth brethren, ſiſters, and Collaterals in blood: It judgeth of ſmall journeys, and fidelities of men. The fourth Houſe ſignifies fathers and grandfathers, patrimony and inheritance, poſſeſſions, buildings, fields, treaſure, and things hidden: It giveth alſo the deſcription of thoſe who want any thing by theft, loſing, or negligence. The fifth Houſe giveth judgement of Legats, Meſſengers, Rumours, News; of Honour, and of accidents after death: and of Queſtions that may be propounded concerning women with childe, or creatures pregnant. The ſixth Houſe giveth Judgement of infirmities, and medicines; of familiars and ſervants; of cattel and domeſtick animals. The ſeventh Houſe ſignifies wedlock, whoredom, and fornication; tendreth Judgement of friends, ſtrifes, and controverſies; and of matters acted before Judges. The eighth hath ſignification of death, and of thoſe things which come by death of Legats, and hereditaments; of the dowry or portion of a wife. The ninth Houſe ſheweth journeys, faith, and conſtancie; dreams, divine Sciences, and Religion. The tenth Houſe hath ſignification of Honours, and of Magiſterial Offices. The eleventh Houſe ſignifies friends, and the ſubſtance of Princes. The twelfth Houſe ſignifies enemies, ſervants, impriſonment, and misfortune, and whatſoever evil can happen beſides death and ſickneſs, the Judgements whereof are to be required in the ſixth Houſe, and in the eighth.

It reſts now, that we ſhew you what every Figure before ſpoken of ſignifieth in theſe places; which we ſhall now unfold.

Fortuna

Fortuna major being found in the firſt Houſe, giveth long *The grea-* life, and freeth from the moleſtation of Diſeaſes : it demon- *ter For-* ſtrateth a man to be noble, magnanimous, of good manners, *tune.* mean of ſtature, complexion ruddy, hair curling, and his ſu-periour members greater then his inferiour. In the ſecond Houſe, he ſignifies manifeſt riches and manifeſt gain,good for-tune,and the gaining of any thing loſt or miſ-laid ; the taking of a thief,and recovery of things ſtollen. In the third Houſe, he ſignifies brethren and kinſmen, Nobles, and perſons of good converſation ; journeys to be proſperous and gainful with honour: it demonſtrateth men to be faithful, and their friendſhip to be unfeigned. In the fourth Houſe, he repre-ſents a father to be noble,and of good reputation,and known by many people : He enlargeth poſſeſſions in Cities, increa-ſeth Patrimonies, and diſcovereth hidden treaſures. In this place he likewiſe ſignifies theft, and recovers every thing loſt. In the fifth Houſe, he giveth joy by children, and cauſeth them to attain to great Honours : Embaſſages he rendereth proſperous ; but they are purchaſed with pains,and prayers : He noteth rumours to be true : he beſtoweth publike Ho-nours,and cauſeth a man to be very famous after death: fore-ſheweth a woman with childe to bring forth a man-childe. In the ſixth Houſe, he freeth from diſeaſes ; ſheweth thoſe that have infirmities ſhall in a ſhort time recover ; ſignifieth a Phyſitian to be faithful and honeſt to adminiſter good Phy-ſick, of which there ought to be had no ſuſpicion; houſhold-ſervants and miniſters to be faithful : and of animals, he chiefly ſignifies Horſes. In the ſeventh Houſe, he giveth a wife rich, honeſt, and of good manners ; loving and plea-ſant: he overcometh ſtrifes and contentions. But if the Que-ſtion be concerning them, he ſignifieth the adverſaries to be very potent,and great favourites. In the eighth Houſe, if a Queſtion be propoſed of the death of any one, it ſignifies he ſhall live : the kinde of death he ſheweth to be good and natural ; an honeſt burial, and honourable Funerals : He foreſheweth a wife to have a rich dowry, legacies and inheri-tance. In the ninth Houſe, he ſignifies journeys to be pro-

ſpe-

fperous ; and by land on horfeback, rather then on foot, to
be long, and not foon accomplifhed : He fheweth the return
of thofe that are abfent ; fignifies men to be of good faith,
and conftant in their intentions ; and religious ; and that
never change or alter their faith : Dreams he prefageth to be
true ; fignifieth true and perfect Sciences. In the tenth
Houfe, he forefheweth great Honours , beftoweth publike
Offices, Magiftracie, and Judgements ; and honours in the
Courts of Princes : fignifieth Judges to be juft, and not corrupted with gifts : bringeth a Caufe to be eafily and foon ex-
pedited : fheweth Kings to be potent, fortunate, and victorious : denoteth Victory to be certain : fignifieth a mother
to be noble, and of long life. In the eleventh houfe, he fignifies true friends, and profitable ; a Prince rich and liberal ;
maketh a man fortunate, and beloved of his Prince. In the
twelfth Houfe , if a Queftion be propofed of the quality of
enemies, it demonftrateth them to be potent and noble, and
hardly to be refifted : But if a Queftion fhall be concerning
any other condition or refpect to the enemies, he will deliver from their treacheries. It fignifieth faithful fervants ; reduceth fugitives ; hath fignification of animals, as horfes, lions, and bulls ; freeth from imprifonments ; and eminent
dangers he either mitigateth or taketh away.

The leffer   *Fortuna minor* in the firft houfe, giveth long life, but incum-
Fortune.   bred with divers moleftations and ficknesses : it fignifieth a
perfon of fhort ftature, a lean body , having a mold or mark
in his forehead or right eye. In the fecond Houfe, he fignifies fubftance, and that to be confumed with too much prodigality : hideth a thief ; and a thing ftoln is fcarcely to be recovered, but with great labour. In the third Houfe, he caufeth difcord amongft brethren and kinsfolks ; threatneth
danger to be in a journey, but efcapeth it : rendreth men to
be of good faith, but of clofe and hidden mindes. In the
fourth Houfe, he prejudiceth Patrimonies and Inheritances ;
concealeth treafuries ; and things loft cannot be regained, but
with great difficulty : He fignifieth a father to be honeft, but
a fpender of his eftate through prodigality, leaving fmall por-
tions

tions to his children. *Fortuna minor* in the fifth Houſe
giveth few children; a woman with childe he ſignifies ſhall
have a woman-childe ; ſignifies Embaſſages to be honourable, but little profitable ; raiſeth to mean honours ; giveth
a good fame after death, but not much divulged; nor of laſt-
ing memory. In the ſixth Houſe, he ſignifies diſeaſes, both
Sanguine and Cholerick ; ſheweth the ſick perſon to be in
great danger, but ſhall recover : ſignifies faithful ſervants,but
ſlothful and unprofitable : And the ſame of other animals.
In the ſeventh Houſe, he giveth a wife of a good progenie
deſcended ; but you ſhall be incumbred with many troubles
with her: cauſeth love to be anxious & unconſtant : prolongeth contentions, and maketh ones adverſary to circumvent
him with many cavillations ; but in proceſs of time he giveth
victory. In the eighth Houſe, he ſheweth the kind of death
to be good and honeſt ; but obſcure, or in a ſtrange place, or
pilgrimage : diſcovereth Legacies and Poſſeſſions ; but to be
obtained with ſuit and difficulty: denoteth Funerals and
Buryings to be obſcure ; the portion of a wife to be hardly
gotten, but eaſily ſpent. In the ninth Houſe, he maketh
journeys to be dangerous; and a party abſent ſlowly to re-
turn:cauſeth men to be occupied in offices of Religion:ſhew-
eth Sciences to be unaccompliſhed ; but keepeth conſtancy
in faith and Religion. In the tenth Houſe, he ſignifieth
Kings and Princes to be potent ; but to gain their power
with war and violence : baniſhed men he ſheweth ſhall ſoon
return: it likewiſe diſcovereth Honors, great Offices and benefits ; but for which you ſhall continually labour and ſtrive,
and wherein you ſhall have no ſtable continuance : A Judge
ſhall not favour you : Suits and contentions he prolongeth :
A father and mother he ſheweth ſhall ſoon die , and always
to be affected with many diſeaſes. In the eleventh Houſe,
he maketh many friends ; but ſuch as are poor and unprofitable, and not able to relieve thy neceſſities : it ingratiates
you with Princes, and giveth great hopes, but ſmall gains ;
neither long to continue in any benefice or offices beſtowed
by a Prince. In the twelfth Houſe, he ſheweth enemies to
be

be crafty, subtil, and fraudulent, and studying to circumvent you with many secret factions: signifies one in prison to be long detained, but at length to be delivered : Animals he sheweth to be unfruitful, and servants unprofitable ; and the changes of fortune to be frequent, from good to evil, and from bad to good.

Way.

Via in the first House, bestoweth a long and prosperous life; giveth signification of a stranger; lean of body, and tall of stature; fair of complexion, having a small beard : a person liberal and pleasant ; but slowe, and little addicted to labour. In the second, he increaseth substance and riches; recovereth any thing that is stolen or lost ; but signifies the thief to be departed without the City. In the third, he multiplies brethren and kinsfolks ; signifies continual journeys, and prosperous ; men that are publikely known, honest, and of good conversation. *Via* in the fourth House, signifies the father to be honest ; increaseth the Patrimony and Inheritance ; produceth wealthy fields ; sheweth treasure to be in the place enquired after; recovereth any thing lost. In the fifth, he increaseth the company of male-children; sheweth a woman with childe to bring forth a male-childe ; sendeth Embassages to strange and remote parts; increaseth publike honours ; signifieth an honest kinde of death, and to be known thorow many Provinces   In the sixth House, *Via* preserveth from sicknefs ; signifies the diseased speedily to recover · giveth profitable servants, and animals fruitful and profitable. In the seventh House, he bestoweth a wife fair and pleasant, with whom you shall enjoy perpetual felicity : causeth strifes and controversies most speedily to be determined ; adversaries to be easily overcome, and that shall willingly submit their controversies to the Arbitration of good men. In the eighth House, he sheweth the kinde of death to proceed from Phlegmatick diseases ; to be honest, and of good report : discovereth great Legacie , and rich Inheritances to be obtained by the dead : And if any one hath been reported to be dead, it sheweth him to be a-live. In the ninth House, *Via* causeth long journeys by water, espe-

especially by Sea , and portendeth very great gains to be acquired thereby : he denoteth Priesthoods, and profits from Ecclesiastical employments ; maketh men of good Religion, upright, and constant of faith : sheweth dreams to be true, whose signification shall suddenly appear : increaseth Philosophical and Grammatical Sciences , and those things which appertain to the instruction and bringing up of children. In the tenth House if *Via* be found, he maketh Kings and Princes happie and fortunate, and such as shall maintain continual peace with their Allies ; and that they shall require amity and friendship amongst many Princes by their several Embassages : promoteth publike Honours, Offices, and Magistracie amongst the vulgar and common people ; or about things pertaining to the water, journeys, or about gathering Taxes and Assesments : sheweth Judges to be just and merciful, and that shall quickly dispatch Causes depending before them : and denotes a mother to be of good repute, healthy, and of long life. In the eleventh House , he raiseth many wealthy friends, and acquireth faithful friends in forraign Provinces and Countries, and that shall willingly relieve him that requires them, with all help and diligence : It ingratiates persons with profit and trust amongst Princes, employing him in such Offices, as he shall be incumbred with continual travels. *Via* in the twelfth House, causeth many enemies , but such as of whom little hurt or danger is to be feared : signifies servants and animals to be profitable : whosoever is in prison, to be escaped, or speedily to be delivered from thence : and preserveth a man from the evil accidents of Fortune.

Populus being found in the first House, if a Question be **People.** propounded concerning that House, sheweth a mean life, of a middle age, but inconstant, with divers sicknesses , and various successes of Fortune : signifies a man of a middle stature, a gross body, well set in his members ; perhaps some mold or mark about his left eye. But if a Question shall be propounded concerning the figure of a man, and to this figure if there be joyned any of the figures of *Saturn* or *Rubeus*, it sheweth the man to be monstrously deformed ; and that deformity

formity he fignifies to proceed from his birth : but if in the fifth Houfe , if he be encompaffed with malevolent Afpects, then that monftroufnefs is to come. In the fecond Houfe, *Populus* fheweth a mean fubftance, and that to be gotten with great difficulty : maketh a man alfo always fenfible of laborious toyl : things ftoln are never regained : what is loft fhall never be wholly recovered:that which is hidden fhall not be found. But if the Queftion be of a thief, it declareth him not yet to be fled away , but to lie lurking within the City. In the third Houfe, *Populus* raifeth few friends, either of brethren or kindred : forefheweth journeys , but with labour and trouble ; notwithftanding fome profit may accrue by them : denotes a man unftable in his faith, and caufeth a man often to be deceived by his companions. In the fourth Houfe, it fignifies a father to be fickly, and of a laborious life, and his earthly poffeffions and inheritances to be taken away: fheweth profit to be gained by water : fheweth treafure not to be hid ; or if there be any hidden, that it fhall not be found : A patrimony to be preferved with great labour. In the fifth Houfe, he fheweth no honeft Meffages, but either maketh the meffengers to be Porters, or publike Carryers: he divulgeth falfe rumours, which notwithftanding have the likenefs of fome truth , and feem to have their original from truth, which is not reported as it is done : It fignifies a woman to be barren, and caufeth fuch as are great with childe to be abortives: appointeth an inglorious Funeral, and ill report after death. In the fixth Houfe, *Populus* fheweth cold fickneffes ; and chiefly affecteth the lower parts of the body : A Phyfician is declared to be carelefs and negligent in adminiftring Phyfick to the fick, and fignifies thofe that are affected with ficknefs to be in danger of death, and fcarcely recover at all : it notes the deceitfulnefs of fervants, and detriment of cattel. In the feventh Houfe, it fheweth a wife to be fair and pleafant, but one that fhall be follicited with the love of many wooers : fignifies her loves to be feigned and diffembling: maketh weak and impotent adverfaries foon to defert profecuting. In the eighth Houfe, it denotes

notes sudden death without any long sicknefs or anguish, and oftentimes sheweth death by the water ; giveth no inheritance, poffeffion or legacy from the dead ; and if any be, they shall be loft by fome intervening contention, or other difcord : he fignifies the dowry of a wife to be little or none.

Populus in the ninth Houfe, sheweth falfe dreams, perfonates a man of rude wit, without any learning or fcience ; In religion he fignifies inferiour Offices, fuch as ferve either to cleanfe the Church, or ring the bells ; and he fignifies a man little curious or ftudious in religion, neither one that is troubled with much confcience. In the tenth Houfe he fignifies fuch Kings and Princes, as for the moft part are expulfed out of their Rule and Dominions, or either fuffer continual trouble and detriment about them : he fignifies Offices and Magiftracy, which appertain to matters concerning the waters, as about the Navy, bridges, fifhings, fhores, meadows, & things of the like fort ; maketh Judges to be variable and flowe in expediting of Caufes before them ; declareth a Mother to be fickly, and of a fhort life. In the eleventh Houfe he giveth few friends, and many flatterers ; and with Princes giveth neither favour nor fortune. In the twelfth Houfe he sheweth weak and ignoble enemies ; declareth one in prifon not to be delivered ; difcovereth dangers in waters, and watry places.

Acquifitio found in the firft Houfe, giveth a long life and *Gain.* profperous old age ; fignifies a man of a middle ftature, and a great head, a countenance very well to be diftinguifhed or known, a long nofe, much beard, hair curling, and fair eyes, free of his meat and drink, but in all things elfe fparing and not liberal. In the fecond Houfe, he fignifies very great riches, apprehendeth all theeves, and caufeth whatfoever is loft to be recovered. In the third Houfe, many brethren, and they to be wealthy ; many gainful journies ; fignifies a man of good faith. In the fourth is fignified a Patrimony of much riches, many poffeffions of copious fruits ; he fignifieth that treafure hid in any place fhall be found ; and sheweth a Father to be rich, but covetous. In the fifth Houfe, *Acquifitio* fignifies

D

fies

fies many children of both Sexes, but more Males then Females; sheweth a woman to be with child, and that she shall be delivered without danger: and if a question be propounded concerning any Sex, he signifies it to be Masculine ; encreaseth gainful profitable Embassages and Messages, but extendeth fame not far after death, yet causeth a man to be inherited of his own, and signifieth rumours to be true. In the sixth House he signifies many and grievous sicknesses, and long to continue, maketh the sick to be in danger of death, and often to die : yet he declareth a Physitian to be learned and honest ; giveth many servants and chattel, and gains to be acquired from them. In the seventh House he signifies a wife to be rich, but either a widow, or a woman of a well-grown age; signifies suits and contentions to be great and durable, and that love and wedlock shall be effected by lot. In the eighth House, if a man he enquired after, it sheweth him to be dead, signifieth the kinde of death to be short, and sickness to last but a few dayes ; discovereth very profitable legacies and inheritances, and signifieth a wife to have a rich dowry. In the ninth House he signifies long and profitable journeys ; sheweth if any one be absent he shall soon return ; causeth gain to be obtained from Religious and Ecclesiastical Persons or Scholars , and signifies a man of a true and perfect Science. In the tenth House, he maketh Princes to inlarge their Dominions; a Judge favourable, but one that must be continually presented with gifts ; causeth Offices and Magistracy to be very gainful ; signifieth a Mother rich and happy. In the eleventh House, *Acquisitio* multiplieth friends, and bringeth profit from them, and increaseth favour with Princes. In the twelfth House he signifieth a man shall have many powerful or potent enemies ; reduceth and bringeth home servants fled away, and cattel strayed ; and signifies he that is in prison shall not be delivered.

Joy.   *Lætitia* in the first House signifies long life with prosperity, and much joy and gladness, and causeth a man to out-live and be more victorious then all his brethren ; signifies a man of a tall stature, fair members, a broad forehead, having great and
broad

broad teeth ; and that hath a face comely and well coloured. In the second House it signifies riches and many gains, but great expences and various mutations of ones state and condition ; theft and any thing lost is recovered and returned : but if the Question be of a theef, it declareth him to be fled away. In the third House *Latitia* sheweth brethren to be of a good conversation, but of short life ; journeys pleasant and comfortable ; men of good credit and faith. In the fourth he signifies happy Patrimonies and possessions, a Father to be noble,and honoured with the dignity of some princely office; sheweth treasure to be in the place enquired after,but of less worth and value then is suppofed,and causeth it to be found. In the fifth House he giveth obedient children, endued with good manners, and in whom shall be had the greatest joy and comfort of old age ; signifies a woman with child to bring forth a daughter ; sheweth honourable Embassages, and declares rumours and news to be altogether true , and leaveth a good and ample fame after death. In the sixth House it sheweth the sick shall recover, denoteth good servants, good and profitable cattel and animals. In the seventh House *Latitia* giveth a wife fair, beautiful and young ; overcometh strifes and contentions, and rendereth the successes thereof to be love. *Latitia* in the eighth House giveth Legacies and possessions, and a commendable portion with a wife : if a Question be proposed concerning the condition of any man, it signifies him to be alive, and declares an honest, quiet, and meek kinde of death. In the ninth House *Latitia* signifies very few journies, and those that do apply themselves to travail, their journyes either are about the Messages and Embassages of Princes,or Pilgrimages to fulfil holy vows : sheweth a man to be of a good religion,of indifferent knowledge, and who easily apprehendeth all things with natural ingenuity. In the tenth House,it raiseth Kings and Princes to honour and great renown; maketh them famous by maintaining peace during their times; signifies Judges to be cruel & severe ; honest Offices and Magistracy ; signifies those things which are exercised either about Ecclesiastical affairs, schools, or the

D 2   ad-

administration of justice; sheweth a mother if she be a widow, that she shall be married again. In the eleventh House *Lætitia* increaseth favour with Princes, and multiplies friends. And in the twelfth House *Lætitia* giveth the victory over enemies; causeth good servants and families, delivereth from imprisonment, and preserveth from future evils.

Maid. *Puella* in the first House signifies a person of a short life, weak constitution of body, middle stature, little fat, but fair, effeminate and luxurious, and one who will incur many troubles and dangers in his ife-time for the love of women. In the second House, it neither encreaseth riches, nor diminisheth poverty; signifies a theef not to be departed from the City, and a thing stollen to be alienated and made away: if a Question be of treasure in a place, it is resolved there is none. In the third House *Puella* signifies more sisters then brethren, and encreaseth and continueth good friendship and amity amongst them; denoteth journies to be pleasant and joyous, and men of good conversations. In the fourth House *Puella* signifies a very small patrimony, and a Father not to live long, but maketh the fields fertile with good fruits. In the fifth House a woman with-child is signified to bring forth a woman-child; denotes no Embassages, causeth much commerce with women, and some office to be obtained from them. *Puella* in the sixth House signifies much weaknefs of the sick, but causeth the sick shortly to recover; and sheweth a Physician to be both unlearned and unskilful, but one who is much esteemed of in the opinion of the vulgar people; giveth good servants, handmaids, cattel and animals. In the seventh House *Puella* giveth a wife fair, beautiful and pleasant, leading a peaceable and quiet conversation with her husband, notwithstanding one that shall burn much with lust, and be coveted and lusted after of many men; denoteth no suits or controversies, which shall depend before a Judge, but some jarres and wranglings with the common people one amongst another, which shall be easily dissolved and ended. In the eighth House, if a Question be of one reputed to be dead, *Puella* declareth him to be alive: giveth a small portion with

2

a wife, but that which contenteth her husband. In the
ninth Houſe *Puella* ſignifies very few journeys,ſheweth a man
of good religion, indifferent skill or knowledge in ſciences,
unleſs happily Muſick, aſwel vocal as inſtrumental. In the
tenth Houſe *Puella* ſignifies Princes not to be very potent,
but notwithſtanding they ſhall govern peaceably within their
Dominions, and ſhall be beloved of their Neighbours and
Subjects; it canſeth them to be affable,milde and courteous,
and that they ſhall alwayes exerciſe themſelves with continual mirth, plays, and huntings; maketh Judges to be good,
godly and merciful; giveth Offices about women, or eſpecially from noble women. In the eleventh Houſe *Puella*
giveth many friends, and encreaſeth favour with women.
In the twelfth Houſe *Puella* ſignifies few enemies, but contention with women; and delivereth Priſoners out of priſon
through the interceſſion of friends.

    Amiſſio in the firſt Houſe ſignifies the ſick not to live long, *Loſs.*
and ſheweth a ſhort life; ſignifies a man of diſproportioned
members of his body, and one of a wicked life and coverſa-
tion, and who is marked with ſome notorious and remarkable defect in ſome part of his body,as either lame,or maimed,
or the like. *Amiſſio* in the ſecond Houſe conſumeth all ſubſtance, and maketh one to ſuffer and undergo the burden of
miſerable poverty;neither theef,nor the thing ſtollen ſhall be
found; ſignifies treaſure not to be in the place ſought after,
and to be ſought for with loſs and damage. In the third
Houſe *Amiſſio* ſignifies death of brethren, or the want of
them,and of kindred and friends; ſignifieth no journeys,and
cauſeth one to be deceived of many. In the fourth Houſe
Amiſſio ſignifies the utter deſtruction of ones Patrimony,
ſheweth the Father to be poor, and Son to die. *Amiſſio* in
the fifth Houſe ſheweth death of children, and afflicts a man
with divers ſorrows; ſignifieth a woman not to be with
child,or elſe to have miſcarried; raiſeth no fame or honours,
and diſperſeth falſe rumors. In the ſixth Houſe *Amiſſio* ſignifies the ſick to be recovered,or that he ſhall ſoon recover; but
cauſeth loſs and damage by ſervants and cattels. In the ſeventh

venth House *Amiſſio* giveth an adulterous wife, and contrarying her husband with continual contention ; neverthelefs fhe fhall not live long ; and it caufeth contentions to be ended.   In the eighth Houfe *Amiſſio* fignifies a man to be dead, confumeth the dowry of a wife ; beſtoweth or fendeth no inheritances or legacies.   In the ninth Houfe *Amiſſio* caufeth no journies, but fuch as fhall be compaſſed with very great lofs ; fignifies men to be inconſtant in Religion, and often changing their opinion from one feʤ to another, and altogether ignorant of learning.   In the tenth Houfe *Amiſſio* rendereth Princes to be moſt unfortunate , and fheweth that they fhall be compelled to end their lives in exile and banifhment ; Judges to be wicked ; and fignifies Offices and Magiſtracy to be damageable , and fheweth the death of a Mother.   In the eleventh Houfe *Amiſſio* fignifies few friends, and caufeth them to be eafily loſt, and turned to become enemies ; and caufeth a man to have no favour with his Prince, unlefs it be hurtful to him.   In the twelfth Houfe *Amiſſio* deſtroyeth all enemies, detaineth long in prifon, but preferveth from dangers.

Conjun-
ʤion.   *Conjunʤio* in the firſt Houfe maketh a profperous life, and fignifies a man of a middle ſtature, not lean nor fat, long face, plain hair, a little beard, long fingers and thighs, liberal, amiable, and a friend to many people.   In the fecond Houfe *Conjunʤio* doth not fignifie any riches to be gotten, but preferveth a man fecure and free from the calamities of poverty ; deteʤeth both the theef and the thing ſtolen, and acquireth hidden treafure.   In the third Houfe he giveth various journeys with various fuccefs , and fignifieth good faith and conſtancy.   In the fourth Houfe *Conjunʤio* fheweth a mean Patrimony ; caufeth a Father to honeſt, of good report, and of good underſtanding. In the fifth Houfe he giveth Children of fubtile ingenuity and wit, fheweth a woman pregnant to have a male-child , and raifeth men to honours by their own meer proper wit and ingenuity, and difperfeth their fame and credit far abroad ; and alfo fignifies news and rumours to be true. In the fixth Houfe *Conjunʤio* fignifies ficknefſes to be tedious

dious and of long continuance; but foresheweth the Physitian to be learned and well experienced; and sheweth servants to be faithful and blameless, and animals profitable In the seventh House he giveth a wife very obedient, conformable, and dutiful to her husband, and one of a good wit and ingenuity; causeth difficult suits and controversies, and crafty, subtil and malicious adversaries. In the eighth House, him of whom a Question is propounded, *Conjunctio* signifies him to be dead, & pretendeth some gain to be acquired by his death; sheweth a wife shall not be very rich. In the ninth House he giveth a few journeys, but long and tedious, and sheweth one that is absent shall after a long season return. *Conjunctio* in this House increaseth divers Arts, Sciences, and Mysteries of Religion; and giveth a quick, perspicuous, and efficacious wit. In the tenth House *Conjunctio* maketh Princes liberal, affable and benevolent, and who are much delighted and affected with divers Sciences, and secret Arts, and with men learned therein; causeth Judges to be just, and such who with a piercing and subtil speculation, do easily discern causes in controversie before them; enlargeth Offices which are concerned about Letters, Learning, sound Doctrines and Sciences; and signifies a Mother to be honest, of good ingenuity and wit, and also one of a prosperous life. In the eleventh House *Conjunctio* signifies great encrease of friends; and very much procureth the grace and favour of Princes, powerful and noble Men. In the twelfth House *Conjunctio* signifies wary and quick-witted enemies; causeth such as are in prison to remain and continue so very long, and causeth a man to eschew very many dangers in his life.

Albus in the first House signifies a life vexed with continual *White.* sickness and greivous diseases; signifies a man of a short stature, broad brest, and gross arms, having curled or crisped hair, one of a broad full mouth, a great talker and babler, given much to use vain and unprofitable discourse, but one that is merry, joyous and jocond, and much pleasing to men. In the second House *Albus* enlargeth and augmenteth substance gained by sports, playes, vile and base arts and exercises,

cifes, but such as are pleafing and delightful ; as by playes, paftimes, dancings and laughters : he difcovereth both the theef, and the cheft or thing ftollen, and hideth and concealeth treafure. In the third Houfe *Albus* fignifies very few brethren ; giveth not many, but tedious and wearifome journyes, and fignifies all deceivers. In the fourth Houfe he fheweth very fmall or no Patrimony, and the Father to be a man much known ; but declareth him to be a man of fome bafe and inferiour Office and Imployment. In the fifth Houfe *Albus* giveth no children, or if any, that they fhall foon die ; declareth a woman to be fervile, and caufeth fuch as are with young to mifcarry, or elfe to bring forth Monfters ; denoteth all rumours to be falfe, and raifeth to no honour. In the fixth Houfe *Albus* caufeth very tedious ficknefles and difeafes ; difcovereth the fraud, deceit and wickednefs of fervants, and fignifies difeafes and infirmities of cattel to be mortal, and maketh the Phyfitian to be fufpected of the fick Patient. *Albus* in the feventh Houfe giveth a barren wife, but one that is fair and beautiful ; few fuits or controverfies, but fuch as fhall be of very long continuance. In the eighth Houfe if a queftion be propounded of any one, *Albus* fhews the party to be dead ; giveth little portion or dowry with a wife, and caufeth that to be much ftrived and contended for. In the ninth Houfe *Albus* denoteth fome journyes to be accomplifhed, but with mean profit ; hindereth him that is abfent, and fignifies he fhall not return ; and declareth a man to be fuperftitious in Religion, and given to falfe and deceitful Sciences. In the tenth *Albus* caufeth Princes and Judges to be malevolent; fheweth vile and bafe Offices and Magiftracies ; fignifies a Mother to be a whore, or one much fufpected for adultery. In the eleventh Houfe *Albus* maketh diffembling and falfe friends ; caufeth love and favour to be inconftant. *Albus* in the twelfth Houfe denoteth vile, impotent and ruftical enemies ; fheweth fuch as are in prifon fhall not efcape, and fignifies a great many and various troubles and difcommodities of ones life.

Child.   *Puer* in the firft Houfe giveth an indifferent long life, but
la-

laborious;raiſeth men to great fame through military dignity;
ſignifies a perſon of a ſtrong body, ruddy complexion, a fair
countenance, and black hair. In the ſecond Houſe *Puer* increaſeth ſubſtance, obtained by other mens goods, by plunderings, rapines, confiſcations, military Laws, and ſuch like ;
he concealeth both the theef and the thing ſtolen, but diſcovereth no treaſure. In the third Houſe *Puer* raiſeth a man
to honour above his brethren, and to be feared of them ;
ſignifies journies to be dangerous, and denoteth perſons of
good credit. In the fourth Houſe *Puer* ſignifies dubious inheritances and poſſeſſions, and ſignifies a Father to attain
to his ſubſtance and eſtate through violence. In the fifth
Houſe *Puer* ſheweth good children, and ſuch as ſhall attain to
honors and dignities ; he ſignifies a woman to have a male-
child, and ſheweth honors to be acquired by military diſcipline, and great and full fame. In the ſixth Houſe *Puer* cauſeth
violent diſeaſes and infirmities, as wounds, falls, contuſions,
bruiſes, but eaſily delivereth the ſick, and ſheweth the Phyſitian and Chirurgion to be good ; denoteth ſervants and a-
nimals to be good, ſtrong and profitable. In the ſeventh
Houſe *Puer* cauſeth a wife to be a virago, of a ſtout Spirit, of
good fidelity, and one that loveth to bear the Rule and Government of a houſe ; maketh cruel ſtrifes and contentions,
and ſuch adverſaries, as ſhall ſcarcely be reſtrain'd by Juſtice.
Puer in the eighth Houſe ſheweth him that is ſuppoſed to be
dead to live, ſignifieth the kinde of death not to be painful, or
laborious, but to proceed from ſome hot humour, or by iron,
or the ſword, or from ſome other cauſe of the like kinde; ſheweth a man to have no legacies or other inheritance. In the
ninth Houſe *Puer* ſheweth journeys not to be undergone
without peril and danger of life, yet neverthelefs declareth
them to be accompliſhed proſperouſly and ſafely ; ſheweth
perſons of little Religion, and uſing little conſcience, notwithſtanding giveth the knowledge of natural philoſophy
and phyſick, and many other liberal and excellent Arts. *Puer*
in the tenth Houſe ſignifies Princes to be powerful, glorious,
and famous in warlike atchievements, but they ſhall be un-

con-

conſtant and unchangeable, by reaſon of the mutable and various ſucceſs of victory. *Puer* in this Houſe cauſeth Judges to cruel and unmerciful ; increaſeth offices in warlike affairs ; ſignifies Magiſtracy to be exerciſed by fire and ſword ; hurteth a Mother, and endangereth her life. In the eleventh Houſe *Puer* ſheweth Noble friends, and Noble men, and ſuch as ſhall much frequent the Courts of Princes, and follow after warfare ; and cauſeth many to adhere to cruel men : nevertheleſs he cauſeth much eſteem with Princes ; but their favour is to be ſuſpected. *Puer* in the twelfth Houſe cauſeth Enemies to be cruel and pernicious ; thoſe that are in Priſon ſhall eſcape, and maketh them to eſchew many dangers.

Red.   *Rubeus* in the firſt Houſe, ſignifies a ſhort life, and an evil end ; ſignifies a man to be filthy, unprofitable , and of an evil, cruel and malicious countenance, having ſome remarkable and notable ſigne or ſcar in ſome part of his body. In the ſecond Houſe *Rubeus* ſignifies poverty , and maketh theeves and robbers , and ſuch perſons as ſhall acquire and ſeek after their maintenance and livelihoods by uſing falſe, wicked, and evil , and unlawful Arts ; preſerveth theeves, and concealeth theft ; and ſignifies no treaſure to be hid nor found. In the third Houſe *Rubeus* renders brethren and kinſmen to be full of hatred, and odious one to another, and ſheweth them to be of evil manners,& ill diſpoſition ; cauſeth journeys to be very dangerous , and foreſheweth falſe faith and treachery. In the fourth Houſe he deſtroyeth and conſumeth Patrimonies , and diſperſeth and waſteth inheritances , cauſeth them to come to nothing ; deſtroyeth the fruits of the field by tempeſtuous ſeaſons, and malignancy of the earth ; and bringeth the Father to a quick and ſudden death. *Rubeus* in the fifth Houſe giveth many children, but either they ſhall be wicked and diſobedient , or elſe ſhall afflict their Parents with grief, diſgrace and infamy. In the ſixth Houſe *Rubeus* cauſeth mortal wounds, ſickneſſes and diſeaſes ; him that is ſick ſhall die ; the Phyſitian ſhall erre, ſervants prove falſe and treacherous, cattel and beaſts ſhall produce hurt and danger. In the ſeventh Houſe *Rubeus* ſignifies a wife

wife to be infamous, publickly adulterate, and contentious; deceitful and treacherous adverfaries, who fhall endeavour to overcome you, by crafty and fubtil wiles and circumventions of the Law. In the eighth Houfe *Rubeus* fignifies a violent death to be inflicted, by the execution of publike Juftice; and fignifies,if any one be enquired after,that he is certainly dead; and a wife to have no portion or dowry. *Rubeus* in the ninth Houfe fheweth journeys to be evil and dangerous, and that a man fhall be in danger either to be fpoiled by theeves and robbers, or to be taken by plunderers and robbers; declareth men to be of moft wicked opinion; in Religion, and of evil faith, and fuch as will often eafily be induced to deny and go from their faith for every fmall occafion; denoteth Sciences to be falfe and deceitful, and the profeffors thereof to be ignorant. In the tenth Houfe *Rubeus* fignifies Princes to be cruel and tyrannical,and that their power fhall come to an evil end, as that either they fhall be cruelly murdered and deftroyed by their own Subjects, or that they fhall be taken captive by their conquerers, and put to an ignominious and cruel death,or fhall miferably end their lives in hard imprifonment; fignifies Judges and Officers to be falfe, theevifh, and fuch as fhall be addicted to ufury; fheweth that a mother fhall foon die, and denoteth her to be blemifht with an evil fame and report. In the eleventh Houfe *Rubeus* giveth no true, nor any faithful friends; fheweth men to be of wicked lives and converfations, and caufeth a man to be rejected and caft out from all fociety and converfation with good and noble perfons. *Rubeus* in the twelfth Houfe maketh enemies to be cruel and traiterous, of whom we ought circumfpectly to beware; fignifies fuch as are in prifon fhall come to an evil end; and fheweth a great many inconveniences and mifchiefs to happen in a mans life.

Carcer in the firft Houfe being pofited,giveth a fhort life; *Prifon.* fignifies men to be moft wicked, of a filthy and cruel unclean figure and fhape, and fuch as are hated and defpifed of all men. *Carcer* in the fecond Houfe caufeth moft cruel and

mife-

miserable poverty ; signifies both the theef and thing stollen to be taken and regained ; and sheweth no treasure to be hid.   In the third House *Carcer* signifieth hatred and dissention amongst brethren; evil journeys, most wicked faith and conversation.   *Carcer* in the fourth House signifieth a man to have no possessions or inheritances, a Father to be most wicked, and to die a sudden and evil death.   In the fifth House *Carcer* giveth many children ; sheweth a woman not to be with child, and provoketh those that are with child to miscarry of their own consent, or slayeth the child ; signifieth no honours, and disperseth most false rumours.   In the sixth House *Carcer* causeth the diseased to undergo long sickness; signifieth servants to be wicked, rather unprofitable ; Physitians ignorant.   In the seventh House *Carcer* sheweth the wife shall be hated of her husband, and signifies suits and contentions to be ill ended and determined.   In the eighth House *Carcer* declareth the kinde of death to be by some fall, mischance, or false accusation, or that men shall be condemned in prison, or in publike judgement, and sheweth them to be put to death, or that they shall often lay violent and deadly hands upon themselves ; denieth a wife to have any portion and legacies.   *Carcer* in the ninth House, sheweth he that is absent shall not return, and signifieth some evil shall happen to him in his journey ; it denotes persons of no Religion, a wicked conscience, and ignorant of learning.   In the tenth House *Carcer* causeth Princes to be very wicked, and wretchedly to perish, because when they are established in their power, they will wholly addict themselves to every voluptuous lust, pleasure, and tyranny ; causeth Judges to be unjust and false ; declareth the Mother to be cruel, and infamous, and noted with the badge of adultery ; giveth no Offices nor Magistracies, but such as are gotten and obtained either by lying, or through theft, and base and cruel robbery.   In the eleventh House *Carcer* causeth no friends, nor love, nor favour amongst men.   In the twelfth House it raiseth enemies, detaineth in prison, and inflicteth many evils.

Sorrow   *Tristitia* in the first House doth not abbreviate life, but
                                                                      afflict-

afflicteth it with many moleſtations ; ſignifieth a perſon of good manners and carriage, but one that is ſolitary,and ſlow in all his buſineſs and occaſions ; one that is ſolitary, melancholly, ſeldom laughing, but moſt covetous after all things. In the ſecond Houſe it giveth much ſubſtance and riches, but they that have them,ſhall not enjoy them,but ſhall rather hide them,and ſhall ſcarce afford to themſelves food or ſuſtenance therefrom ; treaſure ſhall not be found, neither ſhall the theef nor the theft. *Triſtitia* in the third Houſe ſignifieth a man to have few brethren, but ſheweth that he ſhall outlive them all ; cauſeth unhappy journeys, but giveth good faith. In the fourth Houſe *Triſtitia* conſumeth and deſtroyeth fields, poſſeſſions and inheritances ; cauſeth a Father to be old and of long life, and a very covetous hoorder up of money. In the fifth Houſe it ſignifies no children, or that they ſhall ſoon die ; ſheweth a woman with child to bring forth a womanchild, giveth no fame nor honors. In the ſixth Houſe *Triſtitia* ſheweth that the ſick ſhall die ; ſervants ſhall be good, but ſlothful ; and ſignifies cattel ſhall be of a ſmall price or value. In the ſeventh Houſe *Triſtitia* ſheweth that the wife ſhall ſoon die;and declareth ſuits and contentions to be very hurtful, and determining againſt you. In the eighth Houſe it ſignifies the kinde of death to be with long and grievous ſickneſs, and much dolour and pain ; giveth legacies and an inheritance, and indoweth a wife with a portion. *Triſtitia* in the ninth Houſe, ſheweth that he that is abſent ſhall periſh in his journey ; or ſignifies that ſome evil miſchance ſhall happen unto him ; cauſeth journeys to be very unfortunate, but declareth men to be of good Religion,devout, and profound Scholars. In the tenth Houſe *Triſtitia* ſignifies Princes to be ſevere, but very good lovers of juſtice ; it cauſeth juſt Judges, but ſuch as are tedious and ſlow in determining of cauſes ; bringeth a Mother to a good old age, with integrity and honeſty of life, but mixt with divers diſcommodities and miſ-fortunes ; it raiſeth to great Offices, but they ſhall not be long enjoyed nor perſevered in ; it ſignifies ſuch Offices as do appertain to the water, or tillage, and manuring

of

of the Earth, or such as are to be imployed about matters of Religion and wisdom. In the eleventh House *Tristitia* signifies scarcity of friends, and the death of friends ; and also signifies little love or favour. In the twelfth House it sheweth no enemies ; wretchedly condemneth the imprisoned ; and causeth many discommodities and disprofits to happen in ones life.

Dragons head.

Caput Draconis in the first House augmenteth life and fortune. In the second House he increaseth riches and substance ; saveth and concealeth a theef; and signifies treasure to be hid. In the third House *Caput Draconis* giveth many brethren ; causeth journeys, kinsmen, and good faith and credit. In the fourth House he giveth wealthy inheritances; causeth the Father to attain to old age. In the fifth House *Caput Draconis* giveth many children ; signifies women with child to bring forth women-children, and oftentimes to have twins ; it sheweth great honours and fame ; and signifies news and rumours to be true. *Caput Draconis* in the sixth House increaseth sicknesses and diseases ; signifieth the Physitian to be learned ; and giveth very many servants and chattel. In the seventh House he signifieth a man shall have many wives ; multiplies and stirreth up many adversaries and suits. In the eight House he sheweth the death to be certain, increaseth Legacies and inheritances, and giveth a good portion with a wife. In the ninth House *Caput Draconis* signifies many journeys, many Sciences, and good Religion; and sheweth that those that are absent shall soon return   In the tenth House he signifies glorious Princes, great and magnificent Judges, great Offices, and gainful Magistracy. In the eleventh House he causeth many friends, and to be beloved of all men. In the twelfth House *Caput Draconis* signifieth men to have many enemies, and many women; detaineth the imprisoned, and evilly punisheth them.

Dragons tail.

Cauda Draconis, in all and singular the respective Houses aforesaid, giveth the contrary judgement to *Caput*. And these are the natures of the figures of Geomancy, and their judgments, in all and singular their Houses, upon all maner of
Questions

Queſtions to be propounded, of or concerning any matter or thing whatſoever.

But now in the maner of proceeding to judgement, this you are eſpecially to obſerve; That whenſoever any Queſtion ſhall be propoſed to you, which is contained in any of the Houſes, that you ſhall not onely anſwer thereunto by the figure contained in ſuch a Houſe; but beholding and diligently reſpecting all the figures, and the Index it ſelf in two Houſes, you ſhall ground the face of judgement. You ſhall therefore conſider the figure of the thing queſited or enquired after, if he ſhall multiply himſelf by the other places of the figure, that you may cauſe them alſo to be partakers in your judgement : as for example, if a Queſtion ſhall be propounded of the ſecond Houſe concerning a theef, and the figure of the ſecond Houſe ſhall be found in the ſixth, it declareth the theef to be ſome of ones own houſhold or ſervants : and after this maner ſhall you judge and conſider of the reſt ; for this whole Art conſiſteth in the Commixtures of the figures, and the natures thereof; which whoſoever doth rightly practice, he ſhall alwaies declare moſt true and certain judgements upon every particular thing whatſoever.

Of

Of Occult Philosophy,
or
Of Magical Ceremonies:
The Fourth Book.

Written by *Henry Cornelius Agrippa.*

N our Books of Occult Philoſophy, we have not ſo compendiouſly, as copiouſly, declared the principles, grounds, and reaſons of Magick it ſelf, and after what maner the experiments thereof are to be choſen, elected, and compounded, to produce many wonderful effects ; but becauſe in thoſe books they are treated of, rather Theorically, then Practically ; and ſome alſo are not handled compleatly and fully, and others very figuratively, and as it were Enigmatically and obſcure Riddles, as being thoſe which we have attained unto with great ſtudy, diligence, and very curious ſearching and exploration, and are heretofore ſet forth in a more

more rude and unfashioned maner. Therefore in this book, which we have compoſed and made as it were a Complement and Key of our other books of Occult Philoſophy, and of all Magical Operations, we will give unto thee the documents of holy and undefiled verity, and Inexpugnable and Unreſiſtable Magical Diſcipline, and the moſt pleaſant and deleʒable experiments of the ſacred Deities. So that as by the reading of our other books of Occult Philoſophy, thou maiſt earneſtly covet the knowledge of theſe things; even ſo with reading this book, thou ſhalt truely triumph. Wherefore let ſilence hide theſe things within the ſecret cloſets of thy religious breaſt, and conceal them with conſtant Taciturnity.

This therefore is to be known, That the names of the intelligent preſidents of every one of the Planets are conſtituted after this maner : that is to ſay, By collecting together the letters out of the figure of the world, from the riſing of the body of the Planet, according to the ſucceſſion of the Signes through the ſeveral degrees ; and out of the ſeveral degrees, from the aſpects of the Planet himſelf, the calculation being made from the degree of the aſcendant. In the like maner are conſtituted the names of the Princes of the evil ſpirits; they are taken under all the Planets of the preſidents in a retrograde order, the projection being made contrary to the ſucceſſion of the ſignes, from the beginning of the ſeventh Houſe. Now the name of the ſupreme & higheſt intelligence, which many do ſuppoſe to be the ſoul of the world, is collected out of the four Cardinal points of the figure of the world, after the maner already delivered : & by the oppoſite and contrary way, is known the name of the great *Dæmon*, or evil ſpirit, upon the four cadent Angles. In the like maner ſhalt thou underſtand the names of the great preſidential ſpirits ruling in the Air, from the four Angles of the ſuccedant Houſes : ſo that as to obtain the names of the good ſpirits, the calculation is to be made according to the ſucceſſion of the ſignes, beginning from the degree of the aſcendant : and to attain to the names of the evil ſpirits, by working the

F   con-

contrary way.

You muſt alſo obſerve, that the names of the evil ſpirits are extracted, aſwel from the names of the good ſpirits, as of the evil : ſo notwithſtanding, that if we enter the table with the name of a good ſpirit of the ſecond order, the name of the evil ſpirit ſhall be extracted from the order of the Princes and Governours ; but if we enter the table with the name of a good ſpirit of the third order, or with the name of an evil ſpirit a Governour, after what maner ſoever they are extracted, whether by this table, or from a celeſtial figure, the names which do proceed from hence, ſhall be the names of the evil ſpirits, the Miniſters of the inferiour order.

It is further to be noted, That as often as we enter this table with the good ſpirits of the ſecond order, the names extracted are of the ſecond order : and if under them we extract the name of an evil ſpirit, he is of the ſuperiour order of the Governours. The ſame order is, if we enter with the name of an evil ſpirit of the ſuperiour order. If therefore we enter this table with the names of the ſpirits of the third order, or with the names of the miniſtring ſpirits, aſwel of the good ſpirits, as of the evil, the names extracted ſhall be the names of the miniſtring ſpirits of the inferiour order.

But many Magicians, men of no ſmall Authority, will have the tables of this kinde to be extended with Latine letters: ſo that by the ſame tables alſo, out of the name of any office or effect, might be found out the name of any ſpirit, aſwel good as evil, by the ſame maner which is above delivered, by taking the name of the office or of the effect, in the columne of letters, in their own line, under their own ſtar. And of this practice *Triſmegiſtus* is a great Author, who delivered this kinde of calculation in Egyptian letters : not unproperly alſo may they be referred to other letters of other tongues, for the reaſons aſſigned to the ſignes ; for truly he only is extant of all men, who have treated concerning the attaining to the names of ſpirits.

Therefore the force, secrecy and power, in what maner the sacred names of spirits are truly and rightly found out, consisteth in the disposing of vowels, which do make the name of a spirit, and wherewith is constituted the true name, and right word. Now this art is thus perfected and brought to pass: first, we are to take heed of the placing the vowels of the letters, which are found by the calculation of the celestial figure, to finde the names of the spirits of the second order, Presidents and Governours. And this in the good spirits, is thus brought to effect, by considering the stars which do constitute and make the letters, and by placing them according to their order: first, let the degree of the eleventh House be substracted from the degree of that star which is first in order; and that which remaineth thereof, let it be projected from the degree of the ascendent, and where that number endeth, there is part of the vowel of the first letter: begin therefore to calculate the vowels of these letters, according to their number and order; and the vowel which falleth in the place of the star, which is the first in order, the same vowel is attributed to the first letter. Then afterwards thou shalt finde the part of the second letter, by substracting the degree of a star which is the second in order from the first star; and that which remaineth, cast from the ascendant. And this is the part from which thou shalt begin the calculation of the vowels; and that vowel which falleth upon the second star, the same is the vowel of the second letter. And so consequently maist thou search out the vowels of the following letters alwaies, by substracting the degree of the following star, from the degree of the star next preceding and going before. And so also all calculations and numerations in the names of the good spirits, ought to be made according to the succession of the signes. And in calculating the names of the evil spirits, where in the names of the good spirits is taken the degree of the eleventh House, in these ought to be taken the degree of the twelfth House. And all numerations and calculations may be made with the succession of the signes, by taking the beginning from the degree of the tenth House.

But in all extractions by tables, the vowels are placed after another maner. In the first place therefore is taken the certain number of letters making the name it self, and is thus numbred from the beginning of the columne of the first letter, or whereupon the name is extracted; and the letter on which this number falleth, is referred to the first letter of the name, extracted by taking the distance of the one from the other, according to the order of the Alphabet. But the number of that distance is projected from the beginning of his columne; and where it endeth, there is part of the first vowel: from thence therefore thou shalt calculate the vowels themselves, in their own number and order, in the same columne; and the vowel which shall fall upon the first letter of a name, the same shall be attributed to that name. Now thou shalt finde the following vowels, by taking the distance from the precedent vowel to the following: and so consequently according to the succession of the Alphabet. And the number of that distance is to be numbered from the beginning of his own columne; and where he shall cease, there is the part of the vowel sought after. From thence therefore must you calculate the vowels, as we have abovesaid; and those vowels which shall fall upon their own letters, are to be attributed unto them: if therefore any vowel shall happen to fall upon a vowel, the former must give place to the latter: and this you are to understand only of the good spirits. In the evil also you may proceed in the same way; except only, that you make the numerations after a contrary and backward order, contrary to the succession of the Alphabet, and contrary to the order of the columnes (that is to say) in ascending.

The name of good Angels, and of every man, which we have taught how to finde out, in our third book of Occult Philosophy, according to that maner, is of no little Authority, nor of a mean foundation. But now we will give unto thee some other ways, illustrated with no vain reasons. One whereof is, by taking in the figure of the nativity, the five places

of

of Hylech : which being noted, the characters of the letters
are projected in their order and number from the beginning
of *Aries* ; and thofe letters which fall upon the degrees of
the faid places, according to their order and dignity difpofed
and afpected, do make the name of an Angel. There is alfo
another way, wherein they do take Almutel, which is the
ruling and governing ftars over the aforefaid five places ; and
the projection is to be made from the degree of the afcendant ; which is done by gathering together the letters
falling upon Almutel: which being placed in order, according to their dignity, do make the name of an Angel. There
is furthermore another way ufed, and very much had in obfervation from the Egyptians, by making their calculation
from the degree of the afcendant, and by gathering together
the letters according to the Almutel of the eleventh Houfe ;
which Houfe they call a good *Dæmon:* which being placed according to their dignities, the names of the Angels are conftituted. Now the names of the evil Angels are known after
the like maner, except only that the projections muft be performed contrary to the courfe and order of the fucceffion of
the fignes, fo that whereas in feeking the names of good fpirits, we are to calculate from the beginning of *Aries* ; con-
trariwife, in attaining the names of the evil, we ought to account from the beginning of *Libra.* And whereas in the
good fpirits we number from the degree of the afcendant ;
contrarily, in the evil, we muft calculate from the degree of
the feventh Houfe. But according to the Egyptians, the
name of an Angel is collected according to the Almutel of the
twelfth Houfe, which they call an evil fpirit. Now all thofe
rites, which are elfewhere already by us dilivered in our third
book of Occult Philofophy, may be made by the characters
of any language. In all which (as we have abovefaid) there
is a myftical and divine number, order and figure ; from
whence it cometh to pafs, that the fame fpirit may be called
by divers names. But others are difcovered from the name
of the fpirit himfelf, of the good or evil, by tables formed
to this purpofe.

Now

Now thefe celeftial characters do confift of lines and heads: the heads are fix, according to the fix magnitudes of the ftars, whereunto the planets alfo are reduced.   The firft magnitude holdeth a Star, with the Sun, or a Crofs.   The fecond with Jupiter a circular point.   The third holdeth with Saturn, a femicircle, a triangle, either crooked, round, or acute. The fourth with Mars, a little ftroke penetrating the line, either fquare, ftraight, or oblique.   The fifth with Venus and Mercury, a little ftroke or point with a tail, afcending or defcending.   The fixth with the Moon, a point made black. All which you may fee in the enfuing table.   The heads then being pofited according to the fite of the Stars in the figure of Heaven, then the lines are to be drawn out, according to the congruency or agreement of their natures.   And this you are to underftand of the fixed Stars.   But in the erecting of the Planets, the lines are drawn out, the heads being pofited according to their courfe and nature amongft themfelves.

	Stars.	Heads.	Lines joyned to the Heads.

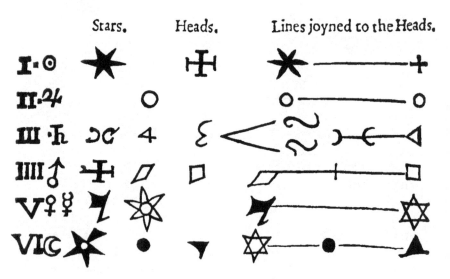

When therefore a character is to be found of any celeftial
Image

Image afcending in any degree or face of a figne , which do confift of Stars of the fame magnitude and nature ; then the number of thefe Stars being pofited according to their place and order, the lines are drawn after the fimilitude of the Image fignified,as copioufly as the fame can be done.

But the Characters which are extracted according to the name of a fpirit, are compofed by the table following , by giving to every letter that name which agreeth unto him, out of the table ; which although it may appear eafie to thofe that apprehend it, yet there is herein no fmall difficulty ; To wit, when the letter of a name falleth upon the line of letters or figures, that we may know which figure or which letter is to be taken. And this may be thus known : for if a letter falleth upon the line of letters, confider of what number this letter may be in the order of the name ; as the fecond, or the third ; then how many letters that name containeth ; as five or feven ; and multiply thefe numbers one after another by themfelves,and treble the product : then caft the whole (being added together) from the beginning of the letters, according to the fucceffion of the Alphabet : and the letter upon which that number fhall happen to fall , ought to be placed for the character of that fpirit. But if any letter of a name fall on the line of figures , it is thus to be wrought. Take the number how many this letter is in the order of the name, and let it be multiplied by that number of which this letter is in the order of the Alphabet ; and being added together, divide it by nine , and the remainder fheweth the figure or number to be placed in the character : and this may be put either in a Geometrical or Arithmetical figure of number ; which notwithftanding ought not to exceed the number of nine,or nine Angles.

The

The Characters of good Spirits.

A ſimple point.   Round.   Starry.

Straight ſtanding line.   Lying.   Oblique.

Line crooked like a bow.   Like waves.   Toothed.

Interſection right.   Inherent.   Adhering ſeparate.

Obliq; interſection ſimple.   Mixt.   Manifold.

Perpendicular right dexter.   Siniſter.   Neuter.

A whole figure.   Broken.   Half.

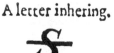

A letter inhering.   Adhering.   Separate.

Cha-

The Characters of evil Spirits.

A right line.	Crooked.	Reflexed.
—		

A simple figure.	Penetrate.	Broken.

A right letter.	Retrograde.	Invers'd.
R	Я	Я

Flame.	Winde.	Water.

A mass.	Rain.	Clay.
	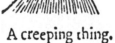	

A flying thing.	A creeping thing.	A serpent.

An eye.	A hand.	A foot.

A crown.	A crest.	Horns.

G A

A fcepter.   A fword.   A fcourge.

But the Characters which are underflood by the revelation
of Spirits, take their vertue from thence ; becaufe they are,
as it were, certain hidden feals, making the harmony of fome
divinity : either they are fignes of a Covenant entred into,
and of promifed and plighted faith, or of obedience. And
thofe Characters cannot by any other means be fearched
out.

Moreover, befides thefe Characters, there are certain familiar Figures & Images of evil Spirits, under which forms they
are wont to appear, and yield obedience to them that invoke
them. And all thefe Characters or Images may be feen by
the table following, according to the courfe of the letters
conflituting the names of Spirits themfelves : fo that if in any
letter there is found more then the name of one Spirit, his
Image holdeth the pre-eminence, the others imparting their
own order ; fo that they which are the firft orders, to them
is attributed the head, the upper part of the body, according
to their own figure : thofe which are the loweft, do poffefs
the thighs and feet ; fo alfo the middle letters do attribute
like to themfelves the middle parts of the body, or give the
parts that fit. But if there happen any contrariety, that letter which is the ftronger in the number fhall bear rule : and
if they are equal, they all impart equal things. Furthermore,
if any name fhall obtain any notable Character or Inftrument
out of the Table, he fhall likewife have the fame character in
the Image.

We may alfo attain to the knowledge of the dignities of the
evil Spirits, by the fame Tables of Characters and Images : for
upon what fpirit foever there falleth any excellent figne or inftrument out of the Table of Characters, he poffeffeth that dignity. As if there fhall be Crown, it fheweth a Kingly dignity ;
if a Creft or Plume, a Dukedome; if a Horn, a County ; if without

out thefe there be a Scepter, Sword, or forked Inftrument, it
fheweth Rule and Authority. Likewife out of the Table of
Images you fhall finde them which bear the chief Kingly
dignity : from the Crown judge dignity ; and from the Inftruments, Rule and Authority. Laftly, they which bear an
humane fhape and figure , have greater dignity then thofe
which appear under the Forms and Images of Beafts ; they
alfo who ride , do excel them which appear on foot. And
thus according to all their commixtures, you may judge the
dignity and excellency of Spirits, one before another. Moreover, you muft underftand, that the Spirits of the inferiour order, of what dignity foever they be, are alwaies fubject to the
Spirits of the fuperiour order : fo alfo, that it is not incongru-
ent for their Kings and Dukes to be Subject and Minifter to
the prefidents of the fuperiour order.

The fhapes familiar to the Spirits of Saturn.

ħ

THey appear for the moft part with a tall, lean, and flender
body , with an angry countenance, having four faces ;
one in the hinder part of the head, one on the former part of
the head, and on each fide nofed or beaked: there likewife appeareth a face on each knee, of a black fhining colour : their
motion is the moving of the winde, with a kinde of earth-
quake : their figne is white earth, whiter then any Snow.

The particular forms are,

A King having a beard, riding on a Dragon.
An Old man with a beard.
An Old woman leaning on a ftaffe.
A Hog.
A Dragon.
An Owl.
A black Garment.
A Hooke or Sickle.
A Juniper-tree.   G 2   *The*

The familiar forms to the Spirits of Jupiter.

♃

THe Spirits of Jupiter do appear with a body sanguine and cholerick, of a middle stature, with a horrible fearful motion; but with a milde countenance, a gentle speech, and of the colour of Iron. The motion of them is flashings of Lightning and Thunder; their signe is, there will appear men about the circle, who shall seem to be devoured of Lions.

Their particular forms are,

　　　　　A King with a Sword drawn, riding on a Stag.
Homo　　A Man wearing a Mitre in long rayment.
mitratus. A Maid with a Laurel-Crown adorned with Flowers.
　　　　　A Bull.
　　　　　A Stag.
　　　　　A Peacock.
Azurino　An azure Garment.
vestis.　A Sword.
Buxus.　A Box-tree.

The familiar forms of the Spirits of Mars.

♂

THey appear in a tall body, cholerick, a filthy countenance, of colour brown, swarthy or red, having horns like Harts horns, and Griphins claws, bellowing like wilde Bulls. Their Motion is like fire burning; their signe Thunder and Lightning about the Circle.

Their particular shapes are,

A King armed riding upon a Wolf.
A Man armed.

A

A Woman holding a buckler on her thigh.
A Hee-goat.
A Horfe.
A Stag.
A red Garment.
Wool.
A Cheeflip.

Shapes familiar to the Spirits of the Sun.

☉

THe Spirits of the Sun do for the moſt part appear in a large, full and great body ſanguine and groſs, in a gold colour, with the tincture of blood. Their motion is as the Lightning of Heaven ; their ſigne is to move the perſon to ſweat that calls them. But their particular forms are,

A King having a Scepter riding on a Lion.
A King crowned.
A Queen with a Scepter.
A Bird.
A Lion.
A Cock.
A yellow or golden Garment.
A Scepter.
Caudatus.

Familiar ſhapes of the Spirits of Venus.

♀

THey do appear with a fair body, of middle ſtature, with an amiable and pleaſant countenance , of colour white or green, the upper part golden. The motion of them is as it were a moſt clear Star. For their ſigne, there will ſeem to be maids playing without the Circle,which will provoke and allure him that calleth them to play. But their particular forms are ,

A

A King with a Scepter riding upon a Camel.
A Maid clothed and dreffed beautifully.
A Maid naked.
A Shee-goat.
A Camel.
A Dove.
A white or green Garment.
Flowers.
The herb Savine.

The familiar forms of the Spirits of Mercury.

☿

THe Spirits of *Mercury* will appear for the moft part in a
body of a middle ftature, cold, liquid and moift, fair, and
with an affable fpeech ; in a humane fhape and form, like unto
a Knight armed ; of colour clear and bright.   The motion
of them is as it were filver-coloured clouds.   For their figne,
they caufe and bring horror and fear unto him that calls them.
But their particular fhapes are,

A King riding upon a Bear.
A fair Youth.
A Woman holding a diftaffe.
A Dog.
A Shee-bear.
A Magpie.
A Garment of fundry changeable colours.
A Rod.
A little ftaffe.

The forms familiar to the Spirits of the Moon.

☽

THey will for the moft part appear in a great and full body,
foft and phlegmatique, of colour like a black obfcure
cloud,

cloud, having a fwelling countenance, with eyes red and full of water, a bald head, and teeth like a wilde boar. Their motion is as it were an exceeding great tempeft of the Sea. For their figne, there will appear an exceeding great rain about the Circle. And their particular fhapes are,

A King like an Archer riding upon a Doe.
A little Boy.
A Woman-hunter with a bow and arrows.
A Cow.
A little Doe.
A Goofe.
A Garment green or filver-coloured.
An Arrow.
A Creature having many feet.

But we now come to fpeak of the holy and facred Pentacles and Sigils. Now thefe pentacles, are as it were certain holy fignes preferving us from evil chances and events, and helping and affifting us to binde, exterminate, and drive away evil fpirits, and alluring the good fpirits, and reconciling them unto us. And thefe pentacles do confift either of Characters of the good fpirits of the fuperiour order, or of facred pictures of holy letters or revelations, with apt and fit verficles, which are compofed either of Geometrical figures and holy names of God, according to the courfe and maner of many of them; or they are compounded of all of them, or very many of them mixt. And the Characters which are ufeful for us to conftitute and make the pentacles, they are the Characters of the good Spirits, efpecially and chiefly of the good fpirits of the firft and fecond order, and fometimes alfo of the third order. And this kinde of Characters are efpecially to be named holy; and then thofe Characters which we have above called holy. What Character foever therefore of this kinde is to be inftituted, we muft draw about him a double circle, wherein we muft write the name of his Angel : and if we will adde fome divine name

con-

congruent with his Spirit and Office, it will be of the greater force and efficacy. And if we will draw about him any angular figure, according to the maner of his numbers, that alfo fhall be lawful to be done. But the holy pictures which do make the pentacles, are they which everywhere are delivered unto us in the Prophets and facred Writings, as well of the old as of the new Teftament. Even as the figure of

The brazen ferpent fet up in the wildernefs. the Serpent hanging on the crofs, and fuch-like ; whereof very many may be found out of the vifions of the Prophets, as of *Efaias, Daniel, Efdras* and others, and alfo out of the revelation of the *Apocalypfe.* And we have fpoken of them in our third book of Occult Philofophy, where we have made mention of holy things. Therefore when any picture is pofited of any of thefe holy Images, let the circle be drawn round about it on each fide thereof, wherein let there be written fome divine name, that is apt and conformed to the effect of that figure, or elfe there may be written about it fome verficle taken out of part of the body of holy Scripture, which may defire to afcertain or deprecate the defired effect. As, if a pentacle were to be made to gain victory or revenge againft ones enemies, afwel vifible as invifible, The figure may be taken out of the fecond book of the *Macchabees :* that is to fay, a hand holding a golden Sword

Accipe gladium fanctum, munus a Deo, in quo concides adverfarios populi mei Ifrael. drawn, about which let there be written the verficle there contained ; To wit, *Take the holy Sword, the gift of God, wherewith thou fhalt flay the adverfaries of my people Ifrael.* Or alfo there may be written about it a verficle of the fifth *Pfalm : In this is the ftrength of thy arm: before thy face there is death;* or fome other fuch-like verficle. But if you will write any divine name about the figure, then let fome name be taken that fignifies Fear, a Sword, Wrath, the Revenge of God, or fome fuch-like name congruent and agreeing with the effect defired. And if there fhall be written any Angular figure, let him be taken according to the reafon and rule of the numbers, as we have taught in our fecond book of Occult Philofophy, where we have treated of the numbers, and of the like operations. And of this fort there are two pentacles of

fub-

sublime vertue and great power, very useful and neceffary to
be ufed in the confecration of experiments and Spirits : one
whereof is that in the firft chapter of *Apocalypfe* ; To wit,
a figure of the Majefty of God fitting upon a Throne, having
in his mouth a two-edged Svvord, as there it is written, about
which let there be written, *I am Alpha & Omega,the beginning*
and the end,which is,and which was, and which is to come, the Al-
mighty.I am the firft and the laft,who am living,and was dead,and
behold I live for ever and ever ; and I have the keys of death and
*hell.*Then there fhall be written about it thefe three verficles.

Ego fum primus & noviffimus, vivus & fui mortuus: & ecce fum vivens in fieula fieulorum , & habeotlaves mortis & inferni.

Manda Deus virtuti tua,&c.

Give commandment, O God, to thy ftrength.
Confirm, Oh God, thy work in us.
Let them be as duft before the face of the winde.   And let the
Angel of the Lord fcatter them.   Let all their wayes be darkneſs
and uncertain. And let the Angel of the Lord perfecute them.

Moreover, let there be written about it the ten general
names, which are, *El, Elohim, Elohe, Zebaoth, Elion, Efcerchie,*
Adonay, Jah, Tetragrammaton, Saday.
    There is another pentacle,the figure whereof is like unto
a *Lambe flain*, *having feven eyes, and feven horns, and under his*
*feet a book fealed with feven feals,*as it is in the 5. chap. of the
Apocalypfe. Whereabout let there be written this verficle :
Behold the Lion hath overcome of the Tribe of Judah , the root
of David.   I will open the book,and unloofe the feven feals thereof.
And one other verficle:*I faw Satan like Ightning fall down from*
heaven.   Behold, I have given you power to tread upon Serpents
and Scorpions, and over all the power of your enemies, and nothing
fhall be able to hurt you.   And let there be alfo written about
it the ten general names, as aforefaid.
    But thofe Pentacles which are thus made of figures and
names, let them keep this order : for when any figure is
pofited, conformable to any number, to produce any certain
effect or vertue, there muft be written thereupon , in all the

H   feveral

feveral Angles, fome Divine name, obtaining the force and efficacie of the thing defired : yet fo neverthelefs, that the name which is of this fort do confift of juft fo many letters, as the Figure may conflitute a number ; or of fo many letters of a name, as joyned together amongft themfelves, may make the number of a Figure ; or by any number which may be divided without any fuperfluity or diminution. Now fuch a name being found, whether it be onely one name or more, or divers names, it is to be written in all the feveral Angles in the Figure : but in the middle of the Figure let the revolution of the name be whole and totally placed, or at leaft principally.

Oftentimes alfo we conftitute Pentacles, by making the revolution of fome kinde of name, in a fquare Table, and by drawing about it a fingle or double Circle, and by writing therein fome holy Verficle competent and befitting this name, or from which that name is extraſted. And this is the way of making the Pentacles, according to their feveral diftinſt forms and fafhions, which we may as we pleafe either multiply or commix together by courfe among themfelves, to work the greater efficacie, and extenfion and enlargement of force and vertue.

As , if a deprecation fhould be made for the overthrow and deftruſtion of ones enemies, then we are to minde and call to remembrance how God deftroyed the whole face of the earth in the deluge of waters ; and the deftruſtion of Sodom and Gomorrha, by raining down fire and brimftone; likewife, how God overthrew Pharaoh and his hoft in the Red-Sea : and to call to minde if any other malediſtion or curfe be found in holy Writ. And thus in things of the like fort. So likewife in deprecating and praying againſt perils and dangers of waters, we ought to call to remembrance the faving of Noah in the deluge of waters, the paffing of the children of Ifrael thorow the Red-fea ; and alfo we are to minde how Chrift walked upon the waters, and faved the fhip in danger to be caft away with the tempeft; and how he commanded the windes and the waves, and they obeyed

him ;

him ; and alſo, that he drew *Peter* out of the water, being in danger of drowning: and the like. And laſtly, with theſe we invoke and call upon ſome certain holy names of God, God ; to wit, ſuch as are ſignificative to accompliſh our deſire, and accommodated to the deſired effect : as, if it be to overthrow enemies, we are to invoke and call upon the names of wrath, revenge, fear, juſtice, and fortitude of God : and if we would avoid and eſcape any evil or danger, we then call upon the names of mercy, defence, ſalvation, fortitude, goodneſs, and ſuch-like names of God. When alſo we pray unto God that he would grant unto us our deſires, we are likewiſe to intermix therewith the name of ſome good ſpirit, whether one onely, or more, whoſe office it is to execute our deſires : and ſometimes alſo we require ſome evil ſpirit to reſtrain or compel, whoſe name likewiſe we intermingle ; and that rightly eſpecially, if it be to execute any evil work ; as revenge, puniſhment, or deſtruction.

Furthermore, if there be any Verſicle in the Pſalms, or in any other part of holy Scripture, that ſhall ſeem congruent and agreeable to our deſire, the ſame is to be mingled with our prayers. Now after Prayer hath been made unto God, it is expedient afterwards to make an Oration to that executioner whom in our precedent prayer unto God we have deſired ſhould adminiſter unto us, whether one or more, or whether he be an Angel, or Star, or Soul, or any of the noble Angels. But this kinde of Oration ought to be compoſed according to the Rules which we have delivered in the ſecond book of Occult Philoſophy, where we have treated of the manner of the compoſition of Inchantments.

You may know further, that theſe kinde of bonds have a threefold difference : for the firſt bond is, when we conjure by Natural things : the ſecond is compounded of Religious myſteries, by Sacraments, Miracles, and things of this ſort: and the third is conſtituted by Divine names, and holy Sigils. And by theſe kinde of bonds, we may binde not onely ſpirits, but alſo all other creatures whatſoever ; as animals, tempeſts, * burnings, floods of waters, and the force and power **Incendia; Envie and Malice.*

of Arms. Oftentimes alfo we ufe thefe bonds aforefaid, not onely by Conjuration, but fometimes alfo ufing the means of Deprecation and Benediction. Moreover, it conduceth much to this purpofe, to joyn fome fentence of holy Scripture, if any fhall be found convenient hereunto : as, in the Conjuration of Serpents, by commemorating the curfe of the Serpent in the earthly Paradife, and the fetting up of the Serpent in the wildernefs ; and further adding that Verficle, *Thou fhalt walk upon the Afp and the Bafilusk,* &c. Superftition alfo is of much prevalency herein, by the tranflation of fome Sacramental Rites, to binde that which we intend to hinder ; as, the Rites of Excommunication, of Sepulchres, Funerals, Buryings, and the like.

Super af-pidem & bafilifcum ambulabis, &c.

And now we come to treat of the Confecrations which men ought to make upon all inftruments and things necef-fary to be ufed in this Art : and the vertue of this Confecration moft chiefly confifts in two things ; to wit, in the power of the perfon confecrating, and by the vertue of the prayer by which the Confecration is made. For in the perfon confecrating, there is required holinefs of Life, and power of fanctifying : both which are acquired by Dignification and Initiation. And that the perfon himfelf fhould with a firm and undoubted faith believe the vertue, power, and efficacie hereof. And then in the Prayer it felf by which this Confecration is made, there is required the like holinefs ; which either folely confifteth in the prayer it felf, as, if it be by divine infpiration ordained to this purpofe, fuch as we have in many places of the holy Bible ; or that it be hereunto infti-tuted through the power of the Holy Spirit, in the ordina-tion of the Church. Otherwife there is in the Prayer a San-ctimony, which is not onely by it felf, but by the commemo-ration of holy things ; as, the commemoration of holy Scriptures, Hiftories, Works, Miracles, Effects, Graces, Promifes, Sacraments and Sacramental things, and the like. Which things, by a certain fimilitude, do feem properly or impro-perly to appertain to the thing confecrated.

There is ufed alfo the invocation of fome Divine names,
with

with the confignation of holy Seals, and things of the like
fort, which do conduce to fanctification and expiation; fuch
as are the Sprinkling with Holy-Water, Unctions with holy
Oyl, and odoriferous Suffumigations appertaining to holy
Worfhip. And therefore in every Confecration there is
chiefly ufed the Benediction and Confecration of Water,
Oyl, Fire, and Fumigations, ufed everywhere with holy Wax-
lights or Lamps burning: for without Lights no Sacrament is
rightly performed. This therefore is to be known, and
firmly obferved, That if any Confecration be to be made of
things profane, in which there is any pollution or defile-
ment, then an exorcifing and expiation of thofe things ought
to precede the confecration. Which things being fo made
pure, are more apt to receive the influences of the Divine
vertues. We are alfo to obferve, that in the end of every
Confecration, after that the prayer is rightly performed, the
perfon confecrating ought to blefs the thing confecrated, by
breathing out fome words, with divine vertue and power of
the prefent Confecration, with the commemoration of his
vertue and authority, that it may be the more duely performed, and with an earneft and intentive minde. And therefore we will here lay down fome examples hereof, whereby
the way to the whole perfection hereof may the more eafily
be made to appear unto you.

So then, in the confecration of water, we ought to commemorate how that God hath placed the firmament in the
midft of the waters, and in what maner that God placed the
fountain of waters in the earthly Paradife, from whence
fprang four holy rivers, which watered the whole earth.
Likewife we are to call to remembrance in what manner God
made the water to be the inftrument of executing his juftice
in the deftruction of the Gyants in the general deluge over
all the earth, and in the overthrow of the hoft of Pharaoh
in the Red-fea; alfo, how God led his own people thorow
the midft of the Sea on dry ground, and through the
midft of the river of Jordan; and likewife how marvel-
oufly he drew forth water out of the ftony rock in the wildernefs;

dernefs; and how at the prayer of Samfon, he caufed a fountain of running water to flow out of the cheek-tooth of the jaw-bone of an afs: and likewife, how God hath made waters the inftrument of his mercy, and of falvation, for the expiation of Original fin: alfo, how Chrift was baptized in Jordan, and hath hereby fanctified and cleanfed the waters. Moreover, certain divine names are to be invocated, which are conformable hereunto; as, that God is a living fountain, living water, the fountain of mercy; and names of the like kinde.

And likewife in the confecration of fire, we are to commemorate how that God hath created the fire to be an inftrument to execute his juftice, for punifhment, vengeance, and for the expiation of fins: alfo, when God fhall come to judge the world, he will command a conflagration of fire to go before him. And we are to call to remembrance in what manner God appeared to Mofes in the burning bufh; and alfo, how he went before the children of Ifrael in a pillar of fire; and that nothing can be duely offered, facrificed, or fanctified, without fire; and how that God inftituted fire to be kept continually burning in the Tabernacle of the Covenant; and how miraculoufly he re-kindled the fame, being extinct, and preferved it elfewhere from going out, being hidden under the waters: and things of this fort. Likewife the Names of God are to be called upon which are confonant hereunto; as, it is read in the Law and the Prophets, that God is a confuming fire: and if there be any of the Divine names which fignifies fire, or fuch-like names; as, the glory of God, the light of God, the fplendor and brightnefs of God.

And likewife in the confecration of Oyl and Perfumes, we are to call to remembrance fuch holy things as are pertinent to this purpofe, which we read in *Exodus* of the holy anoynting oyl, and divine names fignificant hereunto, fuch as is the name Chrift, which fignifies anoynted: and what myfteries there are hereof; as that in the *Revelation,* of the two Olive-trees diftilling holy oyl into the lamps that burn

before

before the face of God : and the like.

And the blessing of the lights, wax, and lamps, is taken from the fire, and the altar which containeth the substance of the flame : and what other such similitudes as are in mysteries ; as that of the seven candlesticks and lamps burning before the face of God.

These therefore are the Confecrations which first of all are necessary to be used in every kinde of devotion, and ought to precede it, and without which nothing in holy Rites can be duely performed.

In the next place now we shall shew unto you the consecration of Places, Instruments, and such-like things.

Therefore when you would confecrate any Place or Circle, you ought to take the prayer of Solomon used in the dedication of the Temple : and moreover, you must bless the place with the sprinkling of Holy-water, and with Fumigations ; by commemorating in the benediction holy mysteries; such as these are : The sanctification of the throne of God, of mount Sinai, of the Tabernacle of the Covenant, of the Holy of holies, of the temple of Jerusalem. Also, the san- *Sanctum* ctification of mount Golgotha, by the crucifying of Christ ; *sanctorum.* the sanctification of the Temple of Christ; of mount Tabor, by the transfiguration and ascension of Christ : and the like. And by invocating divine names which are significant hereunto ; such as the Place of God, the Throne of God, the Chayr of God, the Tabernacle of God, the Altar of God, the Habitation of God, and such-like divine names of this sort, which are to be written about the Circle or place to be confecrated.

And in the confecrations of instruments, and of all other things whatsoever that are serviceable to this Art, you shall proceed after the same manner, by sprinkling the same with Holy-water, perfuming the same with holy Fumigations, anoynting it with holy Oyl, sealing it with some holy Sigil, and blessing it with prayer ; and by commemorating holy things out of the sacred Scriptures, Religion, and Divine names which

which fhall be found agreeable to the thing that is to be confecrated : as for examples fake, in confecrating a fword, we
are to call to remembrance that in the Gofpel , *He that hath*
two coats, &c. and that place in the fecond of the *Macchabees,*
That a fword was divinely and miraculoufly fent to *Judas*
Macchabeus. And if there be any thing of the like in the
Prophets ; as that place, *Take unto you two-edged Swords,* &c.
In like maner you fhall confecrate experiments and books,
and whatfoever of the like nature,as is contained in writings,
pictures , and the like , by fprinkling, perfuming, anointing,
fealing, and bleffing with holy commemorations, and calling
to remembrance the fanctifications of myfteries ; As, the
fanctifying of the Tables of the ten Commandments, which
were delivered to *Mofes* by God in Mount *Sinai* ; The fanctification of the Teftaments of God , the Old and New ;
The fanctificarion of the Law, and of the Prophets,and Scriptures, which are promulgated by the holy Ghoft. Moreover,
there is to be commemorated fuch divine names as are fit
and convenient hereunto ; as thefe are : The Teftament of
God, The book of God, The book of life, The knowledge of
God, The wifdom of God ; and the like. And with fuch
kinde of Rites is the perfonal confecration performed.

There is furthermore, befides thefe, another Rite of confecration , of wonderful power , and much efficacy ; And
this is out of the kindes of fuperfticions : That is to fay, when
the Rite of confecration or collection of any Sacrament in
the Church is transferred to that thing which we would confecrate.

It is to be known alfo, that Vowes, Oblations, and Sacrifice, have the power of confecration, afwel real as perfonal ; and they are as it were certain covenants and conven-
tions between thofe names with which they are made , and
us who make them, ftrongly cleaving to our defire and wifh-
ed effect : As, when we dedicate, offer, and facrifice, with
certain names or things ; as, Fumigations, Unctions, Rings,
Images, Looking-glaffes ; and things lefs material, as Deities,
Sigils , Pentacles , Inchantments , Orations, Pictures, and
Scrip-

Scriptures : of which we have largely fpoken in our third book of Occult Philofophy.

There is extant amongſt thofe Magicians (who do moſt uſe the miniſtery of evil ſpirits) a certain Rite of invocating ſpirits by a Book to be confecrated before to that purpoſe ; which is properly called, *A book of Spirits* ; whereof we *Liber Spi-* ſhall now ſpeak a few words. For this book is to be confe- *rituum.* crated, a book of evil ſpirits,ceremoniouſly to be compofed, in their name and order : whereunto they binde with a certain holy Oath, the ready and prefent obedience of the ſpirit therein written.

Now this book is to be made of moſt pure and clean paper, that hath never been uſed before ; which many do call *Virgin-paper.* And this book muſt be inſcribed after this maner : that is to ſay, Let there be placed on the left ſide the image of the ſpirit, and on the right ſide his character, with the Oath above it, containing the name of the ſpirit, and his dignity and place, with his office and power. Yet very many do compofe this book otherwiſe, omitting the characters or image: but it is more efficacious not to neglect any thing which conduceth to it.

Moreover, there is to be obſerved the circumſtances of places,times,hours, according to the Stars which thefe ſpirits are under, and are ſeen to agree unto, their ſite, rite, and order being applied.

Which book being ſo written, and well bound, is to be a-dorned,garniſhed, and kept fecure,with Regiſters and Seals, leſt it ſhould happen after the confecration to open in ſome place not intented,and indanger the operator. Furthermore, this book ought to be kept as reverently as may be: for irreverence of minde cauſeth it to lofe its vertue,with pollution and profanation.

Now this facred book being thus compofed according to the maner already delivered, we are then to proceed to the confecration thereof after a twofold way : one whereof is, That all and ſingular the ſpirits who are written in the book, be called to the Circle , according to the Rites and Order

I   which

which we have before taught ; and the book that is to be confecrated, let it be placed without the Circle in a triangle. And in the firft place, let there be read in the prefence of the fpirits all the Oathes which are written in that book ; and then the book to be confecrated being placed without the Circle in a triangle there drawn, let all the fpirits be compelled to impofe their hands where their images and characters are drawn, and to confirm and confecrate the fame with a fpecial and common Oath. Which being done, let the book be taken and fhut, and preferved as we have before fpoken, and let the fpirits be licenfed to depart, according to due rite and order.

There is another maner of confecrating a book of fpirits, which is more eafie, and of much efficacie to produce every effect, except that in opening this book the fpirits do not always come vifible. And this way is thus : Let there be made a book of fpirits as we have before before fet forth ; but in the end thereof let there be written Invocations and Bonds, and ftrong Conjurations, wherewith every fpirit may be bound. Then this book muft be bound between two Tables or Lamens, and in the infide thereof let there be drawn the holy Pentacles of the Divine Majeftie, which we have before fet forth and defcribed out of the *Apocalypfe:* then let the firft of them be placed in the beginning of the book, and the fecond at the end of the fame. This book being perfected after this maner, let it be brought in a clear and fair time, to a Circle prepared in a crofs way, according to the Art which we have before delivered ; and there in the firft place the book being opened, let it be confecrated to the rites and ways which we have before declared concerning Confecration. Which being done, let all the fpirits be called which are written in the book, in their own order and place, by conjuring them thrice by the bonds defcribed in the book, that they come unto that place within the fpace of three days, to affure their obedience, and confirm the fame, to the book fo to be confecrated. Then let the book be wrapped up in clean linen, and buried in the middle of the

Cir-

Circle, and there faſt ſtopped up: and then the Circle being deſtroyed, after the ſpirits are licenſed, depart before the riſing of the ſun: and on the third day, about the middle of the night, return, and new make the Circle, and with bended knees make prayer and giving thanks unto God, and let a precious perfume be made, and open the hole, and take out the book; and ſo let it be kept, not opening the ſame. Then you ſhall licenſe the ſpirits in their order, and deſtroying the Circle, depart before the ſun riſe. And this is the laſt rite and maner of conſecrating, profitable to whatſoever writings and experiments, which do direct to ſpirits, placing the ſame between two holy Lamens or Pentacles, as before is ſhewn.

But the Operator, when he would work by the book thus conſecrated, let him do it in a fair and clear ſeaſon, when the ſpirits are leaſt troubled; and let him place himſelf towards the region of the ſpirits. Then let him open the book under a due Regiſter; let him invoke the ſpirits by their Oath there deſcribed and confirmed, and by the name of their character and image, to that purpoſe which you deſire: and, if there be need, conjure them by the bonds placed in the end of the book. And having attained your deſired effect, then you ſhall licenſe the ſpirits to depart.

And now we ſhall come to ſpeak concerning the invocation of ſpirits, as well of the good ſpirits as of the bad.

The good ſpirits may be invocated of us, divers ways, and in ſundry manners do offer themſelves unto us. For they do openly ſpeak to thoſe that watch, and do offer themſelves to our ſight, or do inform us in dreams by oracle of thoſe things which are deſired. Whoſoever therefore would call any good ſpirit, to ſpeak or appear in ſight, it behoveth them eſpecially to obſerve two things: one whereof is about the diſpoſition of the invocant; the other about thoſe things which are outwardly to be adhibited to the invocation, for the conformity of the ſpirits to be called. It behoveth therefore that the invocant himſelf be religi-

ouſly

oufly difpofed for many days to fuch a myftery. In the firft place therefore, he ought to be confeffed and contrite, both inwardly and outwardly, and rightly expiated, by daily wafhing himfelf with holy water. Moreover, the invocant ought to conferve himfelf all thefe days, chafte, abftinent, and to feparate himfelf as much as may be done, from all perturbation of minde, and from all maner of forraign and fecular bufinefs. Alfo, he fhall obferve faftings all thefe days, as much as fhall feem convenient to him to be done. Alfo, let him daily between fun-rifing and fun-fetting, being clothed with a holy linen garment, feven times call upon God, and make a deprecation to the Angels to be called according to the rule which we have before taught. Now the number of days of fafting and preparation, is commonly the time of a whole Lunation. There is alfo another number obferved amongft the Caballifts, which is fourty days.

Now concerning thofe things which do appertain to this Rite of Invocation, the firft is, That a place be chofen, clean, pure, clofe, quiet, free from all maner of noife, and not fubject to any ftrangers fight. This place muft firft be exorcifed and confecrated: and let there be a table or altar placed therein, covered with clean white linen, and fet towards the eaft: and on each fide thereof, let there be fet two confecrated wax-lights burning, the flame whereof ought not to go out all thefe days. In the middle of the altar, let there be placed Lamens, or the holy paper which we have before defcribed, covered with pure fine linen; which is not to be opened until the end of thefe days of the Confecration. You fhall alfo have in readinefs a precious perfume, and pure anointing oyl; and let them be both kept confecrated. There muft alfo a Cenfer be fet on the head of the altar, wherein you fhall kindle the holy fire, and make a perfume every day that you fhall pray. You fhall alfo have a long garment of white linen, clofe before and behinde, which may cover the whole body and the feet, and girt about you with a girdle. You fhall alfo have a veil of pure clean linen, and

and in the fore-part thereof let there be fixed golden or gilded Lamens, with the infcription of the name *Tetragrammaton*; all which things are to be fanctified and confecrated in order. But you muft not enter into the holy place, unlefs it be firft wafhed, and arayed with a holy garment ; and then you fhall enter into it with your feet naked. And when you enter therein, you fhall fprinkle it with holy water: then you fhall make a perfume upon the altar, and afterwards with bended knees pray before the altar as we have directed.

But in the end of thefe days, on the laft day, you fhall faft more ftrictly : and fafting on the day following, at the rifing of the fun, you may enter into the holy place, ufing the ceremonies before fpoken of, firft by fprinkling your felf, then with making a perfume, you fhall figne your felf with holy oyl in the forehead, and anoint your eyes ; ufing prayer in all thefe Confecrations. Then you fhall open the holy Lamen, and pray before the altar upon your knees, as abovefaid : and then an invocation being made to the Angels, they will appear unto you, which you defire ; which you fhall entertain with a benign and chafte communication, and licenfe them to depart.

Now the Lamen which is to be ufed to invoke any good fpirit, you fhall make after this maner ; either in metal conformable, or in new wax, mixt with fpecies and colours conformable : or it may be made in clean paper, with convenient colours: and the outward form or figure thereof may be fquare, circular, or triangular, or of the like fort , according to the rule of the numbers : in which there muft be written the divine names , as well the general names as the fpecial. And in the centre of the Lamen, let there be drawn a character of fix corners ; in the middle whereof, let there be *Hexagonus* written the name and character of the Star, or of the Spirit his governour, to whom the good fpirit that is to be called is fubject. And about this character, let there be placed fo many characters of five corners, as the fpirits we would call *Pentagonus* together at once. And if we fhall call onely one fpirit, neververtheless there shall be made four Pentagones, wherein the name of the spirit or spirits, with their characters, is to be written. Now this table ought to be composed when the Moon is increasing, on those days and hours which then agree to the Spirit. And if we take a fortunate star herewith, it will be the better. Which Table being made in this manner, it is to be consecrated according to the rules above delivered.

And this is the way of making the general Table, serving for the invocation of all good spirits whatsoever. Nevertheless we may make special Tables congruent to every spirit, by the rule which we have above spoken of concerning holy Pentacles.

And now we will declare unto you another Rite more easie to perform this thing : that is to say, Let the man that is to receive any Oracle from the good spirits, be chaste, pure, and confess'd. Then a place being prepared pure and clean, and covered everywhere with white linen, on the Lords day in the new of the moon let him enter into that place, clothed with clean white garments ; and let him exorcize the place, and bless it, and make a Circle therein with a sanctified cole ; and let there be written in the uttermost part of the Circle the names of the Angels, and in the inner part thereof let there be written the mighty names of God : and let him place within the Circle, at the four angles of the world, the Censers for the perfumes. Then let him enter the place fasting, and washed, and let him begin to pray towards the east this whole Psalm : *Beati immaculati in via,&c.* *Blessed are the undefiled in the way,* &c. by perfuming ; and in the end deprecating the Angels, by the said divine names, that they will daign to discover and reveal that which he desireth : and that let him do six days, continuing washed and fasting. And on the seventh day, which is the Sabbath, let him, being washed and fasting, enter the Circle, and perfume it, and anoint himself with holy anointing oyl, by anointing his forehead, and upon both his eyes, and in the palms

Pſal. 119.

palms of his hands, and upon his feet. Then upon his knees let him fay the Pfalm aforefaid, with Divine and Angelical names. Which being faid, let him arife, and let him begin to walk about in a circuit within the faid Circle from the eaft to the weft, until he is wearied with a dizzinefs of his brain: let him fall down in the Circle, and there he may reft ; and forthwith he fhall be wrapt up in an ecftafie, and a fpirit will appear unto him, which will inform him of all things. We muft obferve alfo, that in the Circle there ought to be four holy candles burning at the four parts of the world, which ought not to want light for the fpace of a whole week. And the maner of fafting muft be fuch, that he abftain from all things having a life of Senfe, and from thofe things which do proceed from them : and let him onely drink pure running water : neither let him take any food till the going down of the fun. And let the perfume and the holy anointing oyl be made, as is fet forth in *Exodus* and the other holy books of the Bible. It is alfo to be obferved, that always as often as he enters into the Circle, he have upon his forehead a golden Lamen, upon which there muft be written the name *Tetragrammaton*, as we have before fpoken.

But natural things, and their commixtures, do alfo belong unto us, and are conducing to receive Oracles from any fpirit by a dream : which are either Perfumes, Unctions, and Meats or Drinks : which you may underftand in our firft book of Occult Philofophy.

But he that is willing always and readily to receive the Oracles of a Dream, let him make unto himfelf a Ring of the Sun or of Saturn for this purpofe. There is alfo an Image to be made, of excellent efficacie and power to work this effect ; which being put under his head when he goeth to fleep, doth effectually give true dreams of what things foever the minde hath before determined or confulted on. The Tables of Numbers do likewife confer to receive an Oracle, being duly formed under their own Conftellations. And thefe things thou mayft know in the third book of Occult Philofophy.   Holy

Holy Tables and Papers do alfo ferve to this effect, being fpecially compofed and confecrated : fuch as is the Almadel of *Solomon*, and the Table of the Revolution of the name *Tetragrammaton*. And thofe things which are of this kinde, and written unto thefe things, out of divers figures, numbers, holy pictures, with the infcriptions of the holy names of God and of Angels ; the compofition whereof is taken out of divers places of the holy Scriptures, Pfalms, and Verficles, and other certain promifes of the divine Revelation and Prophecies.

To the fame effect do conduce holy prayers and imprecations, as well unto God, as to the holy Angels and Heroes : the imprecations of which prayers are to be compofed as we have before fhewn, according to fome religious fimilitude of Miracles, Graces, and the like, making mention of thofe things which we intend to do : as, out of the Old Teftament, of the dream of *Jacob*, *Jofeph*, *Pharaoh*, *Daniel*, and *Nebuchadnezzar :* if out of the New Teftament , of the dream of *Jofeph* the husband of the bleffed virgin *Mary* ; of the dream of the three Wife-men ; of *John* the Evangelift fleeping upon the breft of our Lord : and whatfoever of the like kinde can be found in Religion, Miracles , and Revelations ; as, the revelation of the Crofs to *Helen*, the revelations of *Conftantine* and *Charles* the Great, the revelations of *Bridget*, *Cyril*, *Methodius*, *Mechtild*, *Joachim*, *Merhir*, and fuch-like. According to which, let the deprecations be compofed, if when he goeth to fleep it be with a firm intention : and the reft well difpofing themfelves, let them pray devoutly, and without doubt they will afford a powerful effect.

Now he that knoweth how to compofe thofe things which we have now fpoken of, he fhall receive the moft true Oracles of dreams. And this he fhall do ; obferve thofe things which in the fecond book of Occult Philofophy are directed concerning this thing. He that is defirous therefore to receive an Oracle , let him abftain from fupper and from drink, and be otherwife well difpofed, his brain being free from turbulent vapours ; let him alfo have his bed-chamber fair
and

and clean, exorcifed and confecrated if he will ; then let him
perfume the fame with fome convenient fumigation ; and
let him anoint his temples with fome unguent efficacious
hereunto, and put a ring upon his finger, of the things above
fpoken of : let him take either fome image, or holy table, or
holy paper, and place the fame under his head : then having
made a devout prayer, let him go unto his bed, and medi-
tating upon that thing which he defireth to know, let him fo
fleep ; for fo fhall he receive a moft certain and undoubted
oracle by a dream, when the Moon goeth through that figne
which was in the ninth Houfe of his nativity, and alfo when
fhe goeth through the figne of the ninth Houfe of the Revolution of his nativity ; and when fhe is in the ninth figne from
the figne of perfection. And this is the way and means
whereby we may obtain all Sciences and Arts whatfoever,
fuddenly and perfectly, with a true Illumination of our underftanding ; although all inferiour familiar Spirits whatfoever do conduce to this effect ; and fometimes alfo evil
Spirits fenfibly informing us Intrinfecally or Extrinfecally.

But if we would call any evil Spirit to the Circle, it firft
behoveth us to confider, and to know his nature, to which of
the Planets it agreeth, and what Offices are diftributed to
him from that Planet ; which being known, let there be
fought out a place fit and proper for his invocation, according to the nature of the Planet, and the quality of the Offices of the faid Spirit, as near as the fame may be done : as,
if their power be over the Sea, Rivers or Flouds, then let
the place be chofen in the Shore ; and fo of the reft. Then
let there be chofen a convenient time, both for the quality of
the Air, ferene, clear, quiet, and fitting for the Spirits to affume bodies ; as alfo of the quality and nature of the Planet,
and of the Spirit, as to wit, on his day, or the time wherein
he ruleth : he may be fortunate or infortunate, fometimes of
the day, and fometimes of the night, as the Stars and Spirits
do require. Thefe things being confidered, let there be a
Circle framed in the place elected, afwel for the defence of
the Invocant, as for the confirmation of the Spirit. And in

K the

the Circle it felf there are to be written the divine general names, and thofe things which do yeild defence unto us ; and with them, thofe divine names which do rule this Planet, and the Offices of the Spirit himfelf ; there fhall alfo be written therein, the names of the good Spirits which bear rule, and are able to binde and conftrain that Spirit which we intend to call. And if we will any more fortifie and ftrengthen our Circle, we may adde Characters and Pentacles agreeing to the work ; then alfo if we will, we may either within or without the Circle, frame an angular figure, with the infcription of fuch convenient numbers, as are congruent amongft themfelves to our work ; which are alfo to be known, according to maner of numbers and figures: of which in the fecond book of Occult Philofophy it is fufficiently fpoken. Further, He is to be provided of lights, perfumes, unguents and medicines, compounded according to the nature of the Planet and Spirit ; which do partly agree with the Spirit, by reafon of their natural and cœleftial vertue ; and partly are exhibited to the Spirit for religious and fuperftitious worfhip. Then he muft be furnifhed with holy and confecrated things, neceffary afwel for the defence of the Invocant, and his fellows, as alfo ferving for bonds to binde and conftrain the Spirits; fuch as are either holy Papers, Lamens, Pictures, Pentacles, Swords, Scepters, Garments of convenient matter and colour, and things of the like fort. Then when all thefe things are provided, and the Mafter and his fellows being in the Circle, in the firft place let him confecrate the Circle, and all thofe things which he ufeth ; which being performed with a convenient gefture and countenance, let him begin to pray with a loud voice, after this manner. Firft let him make an Oration unto God, and then let him intreat the good Spirits : and if he will read any Prayers, Pfalms, or Gofpel for his defence, they ought to take the firft place. After thefe Prayers and Orations are faid, then let him begin to invocate the Spirit which he defireth, with a gentle and loving Inchantment, to all the coafts of the World, with the commemoration of his own Authority tity and power. And then let him rest a little, looking about him; to see if any Spirit do appear; which if he delay, then let him repeat his invocation, as abovesaid, until he hath done it three times;and if the Spirit be pertinacious,obstinate, and will not appear, then let him begin to conjure with divine power; so also that the conjurations and all his commemorations do agree with the Nature and Offices of the Spirit himself,and reiterate the same three times, from stronger to stronger,usingObjurgations,Contumeries,Cursings, & Punishments,and suspension from his Office and power,and the like.

And after all the courses are finished, then cease a little; and if any Spirit shall appear, let the Invocant turn himself towards the Spirit,and courteously receive him,and earnestly intreating him, let him first require his name, and if he be called by any other name: and then proceeding further, let him ask him whatsoever he will: and if in any thing the Spirit shall shew himself obstinate or lying, let him be bound by covenient conjurations : and if you doubt of any lye, make without the Circle with the consecrated Sword, the figure of a triangle or * *Pentagone*, and compel the Spirit to enter into it • and if thou receivest any promise which thou wouldst have to be confirmed with an Oath, let him stretch the sword out of the Circle, and swear the Spirit, by laying his hand upon the Sword. Then having obtained of the Spirit that which you desire, or are otherwise contented, licenfe him to depart with courteous words, giving command unto him,that he do no hurt : and if he will not depart, compel him by powerful conjurations ; and if need require,expel him by Exorcifmes,and by making contrary fumigations. And when he is departed, go not out of the Circle, but make a stay, making prayer ,and giving of thanks unto God and the good Angels, and also praying for your defence and confervation : and then all those things being orderly performed, you may depart.

But if your hope be frustrated, and no Spirits will appear, yet for this do not despair ; but leaving the Circle, return again at other times, doing as before. And if you shall judge

A Character with five corners.

that

that you have erred in any thing, then that you ſhall amend, by adding or diminiſhing ; for the conſtancy of Reiteration doth often increaſe your authority and power, and ſtriketh terror into the Spirits, and humbleth them to obey.

And therefore ſome uſe to make a Gate in the Circle, whereby they may go in and out, which they open and ſhut as they pleaſe, and fortifie it with holy Names and Pentacles.

This alſo we are to take notice of, That when no Spirits will appear, but the Maſter being wearied hath determined to ceaſe and give over ; let him not therefore depart without licenſing the Spirits : for they that do neglect this, are very greatly in danger, except they are fortified with ſome ſublime defence.

Often imes alſo the Spirits do come, although they appear not viſible, (for to cauſe terror to him that calls them) either in the things which he uſeth, or in the operation it ſelf. But this kinde of licenſing is not given ſimply, but by a kinde of diſpenſation with ſuſpenſion, until in the following terms they ſhall render themſelves obedient. Alſo without a Circle theſe Spirits may be called to appear, according to the way which is above delivered about the conſecration of a book.

But when we do intend to execute any effect by evil Spirits, where an Apparition is not needful ; then that is to be done, by making and forming that thing which is to be unto us as an inſtrument, or ſubject of the experiment it ſelf; as, whether it be an Image, or a Ring, or a Writing, or any Character, Candle, or Sacrifice, or any thing of the like ſort : then the name of the Spirit is to be written therein, with his Character, according to the exigency of the experiment, either by writing it with ſome blood, or otherwiſe uſing a perfume agreeable to the Spirit. Oftentimes alſo making Prayers and Orations to God and the good Angels before we invocate the evil Spirit, conjuring him by the divine power.

There is another kinde of Spirits, which we have ſpoken of in our third book of Occult Philoſophy, not ſo hurtful, and neereſt unto men ; ſo alſo, that they are effected with humane

paſſions

paſſions, and do joy in the converſation of men, and freely do inhabit with them:and others do dwell in the Woods and Deſarts:& others delight in the company of divers domeſtique Animals and wilde Beaſts ; and otherſome do inhabit about Fountains and Meadows. Whoſoever therefore would call up theſe kinde of Spirits, in the place where they abide, it ought to be done with odoriferous perfumes, and with ſweet ſounds and inſtruments of Muſick, ſpecially compoſed for the buſineſs,with uſing of Songs, Inchantments and plea-ſant Verſes, with praiſes and promiſes.

But thoſe which are obſtinate to yeild to theſe things, are to be compelled with Threatnings, Comminations, Cur-ſings, Deluſions, Contumelies, and eſpecially by threatning them to expel them from thoſe places where they are con-verſant.

Further, if need be,thou maiſt betake thee to uſe Exor-ciſmes ; but the chiefeſt thing that ought to be obſerved, is, conſtancy of minde, and boldneſs, free, and alienated from fear.

Laſtly, when you would invocate theſe kinde of Spirits, you ought to prepare a Table in the place of invocation, co-vered with clean linen ; whereupon you ſhall ſet new bread, and running water or milk in new earthen veſſels , and new knives. And you ſhall make a fire, whereupon a perfume ſhall be made. But let the Invocant go unto the head of the Table, and round about it let there be ſeats placed for the Spirits, as you pleaſe ; and the Spirits being called, you ſhall invite them to drink and eat. But if perchance you ſhall fear any evil Spirit, then draw a Circle about it, and let that part of the Table at which the Invocant ſits, be with-in the Circle,and the reſt of the Table without the Circle.

In our third book of Occult Philoſophy, we have taught how and by what means the Soul is joyned to the Body ; and, what hapeneth to the Soul after death.

Thou maiſt know further, That thoſe Souls do ſtill love their relinquiſhed Bodies after death, as it were a certain
affinity

affinity alluring them; such as are the Souls of noxious men, which have violently relinquished their Bodies , and Souls wanting a due burial , which do still wander in a liquid and turbulent Spirit about their dead carkasses ; for these Souls by the known means by which heretofore they were conjoyned to their Bodies,by the like vapors,liquors,and savours, are easily drawn unto them.

From hence it is , that the Souls of the dead are not to be called up without blood, or by the application of some part of their relict Body.

In the raising up of these shadows,we are to perfume with new Blood, with the Bones of the dead , and with Flesh, Egges, Milk , Honey and Oile , and such-like things, which do attribute to the Souls a means apt to receive their Bodies.

It is also to be understood, That those who are desirous to raise up any Souls of the dead , they ought to do it in those places , wherein these kinde of Souls are most known to be conversant , or for some alliance alluring those souls into their forsaken Body ; or for some kinde of affection in times past, impressed in them in their life, drawing the said Soul to certain places, things, or persons ; or for the forcible nature of some place fitted and prepared for to purge or punish these Souls. Which places for the most part are to be known by the experience of visions, mighty incursions, and apparitions, and such-like prodigies seen.

Therefore the places most fitting for these things , are Church-yards. And better then them , are those places wherein there is the execution of criminal judgements. And better then these , are those places, in which of late yeers there have been some publike slaughters of men. Furthermore,that place is better then there , where some dead carkafs , that came by a violent death , is not yet expiated, nor ritely buried , and was lately buried ; for the expiation of those places , is also a holy Rite duly to be adhibited to the burial of the bodies , and oftentimes prohibiteth the souls to come unto their bodies , and expelleth them far off unto the places of judgement.   And

And from hence it is, That the Souls of the dead are not eafily to be raifed up, except it be the Souls of them whom we know to be evil, or to have perifhed by a violent death, and whofe bodies do want a right and due burial.

Now although we have fpoken concerning fuch places of this kinde, it will not be fafe or commodious to go unto them; but it behoveth us to take to what place foever is to be chofen, fome principal part of the body that is relict, and therewith to make a perfume in due maner, and to perform other competent Rites.

It is alfo to be known, That becaufe the Souls are certain fpiritual lights, therefore artificial lights, efpecially if they be framed out of certain competent things, compounded according to a true rule, with congruent infcriptions of Names and Seals, do very much avail to the raifing up of departed Souls.

Moreover, thefe things which now are fpoken of, are not alwaies fufficient to raife up Souls, becaufe of an extranatural portion of underftanding and reafon, which is above, and known onely to the Heaven and Deftinies, and their power.

We ought therefore to allure the faid Souls, by fupernatural and cœleftial powers duely adminiftred, even by thofe things which do move the very harmony of the Soul, afwel imaginative, as rational and intellectual; as are Voices, Songs, Sound, Inchantments: and Religious things; as Prayers, Conjurations, Exorcifmes, and other holy Rites, which may very commodioufly be adminiftred hereunto.

The end of the fourth book of Agrippa.

Heptameron,

Heptameron:

OR,

MAGICAL ELEMENTS

OF

PETER de ABANO

PHILOSOPHER.

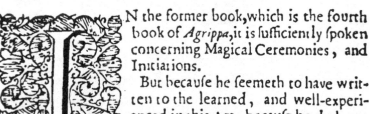

N the former book, which is the fourth
book of *Agrippa,* it is sufficiently spoken
concerning Magical Ceremonies, and
Initiations.

But because he seemeth to have written to the learned, and well-experi-
enced in this Art; because he doth not
specially treat of the Ceremonies, but
rather speaketh of them in general,
it was therefore thought good to adde hereunto the Magical Elements of *Peter de Abano* : that those who are hither-

L

to ignorant, and have not tasted of Magical Superstitions, may have them in readiness, how they may exercise themselves therein. For we see in this book, as it were a certain introduction of Magical vanity;and as if they were in present exercise,they may behold the distinct functions of spirits,how they may be drawn to discourse and communication ; what is to be done every day, and every hour ; and how they shall be read, as if they were described sillable by sillable.

In brief, in this book are kept the principles of Magical conveyances. But because the greatest power is attributed to the Circles ; (For they are certain fortresses to defend the operators safe from the evil Spirits;) In the first place we will treat concerning the composition of a Circle.

Of the Circle, and the composition thereof.

THe form of Circles is not alwaies one and the same ; but useth to be changed, according to the order of the Spirits that are to be called , their places, times, daies and hours. For in making a Circle, it ought to be considered in what time of the year, what day , and what hour , that you make the Circle ; what Spirits you would call, to what Star and Region they do belong, and what functions they have. Therefore let there be made three Circles of the latitude of nine foot, and let them be distant one from another a hands breadth ; and in the middle Circle, first, write the name of the hour wherein you do the work. In the second place, Write the name of the Angel of the hour. In the third place, The Sigil of the Angel of the hour. Fourthly, The name of the Angel that ruleth that day wherein you do the work,and the names of his ministers. In the fifth place, The name of the present time. Sixthly , The name of the Spirits ruling in that part of time,and their Presidents. Seventhly, The name of the head of the Signe ruling in that part of time

time wherein you work. Eighthly, The name of the earth, according to that part of time wherein you work. Ninthly, and for the compleating of the middle Circle, Write the name of the Sun and of the Moon, according to the said rule of time; for as the time is changed, so the names are to be altered. And in the outermost Circle, let there be drawn in the four Angles, the names of the presidential Angels of the Air, that day wherein you would do this work; to wit, the name of the King and his three Ministers. Without the Circle, in four Angles, let *Pentagones* be made. In the inner Circle let there be written four divine names with crosses interposed in the middle of the Circle; to wit, towards the East let there be written *Alpha*, and towards the West let there be written *Omega*; and let a cross divide the middle of the Circle. When the Circle is thus finished, according to the rule now before written, you shall proceed.

Of the names of the hours, and the Angels ruling them.

IT is also to be known, that the Angels do rule the hours in a successive order, according to the course of the heavens, and Planets unto which they are subject; so that that Spirit which governeth the day, ruleth also the first hour of the day; the second from this governeth the second hour; the third, the third hour, and so consequently: and when seven Planets and hours have made their revolution, it returneth again to the first which ruleth the day. Therefore we shall first speak of the names of the hours.

Hours of the day.	Hours of the night.
1. *Yayn.*	1. *Beron.*
2. *Janor.*	2. *Barol.*
3. *Nasnia.*	3. *Thami.*
4. *Salla.*	4. *Athar.*

L 2

5. *Sadedali.*
6. *Thamur.*
7. *Ourer.*
8. *Thamic.*
9. *Neron.*
10. *Jayon.*
11. *Abai.*
12. *Natalon.*

5. *Mathon.*
6. *Rana.*
7. *Netos.*
8. *Tafrac.*
9. *Saſſur.*
10. *Aglo.*
11. *Calerva.*
12. *Salam.*

Of the names of the Angels and their Sigils, it ſhall be ſpoken in their proper places. Now let us take a veiw of the names of the times. A year therefore is fourfold, and is divided into the Spring, Summer, Harveſt and Winter; the names whereof are theſe.

The Spring.　　*Talvi.*
The Summer.　　*Caſmaran.*
Autumne.　　*Ardarael.*
Winter.　　*Farlas.*

The Angels of the Spring.

Caracaſa.
Core.
Amatiel.
Commiſſoros.

The head of the Signe of the Spring.

Spugliguel.

The name of the earth in the Spring.

Amadai.

The

The names of the Sun and Moon in the Spring.

The Sun.	The Moon.
Abraym.	*Agusita.*

The Angels of the Summer.

Gargatel.
Tariel.
Gaviel.

The head of the Signe of the Summer.

Tubiel.

The name of the earth in Summer.

Festativi.

The names of the Sun and Moon in Summer.

The Sun.	The Moon.
Athemay.	*Armatus.*

The Angels of Autumne.

Tarquam.
Guabarel.

The head of the signe of Autumne.

Torquaret.

The name of the earth in Autumne,

Rabianara.

The

The names of the Sun and Moon in Autumne.

The Sun.	The Moon.
Abragini.	*Matasignais.*

The Angels of the Winter.

Amabael.
Ctarari.

The head of the sign of Winter.

Altarib.

The name of the Earth in Winter.

Geremiah.

The names of the Sun and Moon in Winter.

The Sun.	The Moon.
Commutaff.	*Affaterim.*

The Consecrations and Benedictions: and first of the Benediction of the Circle.

WHen the Circle is ritely perfected, sprinkle the same with holy or purging water, and say, *Thou shalt purge me with hysop (O Lord,) and I shall be clean : Thou shals wash me, and I shall be whiter then snow.*

The Benediction of perfumes.

THe God of *Abraham*, God of *Isaac* God of *Jacob*, bleßhere the creatures of these kindes, that they may fill up the power and vertue of their odours ; so that neither the enemy, nor any false imagination, may be able to enter into them: through our Lord *Jesus Christ*, &c. Then let them be sprinkled with holy water.

The Exorcisme of the fire upon which the perfumes are to be put.

THe fire which is to be used for suffumigations , is to be in a new vessel of earth or iron ; and let it be exorcised after this manner. *I exorcise thee, O thou creature of fire , by him by whom all things are made , that forthwith thou cast away every phantasme from thee , that it shall not be able to do any hurt in any thing.* Then say, *Bleß, O Lord, this creature of fire, and sanctifie it , that it may be blessed to set forth the praise of thy holy name , that no hurt may come to the Exercisers or Spectators :* through our Lord *Jesus Christ*, &c.

Of the Garment and Pentacle.

LEt it be a Priests Garment, if it can be : but if it cannot be had, let it be of linen, and clean. Then take this Pentacle made in the day and hour of *Mercury*, the Moon increasing, written in parchment made of a kids skin. But first let there be said over it the Mass of the holy Ghost , and let it be sprinkled with water of baptism.

An

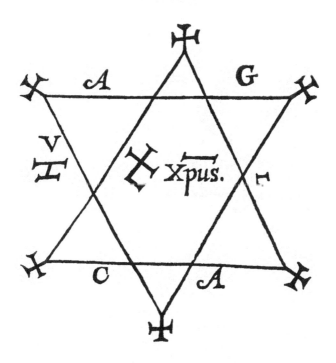

An Oration to be said, when the Vesture is put on.

ANeor, *Amacor, Amides, Theodonias, Anitor,* by the merits of thy Angel, O Lord, I will put on the Garments of Salvation, that this which I desire I may bring to effect : through thee the most holy *Adonay,* whose kingdom endureth for ever and ever. Amen.

                                                        Of

Of the manner of working.

LEt the *Moon* be increafing and equal, if it may then be done, and let her not be combuft.

The Operator ought to be clean and purified by the fpace of nine daies before the beginning of the work, and to be confeffed, and receive the holy Communion. Let him have ready the perfume appropriated to the day wherein he would perform the work. He ought alfo to have holy water from a Prieft, and a new earthen veffel with fire, a Vefture and Pentacle; and let all thefe things be rightly and duly confecrated and prepared. Let one of the fervants carry the earthen veffel full of fire, and the perfumes, and let another bear the book, another the Garment and Pentacle, and let the mafter carry the Sword ; over which there muft be faid one mafs of the Holy Ghoft ; and on the middle of the Sword, let there be written this name *Agla* †, and on the other fide thereof, this name † *On* †. And as he goeth to the confecrated place, let him continually read Letanies, the fervants anfwering. And when he cometh to the place where he will erect the Circle, let him draw the lines of the Circle, as we have before taught : and after he hath made it, let him fprinkle the Circle with holy water, faying, *Afperges me Domine,* &c.

Wafh me O Lord, &c.

The Mafter therefore ought to be purified with fafting, chaftity, and abftinency from all luxury the fpace of three whole dayes before the day of the operation. And on the day that he would do the work, being clothed with pure garments, and furnifhed with Pentacles, Perfumes, and other things neceffary hereunto, let him enter the Circle, and call the Angels from the four parts of the world, which do govern the feven Planets the feven dayes of the week, Colours and Metals; whofe name you fhall fee in their places. And with bended knees invocating the faid Angels particularly, let him fay, *O Angels fupradicti, eftote adjutores mea petitionis,*

M &

& in adjutorium mihi, in meis rebus & petitionibus.

Then let him call the Angels from the four parts of the world, that rule the Air the same day wherein he doth the work or experiment. And having implored specially all the Names and Spirits written in the Circle, let him say, *O vos omnes, adjuro atque contestor per sedem Adonay, per Hagios, ò Theos, Ischyros, Athanatos, Paracletos, Alpha & Omega, & per hæc tria nomina secreta, Agla, On, Tetragrammaton, quòd hodie debeatis adimplere quod cupio.*

These things being performed, let him read the Conjuration assigned for the day wherein he maketh the experiment, as we have before spoken; but if they shall be pertinacious and refractory, and will not yeild themselves obedient, neither to the Conjuration assigned to the day, nor to the prayers before made, then use the Conjurations and Exorcismes following.

An Exorcisme of the Spirits of the Air.

NOs facti ad imaginem Dei, dotati potentia Dei, & ejus facti voluntate, per potentissimum & corroboratum nomen Dei El, forte & admirabile vos exorcizamus (here he shall name the Spirits he would have appear, of what order soever they be) *& imperamus per eum qui dixit, & factum est, & per omnia nomina Dei, & per nomen Adonay, El, Elohim, Elohe, Zebaoth, Elion, Escerchie, Jah, Tetragrammaton, Sadai, Dominus Deus, excelsus, exorcizamus vos, atque potenter imperamus, ut appareatis statim nobis hic juxta Circulum in pulchra forma, videlicet humana, & sine deformitate & tortuositate aliqua.* Venite vos omnes tales, quia vobis imperamus, per nomen Y & V quod Adam audivit, & locutus est : & per nomen Dei Agla, quod Loth audivit, & factus salvus cum sua familia : & per nomen Joth, quod Jacob audivit ab Angelo secum luctantes, & liberatus est de manu fratris sui Esau : and by the name Anephexeton, quod Aaron audivit, & loquens, & sapiens factus est : & per nomen Zebaoth, quod Moses nominavit, & omnia flumina & paludes de terra Ægypti, versa* *verſæ fuerunt in ſanguinem : & per nomen Ecerchie Oriſton, quod Moſes nominavit, & omnes fluvii ebullierunt ranas , & aſcenderunt in domos Ægyptiorum, omnia deſtruentes : & per nomen Elion, quod Moſes nominavit, & fuit grando talis , qualis non fuit ab initio mundi : & per nomen Adonay, quod Moſes nominavit, & fuerunt locuſta , & apparuerunt ſuper terram Ægyptiorum, & comederunt quæ reſidua erant grandini : & per nomen Schemes amathia, quod Joſua vocavit, & remoratus eſt Sol curſum : & per nomen Alpha & Omega, quod Daniel nominavit , & deſtruxit Beel , & Draconem interſecit : & in nomine Emmanuel, quod tres pueri, Sidrach, Miſach & Abdenago , in camino ignis ardentis, cantaverunt, & liberati ſuerunt : & per nomen Hagios, & ſedem Adonay, & per ὁ Theos, Iſcytos, Athanatos, Paracletus; & per hæs tria ſecreta nomina, Agla, On, Tetragrammaton, adjuro, conteſtor, & per hæc nomina , & per alia nomina Domini noſtri Dei Omnipotentis , vivi & veri, vos qui veſtra culpa de Cælis ejecti fuiſtis uſque ad infernum locum, exorcizamus, & viriliter imperamus, per eum qui dixit , & factum eſt , cui omnes obediunt creatura, & per illud tremendum Dei judicium : & per mare omnibus incertum, vitreum, quod eſt ante conſpectum divinæ majeſtatis gradiens, & potentiale : & per quatuor divina animalia T. ante ſedem divinæ majeſta is gradientia, & oculos ante & retrò habentia : & per ignem ante ejus thronum circumſtantem : & per ſanctos Angelos Cælorum, T. & per eam quæ Eccleſia Dei nominatur : & per ſummam ſapientiam Omnipotentis Dei viril ter exorcizamus , ut nobis hic ante Circulum appareatis, ut faciendam noſtram voluntatem, in omnibus prout placuerit nobis : per ſedem Baldachiæ , & per hoc nomen Primeumaton, quod Moſes nominavit, & in cavernis abyſſi ſuerunt profundati vel abſorpti, Datan, Corah & Abiron : & in virtute iſtius nominis Primeumaton, tota Cæli militia compellente, maledicimus vos, privamus vos omni officio, loco & gaudio veſtro, uſque in profundum abyſſi, & uſque ad ultimum diem judicii vos ponimus, & relegamus in ignem æternum, & in ſtagnum ignis & ſulphuris, niſi ſtatim appareatis hic coram nobis, inte Circulum, ad faciendum voluntatem noſtram. In omnibus venite per hæc nomina, Adonay Zebaoth, Adonay Amioram. Venite, venite, imperat vobis Ado-*

nay, Saday, Rex regum potentissimus & tremendissimus, cujus vires nulla subterfugere potest creatura vobis pertinacissimis futuris nisi obedieritis , & appareatis ante hunc Circulum , affabiles subito , tandem ruina flebilis miserabilisque, & ignis perpetuum inextinguibilis vos manet. Venite ergo in nomine Adonay Zebaoth, Adonay Amioram: venite, venite, quid tardatis ? festinate imperat vobis Adonay, Saday, Rex regum, El, Aty, Titeip, Azia, Hyn, Jen, Minosel, Achadan : Vay, Vaa, Ey, Haa, Eye, Exe, à, El, El, El, à, Hy, Hau, Hau, Hau, Va, Va, Va, Va.

A Prayer to God, to be said in the four parts of the world, in the Circle.

A *Morule, Taneha, Latisten, Rabur, Taneha, Latisten, Escha, Aladia, Alpha & Omega, Leyste, Oriston, Adonay: O my most merciful heavenly Father, have mercy upon me, although a sinner ; make appear the arm of thy power in me this day (although thy unworthy child) against these obstinate and pernicious Spirits, that I by thy will may be made a contemplator of thy divine works, and may be illustrated with all wisdom , and alwaies worship and glorifie thy name. I humbly implore and beseech thee, that these Spirits which I call by thy judgement , may be bound and constrained to come, and give true and perfect answers to those things which I shall ask them, and that they may declare and shew unto us those things which by me or us shall be commanded them, not hurting any creature, neither injuring nor terrifying me or my fellows, nor hurting any other creature, and affrighting no man ; but let them be obedient to my requests, in all these things which I command them.* Then let him stand in the middle of the Circle, and hold his hand towards the Pentacle, and say , *Per Pentaculum Salomonis advocavi, dent mihi responsum verum.*

Then let him say , *Beralanensis, Baldachiensis, Paumachiæ & Apologiæ sedes, per Reges potestate'sá magnanimas, ac principes præpotentes, genio, Liachidæ, ministri tartarea sedes: Primac,*

hic

hic princeps fediis Apologiæ nona cohorte : Ego vos invoco, &
invocando vos conjure, atǫ̃ ſuperna Majeſtatis munitus virtute,
potenter impero, per eum qui dixit, & ſattum eſt, & cui obediunt
omnes creaturæ : & per hoc nomen ineffabile, Tetragrammaton
יהוה *Jehovah, in quo eſt plaſmatum omne ſeculum, quo audito*
elementa corruunt, aër concutitur, mare retrograditur, ignis extin-
guitur, terra tremit, omneſǫ̃, exercitus Cœleſtium, Terreſtrium, &
Infernorum tremunt, turbantur & corruunt : quatenus cito &
ſine mora & omni occaſione remota, ab univerſis mundi partibus
veniatis, & rationabiliter de omnibus quacunque interrogavero,
reſpondeatis vos, & veniatis pacifice, viſibiles, & affabiles : nunc
& ſine mora manifeſtantes quod cupimus : conjurati per nomen
æterni vivi & veri Dei Helioren, & mandata noſtra perficientes,
perſiſtentes ſemper uſǫ̃ ad finem, & intentionem meam, viſibiles
nobis, & affabiles, clara voce nobis, intelligibile, & ſine omni am-
biguitate.

Viſions and Apparitions.

Quibus ritè peractis, apparebunt infinita viſiones, & phantaſmata
pulſantia organa & omnis generis inſtrumenta muſica, idǫ̃,
fit à ſpiritibus, ut terrore compulſi ſocii abeant à Circulo, quia nihil
adverſus magiſtrum poſſunt. Poſt hæc videbis infinitos ſagittarios
cum infinita multitudine beſtiarum horribilem : quæ ita ſe com-
ponunt, ac ſi vellent devorare ſocios : & tamen nil timeant.
Tunc Sacerdos ſive Magiſter, adhibens manum Pentaculo, dicat :
Fugiat hinc iniquitas veſtra, virtute vexilli Dei. Et tunc
Spiritus obedire magiſtro coguntur, & ſocii nil am` lius videbunt.

Then let the Exorciſt ſay, ſtretching out his hand to the
Pentacle, *Ecce Pentaculum Salomonis, quod ante veſtram ad-*
duxi præſentiam : ecce perſonam exorcizatoris in medio Exorciſ-
mi, qui eſt optimè à Deo munitus, intrepidus, providus, qui viri-
bus potens vos exorcizando invocavit & vocat. Venite ergo cum
feſtinotione in virtute nominum iſtorum, Aye, Saraye, Aye, Saraye,
Aye Saraye, ne differatis venire, per nomina æterna Dei vivi &
veri Eloy, Archima, Rabur : & per hoc præſens Pentaculum, quod

ſuper

86   *Magical Elements,*

super vos potenter imperat : & per virtutem cœlestium Spirituum dominorum vestrorum : & per personam exorcizatoris,conjurati, festinati venire & obedire præceptori vestro , qui vocatur Ostinomos. His peractis,sibiles in quatuor angulis mundi. Et videbis immediate magnos motus: & cùm videris,dicas : Quid tardatis ? quid moramini? quid facitis? præparate vos & obedite præceptori vestro, in nomine Domini Bathat, vel Vachat super Abrac ruens, superveniens, Abeor super Aberer.

Tunc immediatè venient in sua forma propria. Et quando videbis eos juxta Circulum, ostende illis Pentaculum coopertum syndone sacro,& discooperiatur, & dicat : Ecce conclusionem vestram, nolite fieri inobedientes. Et subito videbis eos in pacifica forma: & dicent tibi,Pete quid vis,quia nos sumus parati complere omnia mandata tua,quia dominus ad hæc nos subjugavit. Cùm autem apparuerint Spiritus , tunc dicas , Bene veneritis Spiritus, vel reges nobilissimi, quia vos vocavi per illum cui omne genu flectitur,cœlestium, terrestrium & infernorum : cujus in manu omnia regna regum sunt , nec est qui sua contrarius esse possit Majestati. Quatenus constringo vos, ut hic ante circulum visibiles , affabiles permanetis, tamdiu tamq, constantes, nec sint licentia mea recedatis, donec meam sine fallacia aliqua & veredicè perficiatis voluntatem, per potentia illius virtutem , qui mare posuit terminum suum, quem præterire non potest, & lege illius potentia, non pertransit fines suos, Dei scilicet altissimi,regis,domini, qui cuncta creavit, Amen. Then command what you will , and it shall be done. Afterwards licenſe them thus : † *In nomine Patris,* † *Filii, &* † *Spiritus sancti, ite in pace ad loca vestra : & pax sit inter nos & vos,parati sitis venire vocati.*

Theſe are the things which *Peter de Abano* hath ſpoken concerning Magical Elements.

But that you may the better know the manner of compoſing a Circle, I will ſet down one Scheme ; ſo that if any one would make a Circle in Spring-time for the firſt hour of Lords day, it muſt be in the ſame manner as is the figure following.

The

The figure of a Circle for the first hour of the Lords day, in Spring-time.

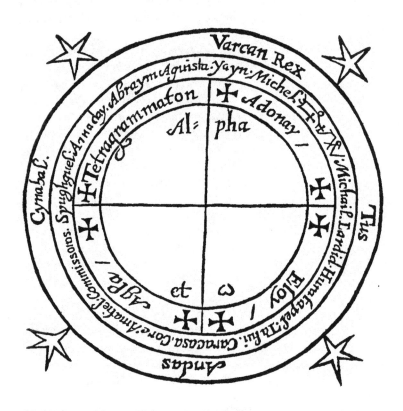

It remaineth now, That we explain the week, the several dayes thereof: and first of the Lords day.

Con-

Confiderations of the Lords day.

THe Angel of the Lords day, his Sigil, Planet, Signe of
the Planet, and the name of the fourth heaven.

Michael.   ☉   ♌

Machen

The Angels of the Lords day.

Michael, Dardiel, Huratapal.

The Angels of the Air ruling on the Lords day.

Varcan, King.

His Minifters.

Tus, Andas, Cynabal.

The winde which the Angels of the Air abovefaid are under.

The North-winde.

The Angel of the fourth heaven, ruling on the Lords day,
which ought to be called from the four parts of the world.

At the Eaft.

Samael.   Baciel.   Atel.
Gabriel.   Vionatraba.   At

At the West.

Ansel. *Pabel.* *Ustael.*
Burchat. *Suceratos.* *Capabili.*

At the North.

Aiel. *Aniel,* vel *Aquiel.* *Masgabriel.*
Sapiel. *Masuyel.*

At the South.

Haludiel. *Machasiel.* *Charsiel.*
Uriel. *Naromiel.*

The perfume of the Lords day.

Red Wheat.

The Conjuration of the Lords day.

COnjuro & confirmo super vos Angeli fortes Dei, & sancti, in nomine Adonay, Eye, Eye, Eya, qui est ille, qui fuit, est & erit, Eye, Abraye: & in nomine Sad y, Cados, Cados, Cados, aliæ sendentis super Cherub n, & per nomen magnum ipsius Dei sortis & potentis, exaltatique super omnes cœlos, Eye, Saraye, plasmatoris seculorum, qui creavit mundum, cœlum, terram, mare, & omnia quæ in eis sunt in primo die, & sigillavit ea sancto nomine suo Phaa : & per nomina sanctorum Angelorum, qui dominantur in quarto exercitu, & serv unt coram potentissimo Salamia, Angelo magno & honorato: & per nomen stellæ, quæ est Sol, & per signum, † per immensum nomen Dei vivi, & per nomina omnia prædicta, conjuro te Michael an ele magne, qui es præposi us D ei Dominicæ : & per nomen Adona, Dei Israel, qui creavit mundum & quicquid in eo est, quod pro melabores, & ad moleas omnem meam petitionem, juxta meum velle & votum meum, in negotio &

N   causa

causa mea. And here thou shalt declare thy cause and busines, and for what thing thou makest this Conjuration.

The Spirits of the Air of the Lords day, are under the North-winde ; their nature is to procure Gold, Gemmes, Carbuncles, Riches ; to cause one to obtain favour and benevolence; to dissolve the enmities of men; to raise men to honors ; to carry or take away infirmities. But in what manner they appear, it's spoken already in the former book of Magical Ceremonies.

Confiderations of Munday.

THe Angel of Munday, his Sigil, Planet, the Signe of the Planet, and name of the first heaven.

Gabriel.

Shamain.

The Angels of Munday.

Gabriel. Michael. Samael.

The Angels of the Air ruling on Munday.

Arcan, King.

His Minsters.

Bilet. Missabu. Abuzaha.

The

The winde which the said Angels of the Air are subject to.

The West-winde.

The Angels of the first heaven, ruling on Munday, which ought to be called from the four parts of the world.

From the East.

Gabriel.   Gabrael.   Madiel.
Deamiel.   Janael.

From the West.

Sachiel.   Zaniel.   Habaiel.
Bachanael.   Corabael.

From the North.

Mael.   Vvael.   Valnum.
Baliel.   Balay.   Humastran.

From the South.

Curaniel.   Dabriel.   Darquiel.
Hanun.   Anayl.   Vetuel.

The Perfume of Munday.

Aloes.

The Conjuration of Munday.

COnjuro & confirmo super vos Angeli fortes & boni, in nomine Adonay, Adonay, Adonay, Eie, Eie, Eie, Cados, Cados,

Cados,

Cados, Achim, Achim, Ja, Ja, Fortis, Ja, qui apparuis monte Sinai, cum glorificatione regis Adonay, Saday, Zebaoth, Anathay, Ya, Ya, Ya, Marinata, Abim, Jeia, qui maria creavit stagna & omnes aquas in secundo die, quasdam super cælos, & quasdam in terra. Sigillavit mare in al o nomine suo, & terminum, quam sibi posuit, non præter b t : & per nomina Angelorum, qui dominantur in primo exercitu, qui serviunt Orphaniel Angelo magno, precioso & honorato: & per nomen Stellæ, quæ est Luna : & per nomina prædicta, super te conjuro, scilicet Gabriel, qui es præpositus diei. Lunæ secundo quod pro me labores & adimpleas, &c. As in the Conjuration of Sunday.

The Spirits of the Air of Munday, are subject to the West-winde, which is the winde of the Moon : their nature is to give silver;to convey things from place to place;to make horses swift, and to disclose the secrets of persons both present and future : but in what manner they appear, you may see in the former book.

Considerations of Tuesday.

THe Angel of Tuesday, his sigil, his Planet, the Signe governing that Planet, and the name of the fifth heaven.

Samael..

Machon.

The Angels of Tuesday.

Samael. Satael. Amabiel.

The

The Angels of the Air ruling on Tuesday.

Samax, King.

His Ministers.

Carmax. Ismoli. Passran.

The winde to which the said Angels are subject.

The East-winde.

The Angels of the fifth heaven ruling on Tuesday, which ought to be called from the four parts of the world.

At the East.

Friagne. Guael. Damael.
Calzas. Arragon.

At the West.

Lama. Astagna. Lobquin.
Soncas. Jazel Isiael.
Irel.

At the North.

Rahumel. Hyniel. Rayel.
Seraphiel. Mathiel. Fraciel.

At the South.

Sacriel. Janiel. Galdel.
Osael. Vianuel. Zaliel.

The

The Perfume of Tuesday.

Pepper.

The Conjuration of Tuesday.

COnjuro & confirmo super vos, Angeli fortes & sancti , per nomen Ya, Ya, Ya, He, He, He, Va, Hy, Hy, Ha, Ha, Ha, Va, Va, Va, An, An, An, Aie, Aie, Aie, El, Ay, Elibra, Eloim, Eloim : & per nomina ipsius alti Dei, qui fecit aquam aridam apparere, & vocavit terram, & produxit arbores , & herbas de ea, & sigillavit super eam cum precioso, honorato, metuendo & sancto nomine suo : & per nomen angelorum dominantium in quinto exercitu , qui serviunt Acimoy Angelo magno, forti, potenti, & honorato : & per nomen Stellæ , quæ est Mars : & per nomina præd Eta conjuro super te Samael, Angele magne , qui prapositus es diei Martis : & per nomina Adonay, Dei vivi & veri, quod pro me labores , & adimpleas , &c. As in the Conjuration of Sunday.*

The Spirits of the Air of Tuesday are under the East-winde : their nature is to cause wars , mortality, death and combustions ; and to give two thousand Souldiers at a time ; to bring death , infirmities or health. The manner of their appearing you may see in the former book.

Considerations of Wednesday.

THe Angel of Wednesday, his Sigil. Planet , the Signe governing that Planet, and the name of the second heaven.

Ra-

The Angels of Wednesday.

Raphael. Miel. Seraphiel.

The Angels of the Air ruling on Wednesday.

Mediat or *Modiat, Rex.*

Ministers.

Suquinos. Sallales.

The winde to which the said Angels of the Air are subject.

The Southwest-winde.

The Angels of the second heaven governing Wednesday, which ought to be called from the four parts of the world.

At the East.

Mathlai. Tarmiel. Baraborat.

At the West.

Jeresous. Mitraton.

At

At the North.

Thiel. Rael. J riahel.
Venahel. Velel. Abuiori.
Ucirnhel.

At the South.

Milliel. Nelapa. Babel.
Caluel. Vel. Laquel.

The Fumigation of Wednesday.
Maſtick.

The Conjuration of Wedneſday.

COnjuro & confirmo vos angeli fortes, ſanĉti & potentes, in nomine fortu, metuendiſſimi & ben diĉti Ja, Adonay, Eloim, Saday, Saday, Saday, Eie, Eie, Eie, Aſanſie, Aſaraie : & in nomine Adonay Dei Iſrael, qui creavit luminaria magna, ad diſtinguendum diem à noĉte : & per nomen omnium Angelorum deſervientium in exercitu ſecundo coram Tetra Angelo majori, atq, ſortu & potenti : & per nomen Stellæ, quæ eſt Mercurius: & per nomen Sigilli, quæ ſigillatur a Deo fortiſſimo & honorato : per omnia prædiĉta ſuper te Raphael Angele magne, conjuro, qui es præpoſitus die: quarta : & per no- en ſanĉtum quod erat ſcrip um in fronte Aaron ſacerdotu alt ſſimi creatoris : & per nomina Angelorum , qu' in gratiam Salvatoris confirmati ſunt: & per nomen ſedu Animalium , habentium ſenas alas , quòd pro me labo et, &c. As in the Conjuration of Sunday.

The Spirits of the Air of Wedneſday are ſubjeĉt to the South-weſt-winde : their nature is to give all Metals ; to reveal all earthly things paſt, preſent and to come ; to pacifie judges, to give victories in war, to re-edifie, and teach experiments and all decayed Sciences, and to change bodies mixt of

Ele-

Elements conditionally out of one into another; to give infirmities or health; ro raife the poor, and caft down the high ones; to binde or lofe Spirits; to open locks or bolts: fuch-kinde of Spirits have the operation of others, but not in their perfect power, but in virtue or knowledge. In what manner they appear, it is before fpoken.

Confiderations of Thurfday.

THe Angel of Thurfday, his Sigil, Planet, the Signe of the Planet, and the name of the fixth heaven.

Sachiel. ♃ ⊕ ♓

Zebul.

The Angels of Thurfday.

Sachiel, Caftiel, Afafiel.

The Angels of the Air governing Thurfday.

Suth, Rex.

Minifters.

Maguth, Guirix.

The winde which the faid Angels of the Air are under.

The South-winde.

But becaufe there are no Angels of the Air to be found a-

O   bove

bove the fifth heaven, therefore on Thursday say the prayers following in the four parts of the world.

At the Eaft.

O Deus magne & excelſe, & honorate, per infinita ſecula.

At the Weſt.

O Deus ſapiens, & clare, & juſte, ac divina clementia : ego rogo te piiſſime Pater, quòd meam petitionem, quòd meum opus, & meum laborem hodie debeam complere, & perfectè intelligere. Tu qui vivis & regnas per infinita ſecula ſeculorum, Amen.

At the North..

O Deus potens, fortis, & ſine principio.

At the South.

O Deus potents & miſericors.

The Perfume of Thurſday.

Saffron.

The Conjuration of Thurſday.

COnjuro & confirmo ſuper vos, Angeli ſancti, per nomen, Ca-dos, Cados, Cados, Eſchereie, Eſchereie, Eſchereie, Hatim Ja, fortis firmator ſeculorum, Cantine, Jaym, Janic, Anic, Cal-bat, Sabbac, Beriſay, Alnaym : & per nomen Adonay, qui cre-avit piſces reptilia in oquis, & aves ſuper faciem terræ, volantes verſus cœlos die quinto : & per nomina Angelorum ſerventium in ſexto exercitu coram paſtore Angelo ſancto & magno & potenti principe : & per nomen ſtellæ, quæ eſt Jupiter : & per nomen Sigilli
ſui:

*fui : & per nomen Adonay, summi Dei, omnium creatoris : &
per nomen omnium stellarum , & per vim & virtutem earum:
& per nomina prædicta, conjuro te Sachiel Angele magne, qui es
præpositus diei Jovis, ut pro me labores,* &c. As in the Conjuration of the Lords day.

The Spirits of the Air of Thursday, are subject to the
South-winde; their nature is to procure the love of women;
to cause men to be merry and joyful ; to pacifie strife and
contentions ; to appease enemies ; to heal the diseased, and
to disease the whole ; and procureth losses, or taketh them
away. Their manner of appearing is spoken of already.

Confiderations of Friday.

THe Angel of Friday, his Sigil, his Planet, the Signe governing that Planet, and name of the third heaven.

Anaël.　　　　　　　　　　　　　*Sagun.*

The Angels of Friday.

Anael. Rachiel. Sachiel.

The Angels of the Air reigning on Friday.

Sarabotes, King.

Ministers.

Amabiel. Aba. Abalidoth. Flaef.

　　　　　　　　The

The winde which the said Angels of the Air are under.

The West-winde.

Angels of the third heaven, ruling on Friday, which are to be called from the four parts of the world.

At the East.

Setchiel. Chedusitaniel. Corat.
Tamael. Tenaciel.

At the West.

Turiel. Coniel. Babiel.
Kadie. . Maltiel. Huphaltiel.

At the North.

Peniel. Penael. Penat.
Raphael. Raniel. Doremiel.

At the South.

Porna. Sachiel. Chermiel.
Samael. Santanael. Famiel.

The Perfume of Friday.

Pepperwort.

The Conjuration of Friday.

COnjuro & confirmo super vos Angeli fortes, sancti atq̃ potentes, in nomine On, Hey, Heya, Ja, Je, Adonay, Saday,
&

& in nomine Saday,qui creavit quadrupedia & anamalia reptilia, & homines in sexto die, & Adæ dedit potestatem super omnia animalia : unde benedictum sit nomen creatoris in locu suo : & per nomina Angelorum servientium in tertio exercitu, coram Dagiel Angelo magno, principe forti atq́, potenti : & per nomen Stellæ quæ est Venus : & per Sigillum ejus, quod quidem est sanctum : & per nomina prædicta conjuro super te Anael, qui es præpositus diei sexta, ut pro me labores, &c. As before in the Conjuration of Sunday.

The Spirits of the Air of Friday are subject to the West-winde ; their nature is to give silver ; to excite men, and incline them to luxury ; to reconcile enemies through luxury ; and to make marriages ; to allure men to love women ; to cause, or take away infirmities ; and to do all things which have motion.

Considerations of Saturday, or the Sabbath day.

THe Angel of Saturday, his Seal, his Planet, and the Signe governing the Planet.

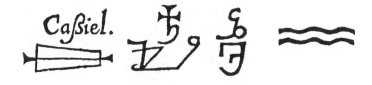

Cassiel.

The Angels of Saturday.

Cassiel. Machatan. Uriel.

The

The Angels of the Air ruling on Saturday.

Maymon, King.

Minifters.

Abumalith. *Affaibi.* *Balidet.*

The winde which the faid Angels of the Air aforefaid are under.

The Southweft-winde.

The Fumigation of Saturday.

Sulphur.

It is already declared in the Confideration of Thurfday, That there are no Angels ruling the Air, above the fifth heaven : therefore in the four Angles of the world, ufe thofe Orations which you fee applied to that purpofe on Thurfday.

The Conjuration of Saturday.

COnjuro & confirmo fuper vos Caphriel vel Caffiel, Machatori, & Seraquiel Angeli fortes & potentes : & per nomen Adonay, Adonay, Adonay, Eie, Eie, Eie, Acim, Acim, Acim, Cados, Cados, Ina vel Ima, Ima, Saclay, Ja, Sar , Domini formatoris feculorum, qui in feptimo die quievt : & per illum qui in beneplacito fuo filiis Ifrael in hareditatem obfervandum dedit, ut eum firmiter cuftodirent, & fanctificarent, ad habendem inde bonam in alio feculo remunerationem : & per nomina Angelorum fervientium in exercitu feptimo Pooel Angelo magno & potenti principi: & per nomen ftella qua eft Saturnus : & per fanctum Sigillum ejus : & per nomina pradicta conjuro fuper te Caphriel, qui
                                                                            prapo-

præpofitus es dici feptima,qua eft dies Sabbati,quòd pro me labores,
&c. As is fet down in the Conjuration of the Lords day.

The Spirits of the Air of Saturday are fubject to the Southweft-winde : the nature of them is to fow difcords, hatred,
evil thoughts and cogitations;to give leave freely, to flay and
kill every one,and to lame or maim every member.Their manner of appearing is declared in the former book.

Tables of the Angels of the Hours, ac-
cording to the courfe of the dayes.

Sunday.

Hours of the day.	Angels of the hours,	Hours of the day.	Angels of the hours.
1. Yayn.	Michael.	7. Ourer.	Samael.
2. Janor.	Anael.	8. Tanic.	Michael.
3. Nafnia.	Raphael.	9. Neron.	Anael.
4. Salla.	Gabriel.	10. Jayon.	Raphael.
5. Sadedali.	Caffiel.	11. Abay.	Gabriel.
6. Thamur.	Sachiel.	12. Natalon.	Caffiel.

Hours of the night.	Angels of the hours,	Hours of the night.	Angels of the hours.
1. Beron.	Sachiel.	7. Netos.	Caffiel.
2. Barol.	Samael.	8. Tafrac.	Sachiel.
3. Tha·u.	Michael.	9. Saffur.	Samael.
4. Athir.	Anael.	10. Aglo.	Michael.
5. Mathun.	Raphael.	11. Calerna.	Anael.
6. Rana.	Gabriel.	12. Salam.	Raphael.

Munday.

MUNDAY.

Hours of the day.	Angels of the hours.	Hours of the night.	Angels of the hours.
1. *Tayn.*	*Gabriel.*	1. *Beron.*	*Anael.*
2. *Janor.*	*Cassiel.*	2. *Barol.*	*Raphael.*
3. *Nasnia.*	*Sachiel.*	3 *Thaun.*	*Gabriel.*
4. *Salla.*	*Samael.*	4. *Athir.*	*Cassiel.*
5. *Sadedali.*	*Michael.*	5. *Mathon.*	*Sachiel.*
6. *Thamur.*	*Anael.*	6. *Rana.*	*Samael.*
7. *Ourer.*	*Raphael.*	7. *Netos.*	*Michael.*
8. *Tanic.*	*Gabriel.*	8. *Tafrac.*	*Anael.*
9. *Neron.*	*Cassiel.*	9. *Saffur.*	*Raphael.*
10. *Jayon.*	*Sachiel.*	10. *Aglo.*	*Gabriel.*
11. *Abay.*	*Samael.*	11. *Calerna.*	*Cassiel.*
12. *Natalon.*	*Michael.*	12. *Salam.*	*Sachiel.*

TUESDAY.

Hours of the day.	Angels of the hours.	Hours of the night.	Angels of the hours.
1. *Tayn.*	*Samael.*	1. *Beron.*	*Cassiel.*
2. *Janor.*	*Michael.*	2. *Barol.*	*Sachiel.*
3. *Nasnia.*	*Anael.*	3. *Thanu.*	*Samael.*
4. *Salla.*	*Raphael.*	4. *Athir.*	*Michael.*
5. *Sadedal.*	*Gabriel.*	5. *Mathon.*	*Anael.*
6. *Thamur.*	*Cassiel.*	6. *Rana.*	*Raphael.*
7. *Ourer.*	*Sachiel.*	7. *Netos.*	*Gabriel.*
8. *Tanic.*	*Samael.*	8. *Tafrac.*	*Cassiel.*
9. *Neron.*	*Michael.*	9. *Suffur.*	*Sachiel.*
10. *Jayon.*	*Anael.*	10. *Aglo.*	*Samael.*
11. *Abay.*	*Raphael.*	11. *Calerna.*	*Michael.*
12. *Natalon.*	*Gabriel.*	12. *Salam.*	*Anael.*

Wednes-

WEDNESDAY.

Hours of the day.	Angels of the hours.	Hours of the night.	Angels of the hours.
1. *Yayn.*	*Raphael.*	1. *Beron.*	*Michael.*
2. *Janor.*	*Gabriel.*	2. *Barol.*	*Anael.*
3. *Nasnia.*	*Cassiel.*	3. *Thanu.*	*Raphael.*
4. *Salla.*	*Sachiel.*	4. *Athir.*	*Gabriel.*
5. *Sadedali.*	*Samael.*	5. *Mathon.*	*Cassiel.*
6. *Thamur.*	*Michael.*	6. *Rana.*	*Sachiel.*
7. *Ourer.*	*Anael.*	7. *Netos.*	*Samael.*
8. *Tanic.*	*Raphael.*	8. *Tafrac.*	*Michael.*
9. *Neron.*	*Gabriel.*	9. *Saffur.*	*Anael.*
10. *Jayon.*	*Cassiel.*	10. *Aglo.*	*Raphael.*
11. *Abay.*	*Sachiel.*	11. *Calerna.*	*Gabriel.*
12. *Neron.*	*Samael.*	12. *Salam.*	*Cassiel.*

THURSDAY.

Hours of the day.	Angels of the hours.	Hours of the night.	Angels of the hours.
1. *Yayn.*	*Sachiel.*	1. *Beron.*	*Gabriel.*
2. *Janor.*	*Samael.*	2. *Barol.*	*Cassiel.*
3. *Nasnia.*	*Michael.*	3. *Thanu.*	*Sachiel.*
4. *Salla.*	*Anael.*	4. *Athir.*	*Samael.*
5. *Sadedali.*	*Raphael.*	5. *Maton.*	*Michael*
6. *Thamur.*	*Gabriel.*	6. *Rana.*	*Anael.*
7. *Ourer.*	*Cassiel.*	7. *Netos.*	*Raphael.*
8. *Tanic.*	*Sachiel.*	8. *Tafrac.*	*Gabriel.*
9. *Neron.*	*Samael.*	9. *Saffur.*	*Cassiel.*
10. *Jayon.*	*Michael.*	10. *Aglo.*	*Sachiel.*
11. *Abay.*	*Anael.*	11. *Calerna.*	*Samael.*
12. *Natalon.*	*Raphael.*	12. *Salam.*	*Michael.*

P

Friday.

FRIDAY.

Hours of the day.	Angels of the hours.	Hours of the night.	Angels of the hours.
1. *Yayn.*	*Anael.*	1. *Beron.*	*Samael.*
2. *Janor.*	*Raphael.*	2. *Barol.*	*Michael.*
3. *Nafnia.*	*Gabriel.*	3. *Thanu.*	*Anael.*
4. *Salla.*	*Caffiel.*	4. *Athir.*	*Raphael.*
5. *Sadedali.*	*Sachiel.*	5. *Maton.*	*Gabriel.*
6. *Thamur.*	*Samael.*	6. *Rana.*	*Caffiel.*
7. *Ourer.*	*Michael.*	7. *Netos.*	*Sachiel.*
8. *Tanic.*	*Anael.*	8. *Tafrac.*	*Samael.*
9. *Neron.*	*Raphael.*	9. *Saffur.*	*Michael.*
10. *Jayon.*	*Gabriel.*	10. *Aglo.*	*Anael.*
11. *Abay.*	*Caffiel.*	11. *Calerna.*	*Raphael.*
12. *Natalon.*	*Sachiel.*	12. *Salam.*	*Gabriel.*

SATURDAY.

Hours of the day.	Angels of the hours.	Hours of the night.	Angels of the hours.
1. *Yayn.*	*Caffiel.*	1. *Beron.*	*Raphael.*
2. *Janor.*	*Sachiel.*	2. *Barol.*	*Gabriel.*
3. *Nafnia.*	*Samael.*	3. *Thanu.*	*Caffiel.*
4. *Salla.*	*Michael.*	4. *Athir.*	*Sachiel.*
5. *Sadedali.*	*Anael.*	5. *Maton.*	*Samael.*
6. *Thamur.*	*Raphael.*	6. *Rana.*	*Michael.*
7. *Ourer.*	*Gabriel.*	7. *Netos.*	*Anael.*
8. *Tanic.*	*Caffiel.*	8. *Tafrac.*	*Raphael.*
9. *Neron.*	*Sachiel.*	9. *Suffur.*	*Gabriel.*
10. *Jayon.*	*Samael.*	10. *Aglo.*	*Caffiel.*
11. *Abay.*	*Michael.*	11. *Calerna.*	*Sachiel.*
12. *Natalon.*	*Anael.*	12. *Salam.*	*Samael.*

But

But this is to be obſerved by the way, that the firſt hour of the day, of every Country, and in every ſeaſon whatſoever, is to be aſſigned to the Sun-riſing, when he firſt appeareth a-riſing in the horizon : and the firſt hour of the night is to be the thirteenth hour, from the firſt hour of the day. But of theſe things it is ſufficiently ſpoken.

FINIS.

Iſagoge,

ISAGOGE:

An Introductory Difcourfe of the nature of fuch Spirits as are exercifed in the
fublunary Bounds; their Original, Names, Offices, Illufions, Power, Prophefies, Miracles ; and how
they may be expelled and driven away.

By *Geo. Pictorius Villinganus* Dr. in Phyfick.

In a Difcourfe between
Castor and Pollux.

Caftor. He *Greeks* do report, that *Caftor & Pollux have both proceeded from one egge*;
but this I fcarcely credit, by reafon of
the difference of your mindes ; for
thou affecteft the heavens , but fhe
meditates upon the earth and flaugh-
ters.

Pollux. And from thence perhaps was derived that argument, *That liberty of lying was alwaies affigned to the Greeks.*

Caftor. Principally. *Pollux.*

Pollux. But it is not to be supposed, that the *Greeks* are vain in all things ; but as many others, when they speak out of a three-footed thing; whereof also the Poet *Ovid* speaks in verse,

———*Nec fingunt omnia Græci.*

Homo ho-   *Castor.* In this proverb I protest they are most true, with-
nini Deus.   out any exception, that is, ἄιθρωπ ᾦ ἀιθρώπυ δαιμόνιον. that is,
One man to another is a devil.

Pollux. Wherefore believest thou this to be most true, *Castor ?*

Homo ho-   *Castor.* Truely, that man to man is a devil and a ravening
mini diabo-   wolf, daily events do most certainly prove , if we do but
lus.   note the treacheries that one man invents daily against another, the robberies, thefts, plunderings, rapes, slaughters, deceits, adulteries, and an hundred vipers of this nature; the fathers persecute the son, with a serpentine and poisonous biting; one friend seeks to devour another , neither can the guest be safe with his host.

Pollux. I confess it is truth thou speakest ; but for ought I hear, thou dost mis understand the Etymologie of the word compared in this Proverb ; for *Dæmon* here is not an horrible or odious name , but the name of one that doth administer
Plin.lib.2. help or succor unto another, and whom *Pliny* calleth a God.
chap.7.

Castor. Therefore dost thou affirm the word *Dæmon* in this Proverb to signifie any other then a cunning and malicious accuser ?

Pollux. Thou hast not shot besides the mark: for, that there are more *Dæmons* then that sublunary one which thou understandest, every one may easily perceive , who hath not negligently read the opinions of the most excellent *Plato.*

Castor. I desire therefore , that thou wouldst not conceal such his writings ; but that I may apprehend the marrow thereof.

Pollux. I will embrace such thy desire, for truely I do delight to treat with thee concerning this subject ; mark therefore, and give attention.   *Plato*

Plato divided the orders of Devils or Spirits into three
degrees, which as they are diſtinct in the greatneſs of their
dignity, ſo alſo they are different in the diſtance and holding
of their places. And the firſt order he aſcribeth to thoſe Spirits whoſe bodies are nouriſhed of the moſt pure element of
Air, wrought and joyned together, in a manner, as it were
with ſplendid threeds, not having ſo much reference to the
element of fire, that they may be perſpicuous to the ſight;
neither do they ſo much participate of the earth, that they
may be touched or felt; and they do inhabit the Cœleſtial
Theater, attending and waiting on their Prince, not to be declared by any humane tongue, or beyond the commands of
the moſt wiſe God.

But the other degree is derived from thoſe Spirits which
Apuleius termeth rational animals, paſſive in their minde, and
eternal in their time, underſtanding the apoſtate Spirits ſpread
abroad from the bounds and borders of the Moon, unto us
under the dominion of their Prince *Beelzebub*, which before the fall of *Lucifer* had pure clarified bodies; and now,
like unto the former, do wander up and down, after their
tranſgreſſion, in the form of an aiery quality.

Castor. Theſe I do not conceive are underſtood in the
Greek Proverb: for theſe do hurt, and are the accuſers and be-
trayers of men. But proceed.

Pollux. The third degree of Spirits is of a divine deitie,
which is called by *Hermes*, A divine miracle to man, if he do
not degenerate from the Kingly habit of his firſt form; whom
therefore of this kinde the *Greeks* and *Plato* have called *Dæ-*
mons, that is, God; and that man may be like unto God, and
profitable and commodious one to another; and ſo alſo (the
Syrian being witneſs) we have known *Plato* himſelf to have
been called *Damon*, becauſe he had ſet forth very many things
of very high matters, for the good of the Commonwealth;
and ſo likewiſe *Ariſtotle*, becauſe he very largely diſputed of
ſublunaries, and all ſuch things as are ſubject to motion and
ſence. *Homer* calleth God and evil Spirits, *Demons*, without
putting a diſcrimination.

Castor.

Castor. Thou haft committed the ship to the waves, *Pollux* ; therefore ceafe not to proceed, and declare fomething more concerning the Office and imployment of thefe Spirits, to whom *Plato* attributeth the fecond degree, and calleth them Lunaries.

Pollux. What fhall I fay ?

Castor. In the firft place, declare wherefore thou haft before termed thefe Spirits cunning and much knowing Accufers.

Why the devil is faid to have much knowledge.

Pollux. Saint *Augustine* unfoldeth this difficulty, and faith, That *a Devil doth fo far fignifie the cunning and much knowing quickneß and vivacity of his deceitful wit, that by the congruent and agreeable feminal permixtures of elements, he doth fo know the fecrets and unknown vertues of men, as thofe things which may be effected and wrought by themfelves fucceffively and leifurely according to the courfe of nature, he by a fpeedy hafting or forcing of the works of nature, or by his own art, fooner bringeth the fame to paß.* An example hereof he giveth in the wife men of *Pharaoh,* who immediately brought forth frogs and ferpents at the commandment of the King, which nature more flowly and leifurely procreateth.

Castor. Thou haft excellently anfwered to the queftion, *Pollux* ; but adde fome thing concerning the original of thofe Spirits which do refut and refufe vertue ; for oftentimes doubting, I have been perfwaded that fuch Erynnes as are from God, do not appear out of the earth.

Pollux. The Ecclefiaftical Scripture everywhere maketh mention of the rifing of them; but I will unfold fuch a doubt: and there do arife many and various opinions of writers, but

Lib.2.
distinct.7.

more commonly *Peter Lombardus* in his book of Sentences, draweth his Allegations out of St. *Augustine* upon *Genefis* ; to wit, That *the Divel was before his fall an Archangel, and had a fine tender body, compofed by God, cut of the ferenity and pureft matter of the Skie and Air ; but then after his fall from an Archangel, he was made an Apoftate, and his body no more fine and fubtil ; but his body was made that it might fuffer the effect of a more groß fubftance, from the quality of the more obfcure, dark, and*

fpiffious

ſpiſſious Air, which body alſo was ſtricken and aſtoniſhed with the raging madneß of pride, did draw away very many which were then *Angels* with him into his ſervice and bondage, that they might be made *Devils,* who for him in this troubleſome world do exerciſe their ſervile courſes for him, and they do compel the inhabitants therein, or rather entice them ; and to this purpoſe they undertake various endeavours, and do attempt various and manifold horrible ſtudies, that are abominable unto God, and they ſerve in ſlavery and thraldom to Beelzebub their Prince, and are held in moſt ſtrong captivity.

Caſtor. What ? Have we the fall of this Archangel no-where elſe in holy writ, but in the writings of St. *Auguſtine ?*

Pollux. We have alſo the fall of other Angels.

Caſtor. Where ?

Pollux. In *Eſaias,* to whom thou ſhalt give the honour of an Evangeliſt, rather then a Prophet, becauſe he ſo fully and plainly foretold of Chriſt and his kingdom: he maketh mention hereof in his 14 Chapter. And we have them alſo ſpoken of by the Apoſtle *Peter,* when he ſaith, *God ſpared not his Angels which ſinned.* 2 Epiſt. 2.

The fall of *Lucifer* in Scripture.

Caſtor. Have the Devils a ſelect place appointed them by God, which they inhabit ?

Pollux. Peter the head of the Church, in the place before quoted, affirmeth *them to be caſt headlong into hell, reſerved in the chains of hell, from whence* (as Corteſius ſaith) *they never go out, unleß it be to tempt, provoke and delude men.* But St. *Auguſtine* the Champion of Chriſt, in his book of *The Agony of a Chriſtian,* teacheth, That *theſe kinde of Spirits do inhabit in the ſublunary region.* And in his 49 Epiſt. he ſets forth, That *the moſt dark and obſcure part of the Air, is prodeſtinated unto them as a priſon, that they may the more neerly caſt their nets of enticing and detaining.*

What place the devils have appointed.

Caſtor. Origen hath taught, That *the puniſhments of the Devils are appointed for a time* ; what ſaiſt thou to this?

Pollux. What ſhall I ſay ? unleſs I ſhould bewail and deplore the opinion of ſo great a man.

The torments of the devils are everlaſting.

Caſtor. Wherefore ſhouldſt thou do ſo?

Q

Pol. Truely if they have hardened themselves in wickedness, time cannot purge nor cleanse them; or if they never so much desire it, they can never be able to accomplish it; for there is no space of repentance, nor time to recal that which is past, given unto them.

Castor. Thou hast now declared that the Archangel that became an apostate, did draw away very many other Angels with him in his fall, that they might become Devils: could not he of his own proper inseparate malice after his fall sufficiently rule over his own Province, without the Angels that fell with him?

Why the Devil hath familiars.

Pol. He could: but being allured by that pride, which made him so arrogantly affect the Majesty of God, he did so far strive to be like unto God, that he chose very many Ministers unto himself, to which in general he doth not commit all things he would have effected, but diverse things to divers Ministers, as may be gathered from the *Hebrew* Astronomers.

Dæmons Jovii or Antemerid.

Those which we call *Jovii, & Antemeridianii,* which are false Gods, that is, lyers, which desire to be esteemed and adored for Gods, and they are appointed as Servants and slaves to the Devil their Prince, that they might allure the people of the earth into a common love of themselves, which *Plato* saith, *Is the fountain of all wickedness, that they may aspire to authority and greatness, covet to be gorgeously clothed, to be called Monarchs of the earth in perpetual power, and Gods upon earth.* It

Mat.4.

is said, That it was one of these that spoke to our Saviour, shewing him all the Kingdoms of the earth, saying, *All these things will I give thee, if thou wilt fall down and worship me.*

The Southern Spirits.

Castor. Certainly these *Meridiani,* I have almost declared to appear a madness in *Libicus, Sappho,* and *Dioclesian* the Emperour, who accounted, the utmost degree of blessedness was, to be reputed for Gods.

Libicus, Sapho and Dioclesian, Gods. The Comment of Sapho.

Pol. Truely, this is a certain natural foolishness of the minde, and of humane nature: he began, having taken certain little birds to teach them by little and little to pronounce humane words, & say, μιγαι Θεός Ψιзor, that is, *Sapho is a great God.* Which birds when they could pronounce the words

per-

perfectly, he fent them abroad for this end and purpofe, that flying everywhere abroad, they might repeat thofe words; and the people which were ignorant of his deceitful invention, were drawn to believe, that thofe words were fpoken by divine inftinct, and thereupon adore and worfhip him for a God. The other would compel his Subjects hereunto, that proftrating themfelves down, and lifting up their hands, they fhould worfhip him as Almighty.

Caftor. But are not they the captives of the Devil, who ftir up wars, which are called *bloody men* in Scripture? *Pfalm·55.*

Pol. The Martialifts of the North part of the world, are called Executioners of vengeance, Authors of devaftations, and fowers of evil, working and executing judgement with *Afmodeus*, for their King *Abaddon* or *Apollyon*, whom St. *John* in his *Revelation*, mentioneth to be banifhed and expelled; for thefe Spirits have committed to them rapines, hatred, envy, robberies, wrath, anger, the excitements and provocations to fin, war and fury; fometimes making the Meridional Spirits their Meffengers. And *Arioch* the Spirit of vengeance, whofe work is to caufe difcord among brethren, to break wedlock, and diffolve conjugal love, that it's impoffible to be renewed; of thefe mention is made in the 39 Chapter of *Ecclefiafticus.* And *Efaias* the heavenly Prophet fpeaketh of other Spirits fent from God to the *Ægyptians* to make them erre, which were Spirits of darknefs, that is, of lyes; and this kinde of Spirit they call *Bolichim.*

The Spirits of the North.

Merid·an Spirit.

Ecclus. 39. 28.

Spirits of darknefs.

Caftor. Is unlawful venery, and exceffive gluttony, alfo to be imputed to the Devils?

Pol. Yes chiefly; for *Iamblichus* doth affert, That *the Spirits of the water, of the weftern part of the world, and fome meridional Spirits, are predeftinated to this purpofe; fuch as* Nefrach *and* Kellen, *that do fo frame and contrive unlawful loves, which produce fhame and difhonefty, revellings and gurmandizings, furfetings with exceffive drunkennefs, wanton dances, gluttony and vomiting: they wander about lakes, fifh-ponds and rivers, and which are the worft, foul and moft fraudulent kinde of Spirits: and by* Alcinach *an occidental Spirit, he caufeth fhipwracks, tem-*

Occidental Spirits.

pefts,

pests, earthquakes, hail, rain, and frequently subverteth and o-
verturneth ships : and if he will appear visible, he appeareth and
is seen in the shape of a woman. The *Hebrew* Astronomers before

The spirits
of the air
do infect
the air.
spoken of, do say, That *the Spirits of the Air do cause thunders,
lightnings and thunderbolts, that so they might corrupt and infect
the Air, and produce pestilence and destruction.* Of such kinde
of Spirits St. *John* makes mention in the 9 Chapter of the
Revelation, having *Meceris* for their tutelar, which is a Spirit
causing heat in the time of noon. St. *Paul* calleth him,
The Prince of the power of the Air, and *the Spirit that ruleth in
the children of disobedience.*

*Ephes.*2.

Castor. Are there so many monsters in *Phlegeton, Pollux* ?

Pol. And many more ; for the same *Hebrew* Assertors do

Spirits of
fire.
declare and maintain, That *there are Spirits of the fiery element,
raging about like the fierce Panthers, which are conversant under
the lunary regions, that whatsoever is committed to them, they
forthwith execute the same.* And there are Spirits of the earth,

Spirits of
the earth.
which inhabit in groves, woods and wildernesses, and are the plague
and mischief of hunters ; and sometimes they frequent open fields,
endeavouring to seduce travellers and passengers out of their right
way, or to deceive them with false and wicked illusions ; or else they
seek to afflict men with a hurtful melancholy, to make them furious
or mad, that they may hurt them, and sometimes almost kill them.
The chief of these are Sanyaab and Achimael, which are oriental
Spirits, a kinde unapt for wickedness, by reason of the constancy of

Subterra-
nean Spi-
rits.
their dispositions. There are also subterranean Spirits, which do
inhabit in dens and cavernes of the earth, and in remote concavi-
ties of mountaines, that they might invade deep pits, and the
bowels of the earth ; these do dig up metals, and keep treasures,
which oftentimes they do transport from one place to another,
lest any man should make use thereof: they stir up windes with flash-
ing flames of fire : they smite the foundations of buildings,
acting frightful daunces in the night, from which they suddenly
vanish away, with making a noise and sounds of bells, thereby causing fear in the beholders ; and sometimes dissembling, and faining
themselves to be the Souls of the dead : notwithstanding they are
ignorant in compassing their deceits upon women ; of which company

ny the Negromancers do fay, is *Gazael, Fegor and Anarazol,*
Meridian Spirits.

Caftor. How warily ought a man to walk, *Pollux,* amongft
fo many ginnes and fnares ?

Pol. A man never walketh fafely, unlefs he forrifie and A man ne-
ftrengthen himfelf with the armour of God,which is, *That his* ver walk-
loynes be girt about with truth, and having on *the breft-plate of* eth fafe.
righteoufnefs, let him walk with his feet fhod with the preparation of Eph 6.
the Gofpel of peace,and let him take the fheild of faith,and the hel-
met of falvation, whereby he *fhall dafh in peices all the darts of his*
adverfary. But hear further:There are alfo befides thefe,other
lying Spirits (although they are all lyers) yet thefe are more
apt to lye; they are called *Pythons,* from whence *Apollo* is called *Pythius.* They have a Prince,of whom mention is made 1 Kings 11.
in the book of the *Kings,*where it is faid, *I will be a lying Spi-*
rit in the mouth of all thy Prophets ; from whom the Spirits of
iniquity do but a little differ, which alfo are called veffels of
wrath. *Belial,*whom they have interpreted to be without any
equal, and *Paul* calleth him an Apoftate or tranfgreffor,is fil-
thily infervient for the worft inventions. *Plato* affirmeth
Theut to have been fuch a one, who was the firft that found
out and invented Playes and Dice : to whom we will joyne
the Monk, who invented the ufe of Gunpowder,in his En- *Pulvis py-*
gins of war. Of thefe *Jacob* makes mention in *Genefis,* where *rium.*
he bleffeth his Sons : he faith, *Simeon and Levi are bloody* Gen. 49.
veffels of iniquity ; *Oh my foul,come not thou into their counfels.*
The *Pfalmift* termeth thefe Spirits, *veffels of death* ; *Efaias* calleth them, *veffels of fury* ; *Jeremiah,* *veffels of wrath* ; and E- Efai.7.
zekiel calleth them, *veffels of death and deftruction.* The Negromancers do call the faid *Belial, Chodar,* *an oriental Spirit,*
which hath under him alfo the Spirits of Juglers, who do imitate
and endeavour to act *miracles,* that they may feduce falfe *Magi-*
cians and wicked perfons. It is apparently manifeft, that the
Serpent which deceived *Eve,* was fuch a feducer, and *Satan*
is his Prince, of whom it is fpoken in the *Revelation,* that *he*
fhould deceive the whole world. And fuch a one was he,that at
Tubinga, in the fight of many people devoured a whole Cha-
riot and fome horfes.   *Caftor.*

Castor. And what shall be the end of these false Prophets, and workers of wickedness? I can scarce believe that there is any angle or corner in the whole fabrick of the world, that is free from them.

Pol. Scarce the smallest mite that may be seen.

The world is the receptacle of *Castor.* Therefore dost thou truely call the world the receptacle of those false lights.

Pol. If it were not most safely purged with the Sword of the word of God, it would forthwith be worse.

Castor. Without doubt.

Pol. Nevertheless I have seen many that remain, whom I have not yet inscribed in this frantique Catalogue.

devils, false accusers, and spies. *Castor.* Who are they?

Pol. False accusers and spies, obedient to *Astaroth,* who is called a Devil among the *Greeks;* and *John* calleth him the accuser of the brethren. Also there are tempters and deceivers that lie in wait to deceive, who are present with every man, and these we term evil Angels, which have *Mammon* for their King, & they do affect men with an insatiable avarice & thirsty desire after authority and dominion. There are others *Lucifugi,* fliers from the light. called *Lucifugi,* which fly from the light, never appearing in the day, but delighting in darkness, maliciously vexing and troubling men, and sometimes by Gods permission, either by some touching, breathing or inspiration, do hurt to them; but truely they are a kind which are unapt for to do much wickedness, because they eschew & fly from any communication with men. *Pliny* the second relates, that *there was such a* A horrible apparition of a Spirit in the house of Anthenodorus. *one at* Athens, *in a certain spacious house, which* Anthenodorus *the Philosopher happened to purchase.* And *Suetonius* in his sixth book of *Cæsar,* makes mention of another to have long continued in the garden of *Lamianus.*

Castor. I desire, if it be not too irksome to thee, declare unto me what *Pliny* speaketh concerning this Spirit of *Anthenodorus.*

Pol. The story is something long and prolixious, yet it shall not much trouble me to relate it. It is thus: *Pliny* in the seventh book of his *Epistles* writeth, *Of a certain large*

spa-

fpacious houſe at Athens, *which no body would inhabit by reaſon of the noɑurnal incurſions of Spirits,which were ſo formidable to the inhabitants, that ſometimes in the day-time, and when they were watching, they would caſt them into dreams, ſo alwayes, that the ſhapes & forms which they then ſaw,were ever preſent in their memory. Where at length a certain Philoſopher named* Anthenodorus *happened to purchaſe that houſe, and prepared and furniſhed the ſame for himſelf to dwell in ; and becauſe all men had an evil ſuſpition of that houſe, he forthwith commanded his ſervants to provide him a bed and tables, that after he had compleated and finiſhed his ſtudy he might go to bed. He therefore(ſaith* Pliny *when he went in (in the evening) and applied himſelf to his ſtudy, ſuddenly heard the locks to ſhake open,and the chains to be moved ; nevertheleß he did not lift up his eyes, nor ſtirred from his book, but ſtopped his ears with his fingers, leſt that furious tumult might work a vain fear upon him ; but the noiſe ſtill approaching neerer unto him, at length he looked up, and ſaw an effigies like unto a finger beckoning and calling unto him, which he little regarded, until it had touched him three times, and the noiſe drew neer unto the table ; and then he locked up, and took a light, and beheld the Spirit, as it were an old man, worn away with withered leanneß and deformity,his beard hanging down long, horrible and deformed hair, his legs and feet were as it were laden with chains and fetters : he went towards a gate which was bolted, and there left the Philoſopher, and vaniſhed away.*

Caſtor. What fearful things thou relateſt,*Pollux !* but what was the event of this ſad ſpectacle ?

Pol. The next day he related the whole matter to the Magiſtrates in order, as he had ſeen the ſame,admoniſhing them that they ſhould dig diligently about the threſhold of the door ; for there it was probable they might finde ſomething, which might cauſe the houſe to be quiet and habitable.

Caſtor. What did they finde ?

Pol. Having digged up the earth, *Pliny* ſaith, *They found a dead carcaß, bound and intangled in chains and fetters, his fleſh being conſumed with devouring time, which without delay they cauſed to be buried, according to the Chriſtian ceremonies.*

Caſtor.

Castor. But this being performed, did the house afterwards become quiet and habitable ?

Pol. Yes, very well.

They are possessed with madness, that destroy Churchyards.

The Spirit Zazalus & Eurynomus.

Castor. What madness therefore possesseth them who prophane and destroy Church-yards , where the sacred Organs of the holy and blessed Spirit do rest ; and do give the bones of the dead for meat to the Spirit *Zazelus*,of whom mention is made in the 3 of the *Kings* ; and we read in *Paufanias,* amongst the Histories of *Delphos* , that he was called *Eurynomus.*

Pol. Thou shalt finde, that the Governours of Cities that were of the opinion and judgement of Christians,did fubvert, deſtroy and prophane these holy places, that herein the youth might dance their mocking interludes,after the furious found of the drum or taber, and fing, *Io pean* ; or, there the poor inferiour old women did fell bafe trumpery or lupines , which God would have to be purged with holy prayers, for the falvation of fouls, or breaking of bread to the hungry.

Castor. But it is an impious and heatheniſh thing fo to have touched the anointed of God.

The Ceremony of burials was in great eſteem amongſt the Heathens.

Pol. And worſe then heatheniſh ; for the heathens did highly eſteem the Rites and Ceremonies of burials, as *Elpinor* is witneſs in *Homer*, where he yeildeth up his life ; and in *Homer* he fpeaketh to *Ulyſſes*, *I intreat thee, O Ulyſſes, to be mindeful of me*, *and not depart away hence and leave me uninterred, leſt that, not being ritely buried, I ſhall be made the wrath of the Gods.* And *Archita* the Philofopher in *Flaccus* , thus fpeaketh to the Mariner :

Horace 1 book of verſes.

Me quoque divexi Rapidus comes rionis
Illyrtsis Notus obruit undis.
Artu Nauta vagæ ne parce malignus harenæ,
Offibus & capiti inhumato.
Particulam dare ; fic quocunque minabitur Eurus
Fluctibus Hesperiis,Venufinæ
Plectantur filuæ, te sofpite multaque merces
Unde poteſt tibi defluat æquo.

Ab

Ab Jove Neptuno, sacri Custode Tarenti.
Negligis immeritis nocituram,
Post modo te natis fraudem committere: fors &,
Debita Jura vicesâ, superbæ
Te manent ipsum præcibus non linquar multis
Teçᵣ piacula nulla resolvent.

And *Palinurus* to *Æneas* in the sixth book of *Virgils Æ-neids.*

Nunc me fluctus habent versantᵣ in littore venti,
Quod te per Cœli jucundum lumen & auras
Per genitorem oro, per spem surgentis Juli.
Eripe me his invicte malis, aut tu mihi terram
Injice namᵣ potes.

Castor. Have the *Gentiles* so greatly esteemed the ceremo-ny of burials?

Pollux. Yes, very much ; for their Religion did hold that the Soul of a body which was uninterred, was void of any intelligible essence, and left to the power and command of a raging furious phansie, and subject to the torment and affliction of corporal qualities ; so that it being an aiery body, somtimes the departed shadow would speak unto his remaining friends, and somtimes evilly vex and torment his enemies with revenge, as in the Poet, *Dido* threatneth *Æneas*, saying,

Omnibus umbra locis adero dabis improbe penas.

The vain Religion of the Gentiles.　　Æneid.4.

Suetonius, as we have shown before, addeth the like concerning the dead body of *C. Caligula* the Emperour in the Garden of *Lamianus*, being not duly buried ; for this body, because it was onely covered with a light turff, did very much disquiet and trouble the possessors of the Garden, with violent incursions in the night ; until by his sisters, who were returned from banishment, it was taken up again and ritely and duly by them buried.

The History of c. caligula.

R　　　　　　　Castor

Castor. And the house wherein the same Emperour died, could by no other way or means be freed from the fury of these shadows or spirits, as History makes mention, but by burning thereof.

Pollux. *Aristotle* speaking of miracles, mentioneth a certain mountain in *Norway*, named *Hechelberg*, environed about with the Sea, that continually sent forth such lamentable voices, like the yelling & howling of infernal devils, insomuch that the noise & clamour of their terrible roaring might be heard almost a mile; and the flocking together of great Ravens and Vultures neer it, did prohibit any access thereunto. And he reporteth that in *Lyppora* neer about the *Æolian* islands, there was a certain Hill from whence in the night there was heard Cymbals, and sounds of tinkling instruments of brass, with certain secret & hidden screechings, laughings and roarings of Spirits. But even now, *Castor*, thou didst make mention of *Zazelus*, whom also thou didst assert to have been called *Eurynomus* by *Pausania*; I desire thee to shew me somthing more largely concerning this Spirit.

Castor. They do declare that he lives altogether by the flesh of the dead; so as sometimes he doth not leave the flesh of bones.

Pollux. The *Saxon* Grammarians, in the fifth book of the *Danish History*, do most truely subscribe their consents and agreements to this thy Assertion; for there they set before our eyes an admirable History of one *Asuitus* and *Asmundus*, which easily proveth all thy sayings.

Castor. I beseech thee declare this unto me, *Pollux.*

Pollux. Give attention; it is thus: *Asuitus* and *Asmundus* had sworn with mutual vows each to other, that he which should live longest of them, would entomb himself alive. Now sickness did consume away *Asuitus* before *Asmundus*; whereupon *Asmundus* for his Oath of friendship sake, with his dog & his horse entombed himself alive in a vast deep den; having carried with him some meat, whereupon a long time he fed. And at length *Ericus* the King of *Suecia* came into that place with an Army, and broke open the tombe of *Asuitus*; (supposing

poſing there had been treaſure hid therein) but when the cave was opened, he drew out *Aſmundus*, and brought him into the light, who was covered with a deformed ſharp countenance, a deadly deformity, and gored with blood flowing from his freſh wounds.

Caſtor. But this ſtory pertaineth not to our purpoſe.

Pollux. Truely it doth, if you diligently mark theſe verſes, which ſet forth the cauſe of his wounds.

Caſtor. Shew me theſe verſes, if thou haſt them.

Pollux. They are theſe which follow.

> *Quid ſtupetis qui reliſtum me Colore cernitis ?*
> *Obſoleſ u nempe vivus omnis inter mortuos ,*
> *Neſcio quo Stygii numinis auſu,*
> *Miſſus ab inferis Spiritus affluit*
> *Sævis alipedem dentibus edit,*
> *Inſandoῷ Canem præbuit ori,*
> *Non contentus equi vel canis eſu,*
> *Mox in me rapidos tranſtulit ungues,*
> *Diſciſſaῷ gena ſuſtulit aurem ;*
> *Huic laceri vultus horret imago,*
> *Emicat inῷ ſero vulnere ſanguis*
> *Haud impune tamen monſtriſer egit ,*
> *Nam ferro ſervi mox caput ejus ,*
> *Perſodiῷ nocens ſtipite Corpus.*

Aſmundus reports of himſelf, that a Spirit eat up his horſe & his dog, and afterwards began to devour him, & that he beat and wounded the Spirit.

Caſtor. I obſerve here, that *Aſmundus* did cut the head of the Spirit *Zazelus* or *Eurynomus*, and ſtruck and pierced his body with a club ; what ? have Spirits bodies, that may be ſeen and handled by men ?

Pollux. *Corteſius* doth not deny, but that their natures may receive the habit and covering of vegetable bodies , and be transformed in ſeveral kindes of ſhapes , whereby they can the more craftily and ſubtilly delude and deceive the improvident wits of men. *Baſilius Magnus* alſo teſtifieth the ſame, and witneſſeth , that they have bodies appropriate to themſelves , as likewiſe alſo have the pure Angels. *Pſellus* a Necromancer doth alſo report the ſame ; and he alſo teacheth,

The devils have bodies.

That

That sometimes they sleep or rest, and do change their places, and shew themselves visible to the sences of men. *Socrates* asserteth, That a Spirit did speak with him, which also sometimes he saw and felt ; but their bodies cannot be discerned to be different in sex. But *Marcus Cherronesius,* an excellent searcher into the natures of Spirits, writeth, That they have simple bodies & that there doth belong a difference of sex to compound bodies ; yet their bodies are easily drawn to motion and flexibility, and naturally apt to receive every configuration. *For,* saith he *, even as the clouds do shew forth the apparition and resemblance sometimes of men, and sometimes of e-. very thing you conceive ; so likewise do the bodies of Spirits receive various shapes as they please , by reason whereof they transforme themselves into the forms sometimes of men, and sometimes of women. Neverthele*ß *this is not free to them all, but onely to the fiery and aiery Spirits.* For he teacheth, That the Spirits of the water have more slow and less active bodies, which by reason of the slowness and softness of that element, they do most especially resemble birds and women ; of which kinde the *Naiades* and *Nereides* are, celebrated by the Poets. *Trimetius* testifies, That *the Devils do desire to a*ß*ume the shapes of men rather then any other form; but when they cannot finde the matter of the air convenient and befitting for that purpose.* And he saith, That *they frame such kinde of apparences to themselves, as the contrary humour or vapour will afford ; and so they are seen sometimes in the form and shape of a Lion, a Wolfe, a Sow, an A*ß*, a Centaure, of a Man horned, having feet like a Goat :* such as it is reported were seen in the mountain of *Thru ngia,* where there was heard a terrible roaring.

The Spirits cannot be discerned by sex.

All Spirits cannot receive several shapes.

Castor. Porphyr us in *Eusebius,* in his fourth book of *Evangelical Preparations,* teacheth, That *some of these are good Spirits, and some bad ;* but I have counted them to be all evil, *Pollux.*

Pollux. Then it seemeth that thou art not seduced with the assertions either of *Porphyrius,* or *Apuleus,* or *Proclus,* or of some other Plattonicks, which are mentioned in St. *Augustines* book of *The City of God,* **1, 2,** and 3 Chapter, who also

alſo do affirm that there are ſome of theſe Spirits good ; for *Euſebius* in the ſaid book and 6 Chapter ; and St. *Auguſtine* concerning the ſame in his book of *The City of God*, the 9 Chapter and the 8, with very great and ſtrong Arguments do convince the Platonicks, that none of theſe *Dæmons* are good, *There is* but all evil;and that we do alſo approve of from their names, *no Dæmon* which are every where ſet forth in holy Scripture ; for the *God.* Devil is called *Diabolus*, that is, flowing downwards: that he *Why he is* which ſwelling with pride, determined to reign in high *called Di-* places, fell flowing downwards to the loweſt parts, like the *abolus.* torrent of a violent ſtream, as *Caſſiodorus* writeth. And he is called *Sathan*,that is,an adverſary;who as St. *Jerome* teſtifieth, *Sathan.* by reaſon of the corruption of his own malice, he continu- ally refiſteth, and is an adverſary againſt God, who is the chiefeſt good. He is called *Behemoth* in the 40 Chapter of *Behemoth.* *Job*, which ſignifieth an Ox ; for even as an Ox defireth hay, ſo he with the teeth of his ſuggeſtions, coveteth to deſtroy the upright lives of ſpiritual men. And *Leviathan* in the *Leviathan.* ſame place, which ſignifies an addition, becauſe the Devil al- waies endeavours to adde evil to evil, and puniſhment to puniſhment. He is alſo called in *Revelation* 1 5. *Apollyon*, *Apollyon.* ſignifying a rooter out, for he rooteth out the vertues which God planteth in the Soul. He is called a *Serpent* in the 1 2 *A Serpent.* of the *Revelation*, by reaſon of his virulency. A *Lion* in the 1 Epiſt.*Peter* and the laſt Chapter,which roareth about ſeek- ing whom he may devour. He is called a cunning Workman *Iſa.*55. becauſe by his malice the veſſels that are elected and approved. He is called, *Iſa.*34. *Onocentaurus Erynus, Piloſus, Syren, Lamia, Ulula, Struthio.* And by *David* in the 90 *Pſal.* an *Aſpe, Baſiliske* and *Dragon.* In the Goſpel *Mammon, the Prince of this world, and Ruler of darkneſs.*

Caſtor. Why therefore have the Divines declared, That the Almighty hath given two kindes of Spirits unto men ; the one good, the keeper and preſerver of their lives, the other evil, refiſting the good : if they are all evil ?

*Pollux.*The holy Doctors do underſtand by the good Spirit a good Angel,ſuch as we read *Raphael* was to *Tobias*,who bound

the

the evil Spirit *Afmodeus* in the wildernefs of the furtheft parts of *Egypt*, that he might be the more fafe.

Caftor. It had been more fafe for every man to have been without the evil Spirits ; what therefore was the will of the heavenly Father concerning them?

Pollux. That by the affiftance of the good Spirits, we might couragioufly wage continual war againft the evil Spirits ; but being clothed with the harnefs of righteoufnefs, like valiant fouldiers we may gird our loyns with truth, and with the fheild of faith refift and fight againft all his darts.

Caftor. If we condefcend unto this warfare of Spirits, it feemeth good to inquire whether the Devils have power of doing hurt, granted unto them by God; or whether of themfelves they can hurt afmuch as they pleafe?

Pollux. If the laft were true, who could compare the end of their hurting? but it is very manifeft, that their authority from on high is of fo great exiftency, that *John* the Evangelift doubteth not to name the Devils the Princes of the earth.

The devils are the Princes of the earth.

Caftor. In what manner therefore do they hurt?

Pollux. Although they be moft mighty and powerful Spirits, yet they can do no hurt unlefs it be by permiffion ; or,as *Damafcenus* faith, *By difpenfation.* And *Chryfoftome* faith, *They have a limited power* ; *for truely without the will of God, they cannot touch a hair of any mans head.* The Devil could not have deceived the Prophets of *Ahab*, if he had not received power from God ; neither could he have brought any detriment upon *Job*, either unto his body or his goods, but by the power God had given him. In the 7 of *Exodus* the Magicians made Frogs and Serpents by the power of the Devil permiffively ; but Lice they could not bring forth, by reafon of the greater power of God prohibiting them. Neither in the Gofpel could the Devils hurt the Swine until Chrift had given them leave.

Caftor. Therefore the Devil is not fo much to be feared, but the Lord our God, that either he would not fuffer him to rage againft us ; or if at any time by his own determinate

counfel

counfel he let loofe his chains, that then he would defend and mercifully preferve us.

Pollux. Thou faieft well; for even as a wilde boare is not to be feared if he be bound, and held with a ftrong chain by a powerful ftrong man, and who is able by his ftrength to reftrain the fiercenefs of the boare; but the man is to be feared, and requefted, that he would not let loofe the boare: So alfo *Satan* is not to be feared, being bound with the cords of the Almighty; but the Almighty rather, who holdeth him with a cord, left at any time he fhould let loofe his cord, for to execute his will againft us.

Caftor. We know that the Devils, after incarnation of the Word, were called the Lords of the earth; but I wonder, where the Word is not yet incarnate, whether they have power alfo over men.

The devils feducemen where the word is not known.

Pollux. If it pleafeth God, they have very much; but take a demonftration thereof, *Caftor,* from the *Caldeans,* amongft whom the Devil raged with fo much power and dominion, that they made no efteem of the true God, but worfhipped the elements. There needeth not a demonftration of the *Greeks*; for the fury of the Devil did fo much reign amongft them, that by his Arguments, they accounted *Saturn* for a very great God, devouring their own proper Children; and *Jupiter,* an adulterer and father of all filthinefs, they named to be the father of Gods and men; *Bacchus,* the moft wicked example of all fervitude and bondage, they called a free father; *Venus* a ftrumpet, they termed a pure virgin; and they worfhipped *Flora* an harlot, as a type or example of virginity. There is no man that is ignorant, that the *Egyptians* have been worfe then the *Greeks*, when they made peculiar Gods to themfelves, by the inanimate perfwafions of the Devil; for one worfhipped a fheep, another a goat, another a calfe, very many did worfhip hoggs, crows, hawkes, vultures, eagles, crocodiles, cats, dogs, wolves, affes, dragons; and things growing alfo, as onyons, garlick, and thornes; as every one that is covetous of reading, fhall finde in *Damafcenus,* in his Hiftory of *Jofaphat* and *Barlaas,* and in *Eufebius,* in the fourth

book

book, and firft Chapter of *Evangelical Preparations*; neither
do I account the *Hebrews* (who glory in being the off-fpring
of their father *Abraham*) to have been better then the former, when alfo by the inftinct of the devil, after their coming
up out of *Egypt*, with cruel hands they violently affaulted the
Prophets and holy men of God, whom at length they alfo
flew : that I may hold my peace, how diligently they have
brought into their Religion the Gods, or rather Devils of the
Gentiles.

Caftor. I perceive by thefe thy affertions, that one Devil,
and another Devil, hath been adored for Gods ; for thou
haft now faid, That the *Greeks*, by the madnefs wherewith
the Devil poffeffed them, have made unto themfelves, *Saturn*,
Jupiter, *Bacchus*, *Venus* and *Flora*, for Gods; which *Lactantius*
in his fourth book *De vera Sapientia*, alfo accounteth for
Devils.

Pollux. Declare, I pray, thee the words of *Lanctantius.*

Caftor. Mark them ; they are thus : *The fame Devils are the
gods of the Gentiles ; but if any one will not believe thefe things of
me ; then let him credit* Homer, *who joyneth the great* Jupiter *to
the great Devils; and the other Poets and Philofophers do call them
fometimes Gods, and fometimes Devils whereof there is one true,
and another falfe : for the moft wicked Spirits when they are conjured, do confeß themfelves to be Devils ; but where they are worfhipped, they declare themfelves to be Gods, that they may
thruft men into errors, and draw them from the worfhip of the
true God; through whom alone eternal death can be efcaped.*

Pollux. It is expedient for me now to be more inquifitive
in this difcourfe ; whether there be power given to the Devils to foretell things to come ? concerning which thing
hitherto I have not been able to dart at the right mark ;
for this queftion feemeth fufficiently doubtful unto me.

Caftor. St. *Auguftine* in his book *De Natura Dæmonum*,
diffolveth this *Gordoneus* knot, and faith, That *the damned Spi-*
rits, being filled full of all manner of impiety and wickedneß, do
sometimes challenge to themfelves power of forefeeing things to
come ; becaufe in the fenfe of their Aiery bodies, they have a far
more

The devils
do foretel
things to
come.

more strong and prevalent power of fore-knowing, then men of earthly bodies can have; or because of the incomparable swiftness of their airy bodies, which wonderfully exceedeth not onely the celerity of men and wilde beasts, but also the flying of birds: by which means, they are able to declare things long before they come to be known; which we, by reason of the earthly slowness of our sense, cease not to wonder at and admire: or because of the benefit of their continual life, they obtain this wonderful experience of things; which we cannot attain to, because of the shortness of our momentaneous life, which is but as it were a bubble.

Poll. This last assertion of S. *Augustine* seemeth unto me to be more true then the rest, because the Series of many yeers doth cause great experience.

Cast. If any one shall deny these opinions of *Augustine,* as erroneous, *Damascenus* setteth a greater witness of these things, without all exception, before our eyes; who in his second book of *Orthodox Faith* saith thus : *That the devils cannot foreknow things to come, for that belongs onely unto God: but so much as they are able to know, they have from the disposition of the celestial and inferiour bodies.* The devils of themselves cannot foreknow things to come.

Poll. Why therefore do the devils so willingly and of their own accord undertake Prophecies, and to answer Oracles? What benefit have they from hence? Why the devils desire to be counted Prophets.

Cast. Nothing, but that hereby they seek to get great estimation, and covet to be counted worthy of admiration, and to be adored in stead of Gods.

Poll. We know that the devil is the father of lyes, *Castor:* from whence we are piously to believe, that those things which he foretelleth, he extracteth from his own lyes.

Cast. Furthermore, the Prophet *Esaias* saith thus: *Shew the things that are to come hereafter, and tell us, that we may know that ye are gods.* And the Apostle *Peter* also saith, *The prophecie came not in old time by the will of man, but holy men of God spake as they were moved by the holy Ghost.* *Isai.41.* *2 Pet.1.*

Poll. No man therefore will deny that they do sometimes foretel things to come.

Cast. No man, certainly: but for what cause that is attained

ned to, *Chrysostome* doth most clearly teach, in these words: *It is granted,* he saith, *that sometimes the devil doth speak truth, that he might commend his own lying with rare verity : whereas,*

Why the devil som times tell truth.

if he should never tell the truth , he could deceive no man, neither would his lying suffice him to tempt with. Thus far *Chrysostome.* Notwithstanding , if he understand that he hath not grace granted unto him of himself to foretel the truth, he foretelleth things nevertheless, but *so obscurely,* saith S. *Augustine,*

The Oracles of the devils are uncertain.

that he always layeth the blame of the things by him so foretold, upon the interpreter thereof. *Porphyrius,* in his book of Oracles, although he be the greatest maintainer of devils , and the most expert teacher of diabolical Arts , nevertheless he saith with the aforesaid Doctors, that *the foreknowledge of things to come, is not onely intricate to men, but also uncertain to the gods ; and full of many obscurities.*

Poll. Thou hast said, that the predictions of the devils are done in this maner, that they may gain authority to themselves amongst the credulous people , and be worshipped in stead of Gods : for what end do the evil spirits work Miracles ?

Cast. What is a Miracle, *Pollux ?*

What a Miracle is. The devils work miracles.

Poll. A new and unwonted accident , which cometh to pass contrary to its course and custome , and draweth men into admiration thereof.

Cast. But do they work Miracles ?

Poll. They do : for whereby dost thou believe that *Æsculapius* was honoured in his Consecration for a god, but onely by the means of a Miracle, when he conveyed a Serpent from *Epidaurus* to *Rome ?* What gave so great authority to *Juno,* but onely the working of a Miracle ? when her Image of wood was asked by *Furius Camillus* whether it would be carried to *Rome,* and it answered with a humane voice, *It would.* Also, from thence *Fortune* was made a goddess , because her *Statua,* in the way to *Latium,* in the hearing of many people, not once, but oftentimes spoke with a humane voice. In the 8 Chapter of the *Acts* of the Apostles, we read of Miracles done by *Simon* the son of *Rachel* ; and in *Exod.* 8. of the

Magici-

Magicians of *Pharaoh*, who in the fight of many people brought forth frogs and ferpents, and turned the waters into blood. *Apuleus* doth teftifie the power of men to be fo great in Inchantments, that the devils do not onely work Miracles by the means of men, but they are able alfo to fubvert Nature, and with a Demoniacal Incantation, make violent ftreams to ftay their courfe, To turn the windes, To make the fun ftand ftill, To break the courfe of the moon, To lay impediments upon the ftars, To prolong the day, and to fhorten the night; as *Lucanus* excellently fheweth.

Ceffavere vices rerum, dilataq̃, longa,
Hæfit noĉte dies, legi non paruit æther
Torruit & præceps audito Carmine mundus.

And *Tibullus* of a certain Demoniacal Charm.

Hanc ego de cœlo ducentem fydera vidi,
Fluminis ac rapidi Carmine vertit ater,
Hæc cantu funditq̃, folum manefq̃, fepulchris
Elicit, & tepido devorat offa rogo.
Cum libet hac trifti depellit lumina cœlo,
Cum libet æftivo convocat orbe nives.

Caft. I do not any more wonder that *Mofes* called God *Wonderful*, that he doth fo connive at this fink of wickednefs, and moft wicked feducers, that he granteth them power to act fuch things fo freely.

Poll. *Firmianus* excellently fheweth why God doth fo, in his laft book but one *of the works of God*, *De opificio Dei :* for he faith, that vertue is not vertue, unlefs it have fome like, in ruling whereof it may fhew and exercife its power : for he faith, *As Victory cannot ftand without Vertue,* fo neither can Vertue fubfift without an Enemy ; which vertue no fooner had the Almighty indued man withal, but he forthwith added unto him an enemy, left that vertue fhould lofe its nature, being ftupified with idlenefs. He faith, that *a man cannot*

S 2　　　　　　　　　　other-

otherwise attain to the highest step, unless he have always an active hand ; and that he shall establish and build up his salvation with a continual warfare and contention : for God will not that mortal men shall come to immortal blessedness with an easie journey, but he must wrestle and strive with sayls and oars against the author and inventor of all evils and errours, who causeth and worketh execrable things and miracles.

Somtimes it comes to pass, that the devil cannot be resisted.
Cast. But sometimes it cometh to pass, that by reason of the subtil snares and stratagems of the devil, which he so craftily prepareth against us, and especially against simple persons, whom he intangleth with vain Religions, so that we cannot resist him ; or if we suppose our selves to be very able to withstand him, yet neverthelefs we shall be very much deceived by him; as we read he oftentimes did to the good, but almost-foolish Pastor, of whom *Tritemius* maketh mention.

Poll. But what happened to this good Pastor, and whom thou termest simple ?

An admirable story of a swineherd.
Cast. *Tritemius* saith, *Insomuch that he was not strong in faith, therefore he made more account of the name of Saint* Blaze, *and attributed more power and custody unto it, then unto the name of God, the best and greatest good.*

Poll. In what maner ?

Cast. He had in his walking-staff, or Pastoral Crook, a Schedule inscribed with the name of St. *Blaze* ; by the power and vertue of which staff, he did believe his swine were safely defended from the ravening of the wolves : and he did attribute so great a Deity to that Schedule, that he would leave his herd of swine to feed in the fields alone: notwithstanding, a certain time coming when the pastor was absent from his flock, and a certain man coming in the mean time, saw the devil keeping them ; and he asked him what he kept here, who is the worst persecutor of the salvation of men ? He answered, *I keep these swine.* The other replied, *By whose command ?* The devil saith, *By the foolish confidence of the pastor : for he included a certain Schedule in his staff, unto which he ascribeth divine vertue, or to the inscription of the name of St.* Blaze ; *and now, contrary to his own law, he believeth that his*

hogs

hogs are thereby defended from the injury of wolves ; inhering to me with a false superstition ; where when he hath been by me called again and again, and hath not appeared, I have taken this custody upon my self, instead of S. Blaze *: for I always freely stand in stead of God and his Saints: so also now most freely do I keep his swine for St.* Blaze *, that I may magnifie and confirm the foolish man in his vain confidence ; and thereby I may seduce him so, that he may esteem of this Schedule more then God.*

Poll. This is a pleasant story : but I do not wonder that the devil should impose so much upon so simple a Pastor, when he doth in many things prevail over the more wise, if they do at themselves to his opportunities ; which the Church contradicteth.

Poll. But are all things wrought and brought to pass by means of the devil which men call Miracles?

Cast. No: for we must give unto Nature that which seem- eth to belong unto her, who is said to be the greatest worker of Miracles ; as that which we have experienced in the stone *Asbestos,* which, as *Solinus* witnesseth, being once set on fire, cannot be quenched : and the root *Baara,* described by *Jo-sephus* in the history of *Jerusalem,* which he testifieth to be of the colour of a flame of fire, splendent and shining in the night ; but so difficult to be taken , that it always flies from under the hand of him that would take it, and deceiveth his eyes so long, until it be sprinkled with the urine of a men-struous woman: and when it is retained by this means , it may not be gathered or plucked up without danger; for pre-sent death followeth him that gathereth or plucketh it up, unless he shall be fortified with a Preservative about his neck, of the same root. For which cause, they who want the same root, do scarifie it round about ; and having bound the root about with a bond, they tie the same to a dog, and suddenly depart away. Whereupon,the dog, too much endeavouring to follow after him, draweth up the root ; and, as if the dog were to perform the turn of his master, he forthwith dies;and afterwards the same root may be taken and handled without any danger to any man. And the same *Josephus* teacheth,that

Some mi-racles are done na-turally.

the

the same root is of such present force for expiations, that also those who are vexed and tormented with unclean spirits, are immediately delivered, if they carry this root about

Art some-
times imi
tateth Na
ture in
working
Miracles.

them. Notwithstanding there is nothing hindereth, but that Art also may imitate Nature in the working of Miracles; as we may read in *Aristotle*, of the Greek fire that would burn in water: of which the said Author, in his singular Treatise concerning this, hath described very many compositions. And concerning the fire which is extinguished with oyl, and kindled with cold water, when it is besprinkled over therewith.

Poll. It sometimes happeneth that the devils do clothe themselves, sometimes in more slender, and sometimes in more gross habits, that thereby they may very much affright and molest men with horrible phantasies, and terrible sights; with Ghosts appearing in divers and several shapes and aspects. What, cannot we be fortified with any thing to force and compel them to flie from us?

How the
devils are
to be dri-
ven away.

Cast. *Origen*, in his book against *Celsus*, saith, that *there is no way more certain, then the naming of JESUS the true God.* For he saith he hath oftentimes seen innumerable spirits so driven away, both from the souls and bodies of men. St. *Athanasius*, in his book *de variis Quæstion.* testifieth, that the most present remedy against the insultation of evil spirits, is the beginning of the 67 Psalm, *Let God arise, and let his enemies be scattered.* *Cyprian*, in his book *Quod idola dii non sint*, commandeth that the devils should be conjured away by the true God. Some men have declared, that Fire, which is the most holy of all elements, and the Creed, and also the instrument whereon the fire was carried, were very profitable for this purpose: from whence, in their sacrifices about the sepulchres of the dead, they diligently observed the use of lights: or else from thence that *Pythagoras* did determine, that God could be in no wise truely worshipped without lights burning. Some others do binde swords for this intent and purpose, taking the same out of the 11 Ode of *Homer*, where he writeth, that *Ulysses*, when he offered a sacrifice to his mo-

The Spi-
rits fear
Swords.

ther,

ther, had a fword drawn prefent by him, wherewith he expelled and drove away the fpirits from the blood of his facrifice. And in the fixth of *Virgil,* when the Sybil led *Æ-
neas* into hell, fhe faith thus :

   ———— ————*Procul, O procul efte profani,*
Tuá, invade viam, vagináq, eripe ferrum.

Philoftratus writeth, that he compelled *Apollonius,* a fpirit,
obvious to him and his companions, to flight, with contumelies and direful imprecations ; that the vifion making a
noife, and with great horrour vanifhed away from them.
Very many do much commend a Perfume of Calamint, Pio-
ny, Mint, Palma Chrifti, and Parfley, to be ufed in this cafe.
Many do keep prefent with them Red Coral, Mugwort, Hy-
pericon, Rue, or Vervin, for this purpofe. Some do ufe for
this bufinefs the tinkling of keys, founding of confecrated
bells, or the terrible ratling of Armour.

   Poll. I have fometimes heard from our Elders, that they   Chara-
made them Sigils infcribed with Pentagones ; by vertue   æters do
whereof, the fpirits might be expelled and driven away.   drive away
What fayft thou to thefe?   Spirits.

   Caft. Averrois writing againft *Algazelus,* affirmeth fuch   Chara-
things to be almoft nothing worth, unlefs to them that have   æters avail
confederated with the fpirits. If therefore *Averrois* faith the   not.
truth, how then can the devils kingdom ftand, divided againft
it felf?

   Poll. But we read that *Solomon,* a fingular man with God,
did make fuch Sigils.

   Caft. We do read truely that *Solomon* did make them; but
it was at fuch time when he worfhipped Idols, and not
when he was in the ftate of falvation. *Tertullian* offereth a
more certain Antidote then all the former, and exhorteth
us, as *Job,* the moft ftrong champion of God, to fight againft
all the affaults of temptations : he admonifheth us to be
clothed with the filken garment of Honefty, the purple robe
of Modefty and Shamefac'dnefs, and the cloak of Patience :
                                 and

and he perfwadeth us to meditate upon all thofe things which the devil doth devife and invent, to overthrow our integrity ; that his falling may be proved the glory of our conftancy, and that we be willing conftantly to war againft all machinations, which are permitted by God for this end. And the Prophet *Jeremiah* teacheth the fame,in thefe words: *The Lord of hofts is the approver of the juft.*

D. *Maximus,* in his book *de charitate*, commandeth us to binde and kill the devils. He faith we do then binde them, when by diligent obfervation of the Commandments of God, we do diminifh and quafh thofe affeâions that do boyl up in us : And we are faid to kill them, when we fo truely mortifie our lufts, that we cut him off from all occafions of accufing ; faying with the Propet , *Depart, O homicide, the Lord the ftrong warriour is with me : thou (halt fall, and fhalt be vanquifhed from me for ever.* *Olympiadorus,* 10 *cap.* when he interpreteth the Ecclefiaftical hiftory,faith, that *all fenfual appetites are to be fhut out, and excluded, fo that the devil may not be admitted, neither by the allurements of the eyes, nor by itching ears, nor by the petulancie and frowardnefs of a hurtful tongue :* for this he accounteth to be the moft abfolute feal againft the power of the devils. Some do admonifh us, in our going forth to war againft the devil, to ufe two forts of weapons: the one is pure Prayer,which may raife up our affeâions unto heaven ; and true and perfeâ Knowledge, which may communicate and fill our underftandings with wholefome doârines, and may fuggeft unto us what we are to pray for, that we may pray ardently, according to St. *James*, and not doubtingly. In the Prophefie of *Ifaiah,* and Epiftles of St. *Paul,* we may finde the fame things ; *Ifai.*59. *Eph.*6. and 1 *Theff.*5. which may be as a remedy againft vain Ghofts, that they may be expelled.

We are to fight against the devil with two forts of armor.

Poll. For a remedy againft Ghofts ? Doft thou conceive that a Ghoft is diverfe and different from a fpirit ?

Caft. I know not truely what I may think hereof : for flowing in fo fpafious a fea of many opinions, I am fo led in doubt, that I cannot eafily attain to a certain Port of judgement :

ment : for there are fome which do fuppofe that thefe Ghofts are devils, by reafon of the great fear and terrour wherewith they ragingly moleft men by night in their houfes; and fometimes for their innate nature do do hurt. There are others that do believe thefe Spirits are deceitful fantafies, deceiving thofe that are of evil belief ; who by their fallacious vifions and imaginations do deceive and frighten the inhabitants in their houfes : and do deny that they are Spirits indeed, becaufe the Spirits have a body without hands and feet; wherefore they can hurt no man, nor make any tumult : being ignorant that the Angel (who alfo hath a body without hands and feet) did carry *Habakkuk* with his whole dinner, by the hair of his head, into *Babylon*, and afterwards brought him back again, and fet him in his own place ; neither confidering that the Spirit of the Lord, alfo without a body, fnatched up *Philip*, and carried him to *Azotus* : that I may forbear to fpeak concerning a certain incorporeal Spirit , which did fo difquiet the houfe of my Grandfather , that by the fpace of almoft thirty yeers he caufed it to be uninhabitable, unlefs it were when a Lamp was burning therein ; neither did that then fufficiently quiet the fame : for going out of the houfe, they did fo moleft them with ftones from above in the ftreets, that they would caft out of their hands the hearts of Pinetrees, which they ufed for torches. Concerning the Ghoft that haunted the houfe of *Anthenodorus* the Philofopher, and the tumultuous fpirit of *C. Caligula* , there may more be fpoken : but thou haft underftood the relations of them already in the foregoing difcourfe. From all which, we may eafily convince the opinions of thofe, who deny that the Spirits can walk, or make any motion ; but of how much truth we may hold the affertions of them, who do fuppofe that thefe tumultuous Spirits are neither devils , nor phantafms, but the fouls of the dead, now hearken unto.

Poll. Are there they who are of that opinion?

Caft. There are they who are of both opinions : for they do declare that thefe are the fouls of them who have departed from their bodies laden and clogged in their fins ;

T   which

which are therefore heard to be more or lefs turbulent in
houfes, according as they have any fenfible ardent fpark of
that fin more or lefs ; fo that except in the mean time they
are expelled and driven away from thence, or expiated by
Alms or Interceffions, they are compelled to a certain bound
of liberty, wandering thereabouts in expeduation of the laft
Judgement.

Poll. Wherefore?

Laftant. of
the   fouls
of the
dead. *Caft.* Becaufe I believe that the fouls of them which fleep
in Chrift, do live with Chrift, and do not wander about the
earth; and the fouls of them who are oppreffed and bur-
dened with the grievous weight of their fins, fince they are
the members of Satan, are bound with Satan in the chains of
darknefs, expeduing judgement in hell.

Poll. But *Firmianus*, a Writer of no mean judgement,
thinketh the contrary, in his Book which he hath written
de Divino præmio.

Caft. How is that?

The opini-
on of *Fir*-
mianus. *Poll.* Thefe are his words : *Let not any man conceive that
the fouls of the dead are judged immediately after death: for they
are all detained in one common cuftody, until the time fhall come,
wherein the Almighty Judge fhall make examination and inquifi-
tion of their deeds. Then they who fhall be found righteous, fhalt
receive the reward of immortality ; but they whofe fins and wickedneß fhall then be deteued, fhall not arife again, but fhall be inclo-
fed with the wicked in darkneß, and deftined to eternal punifhments.*

Caft. St. *Auguftine* fubfcribeth to *Lactantius* in his *Enchiri-
dion,* faying, *That the time which is interpofed between the death
of mankinde and the laft refurreuion, containeth the fouls in fecret hidden receptacles, where every foul receiveth condigne reft
or mifery, for the good or evil which he did in the body while he
lived.*

Poll. Neither doth St. *Ambrofe* difagree from this : in his
fecond book of *Cain* and *Abel,* he faith, that *the foul is loofed
from the body, and after the end of this life, is fufpended to the
ambiguous time of the laft judgement.*

Caft.

Caſt. So alſo ſome have declared, that the ſoul of *Trajanus Cæſar* did wander about; but the ſoul of St. *George* was freed from ſuch ſuffrage.

Poll. Thou haſt even now ſpoke, and that truely, that ſpacious is the ſea of various opinions concerning theſe Spirits; for ſo indeed it is : but what Port thou toucheſt at, I deſire thee it may not ſeem troubleſome to thee to tell me : for I am not as yet ſatisfied of the certainty hereof by our diſcourſe.

Caſt. That which thou deſireſt, I conceive to be this : I hold that theſe tumultuous Spirits are meer images of Satan; which are not to be feared, neither is there any credit to be given to their anſwers : and are in no wiſe the ſouls of the dead, which either live with Chriſt, if they have done well; or elſe are bound in chains with Satan, if they have done evil.

Poll. It remaineth that we ſift out this, *Caſtor :* for it happeneth now ſometimes, that my father appeareth to me in my ſleep; perhaps that may alſo ſeem unto thee to be a Spirit.

Caſt. It may ſeem ſo : but I will not in any thing contradi thee beyond Reaſon: of my ſelf I will adde nothing;but at leaſtwiſe I will annihilate thy opinion with the aſſertions of St. *Auguſtine.*

Poll. What aſſertions are thoſe?

Caſt. In his 11 book, which he intituleth *De mortuorum cura*, he offereth them as a means, ſaying, *Humane infirmity doth ſo believe of himſelf, that when he ſeeth any one that is dead, in his ſleep, he ſuppoſeth that he ſeeth the ſoul of that dead perſon; but when he dreameth of any one that is alive, he then is out of doubt, that neither his ſoul nor his body, but the ſimilitude of the man appeared unto him: As if they could be ignorant,that the ſouls of dead men do not appear unto them in dreams, but onely the ſimilitudes of the perſons deceaſed.* And he proveth both theſe to be done, by two examples which were at *Mediolamus*; whereof the firſt he ſheweth to have been the image of a certain father that was dead, who appeared to his ſon, admoniſhing him that he ſhould not pay again a debt to an

unjuſt

unjuft Creditor,which the father had paid him before : for he
faith the Cafe was thus : The father had paid a debt to a certain Creditor , which after the death of the father, the Creditor endeavoured by force to recover the fame again of his
fon, who was ignorant of the payment thereof: to whom
the image of his father appeared when he was fleeping, and
fhewed him where the Writing was hid, Whereupon, the
fon awaking from his fleep, fought for the Paper in the place
he was directed, and found it, and thereby overthrew the
malice of his deceitful Creditor.   The fecond example is,
whereby the fame St. *Auguftine* fheweth that the living do
appear to the living, in their fleep : for he faith, that *Euro-
logius* the Rhetorician, profeffing the Rhetorick of *Cicero* at
Carthage, he found a difficult and obfcure place that was
not declared to him ; fo that waking and fleeping he vexed
himfelf by reafon of his ignorance : but, in a certain night,
the image of *Aurelius Auguftine* appeared to him, and
taught him in what maner the dark and difficult place was to
be underftood.

Poll. Auguftine doth therefore conclude, without doubt,
that they are not fouls.

Caft. He doth fo conclude : and the greater to ftrengthen
fuch his judgement, he addeth, That if the fouls of the
dead have any intereft or counfel in the affairs of the living,
he undoubtedly knew, that his own pious mother did not
defert him, not for one night, but when fhe was living, followed him both by fea and land : neither did he at any time
fuftain any anguifh of heart, but comforted his forrows.
And that this may not feem too hard a fpeech, the prefident
of Chrift teacheth, that they do not erre, who affirm that
the good Angels, by the appointment of God, and Divine
difpenfation, do fometimes come to, and vifit men, both living and fleeping, and fometimes to the place where fouls
endure punifhment : notwithftanding, it is not unto all, but
onely unto thofe who are fo lived, that God fhall judge them
worthy of this mercy ; or unto thofe upon whom, without
any refpect unto their deferts, God will be pleafed to glorifie

rifie his unfpeakable mercy ; that by the prayers of the living they may obtain pardon of their fins, and deliverance from the prifon of torments.

Poll. I have fometimes read, that the fame St. *Auguftine* did write, that it is better for a man to doubt of fecret things, then to contend about things uncertain.

Caft. That is certainly true ; neither doth he declare himfelf to be an offence to thofe who do leave all thefe things to the unfearchable judgements of God, and labour not to finde out the fecrets thereof.

Poll. Becaufe I have eafily underftood thy anfwers hither-to, I will not defift till thou haft fully refolved me concer-ning this fubject. I defire therefore to know whether all Miracles which the devils perform, are done really, or ima-ginary phantafies.

Whether the devils work Mi-racles re-ally, or not.

Caft. That they perform many things really, and many things onely feemingly, we have already manifefted out of the Writings of St. *Auguftine.* For that great Prelate of the Chriftian Church, writeth, in the 11 Chapter of his book *de Trinitate,* That *it is a very eafie thing for the wicked Spirits, through the aëry fubftance of their bodies, to perform many things which feem wonderful (to the fouls that are oppreffed with earth-ly bodies) to be done.* He alfo faith, That *earthly bodies may be fo qualified with art and exercife, that in publike Theaters they may perform fuch wonderful things, that thofe who never have feen them will not believe them, but that they were done by the affiftance of the devil and his minifters, to make their bodies of fuch an aëry element, that the flefh wonders at.* Or elfe, which is much, he faith alfo, That *they do contrive with occult infpirations, forms, and fantafies of images, to delude humane fenfe ; wherewith, waking or fleeping, they may be deceived.* Thus far *Auguftine.* But, if thou wilt, I will produce alfo another witnefs without exception, *Pollux.*

Poll. I would have thee tell me who that is.

Caft. Abbas Tritemius, in his third Queftion to St. *Maxi-mus Emilianus,* which is fpoken of before, faith thus : *The devils, amongft unfaithful people, do feem to raife up the dead to life,*

life, and to fhew miracles to curious men, that they might as it were fwallow them up with errour in ftead of miracles ; and are altogether pertinacious and obftinate: but they cannot truely and really raife up the dead, but do varioufly deceive the fenfes of men, fhewing them feigned refemblances of the dead. For it is certainly manifeft, that the devils can do all things, but onely in a falfe fimilitude of holy miracles in truth.

Poll. Some fay that the devils are obedient to wicked men, becaufe of the fimilitude of their malice. How feemeth that to thee?

Caft. It feemeth to me, that they are obedient to evil men, but not to all men.

Poll. But to whom?

Caft. To thofe certainly with whom they have contracted and made compacts and covenants ; as thofe women which they call *Pythonifts* are accounted, who have vowed themfelves by promife unto him.

Poll. But although they are compelled to be fo ferviceable unto them, yet is this fervice true or feigned?

Caft. It is feigned, certainly: for they are fubfervient unto men of their own accord, and genuine work, that they may deceive them, and allure them to themfelves. Although we do not deny that their fervice is fometimes true, but onely towards thofe men, whofe faith in the Lord Jefus Chrift, by the merit of his holinefs, hath caufed them to be acceptable, and friends unto him. And that *Lactantius* alfo teftifies, in thefe words, in his fecond book *De origine Erroris,* and 16 Chapter, That the devils do fear the juft, that is, thofe that worfhip God, in whofe Name they are conjured to depart out of bodies, and with whofe words they are beaten as it were with fcourges : and they do not onely confefs that they are devils, but do declare their names: neither can they lye unto the juft. And the fame *Lactantius* in his fourth book *De vera Sapientia*, Chap. 27. faith, That it is neceffary that they who are of the true Chriftian Religion, fhould know the courfe and order of the devils, and underftand their fubtilty, and reftrain their force, and conquer

quer and fubdue them with fpiritual weapons, and force them to obey him.

Poll. I am now by thee fufficiently informed of all things which I have hitherto defired to know ; wherefore I fhall not any further trouble thee with my Queftions, or rather Riddles, but leave thee to thy own occafions.

Caft. Neither have I counted my felf idle in anfwering thee : but let the ufe thereof yeeld us each to other an equal recompence. Farewel therefore.

Poll. And thee alfo.

Gerard

GERARD CREMONENSIS
OF
ASTRONOMICAL GEOMANCY.

Ecaufe Aftronomy is fo tranfcedent and fubtil an Art in it felf, that therein a man ought to have refpect unto fo many things before he can attaine to true judgment thereby, becaufe the eye of the underftanding will not pierce unto the half thereof, and few Doctors of our later time have been found fo experienced therein that they know fufficiently how to judge thereby; Therefore I have compofed this work, which I will have to be named, *Aftronomical Geomancy* ; wherein, I will fufficiently teach how to judge with lefs labour and ftudy. For in this prefent fcience it is not requifite to be hold neither the Afcendant, nor the hour in a Table, as it is in Aftrology.

It is expedient therefore, to make four unequal lines, by the points cafually fet down ; and to joyne together thofe points; and out of the points which are not joyned together, which do remain in the heads of the lines, (as it is done in Geomancie) extract one figure ; and the figne of the *Zodiacke* that anfwereth to that figure, put for the Afcendent, for the words fake. If *Acquifitio* arife from the heads of thofe *Acquifition,*

V   four

four Lines, let *Aries* be placed in the Aſcendent ; If *Lætitia,* or the leſſer Fortune put *Taurus* in the Aſcendent;if *Puer* or *Rubeus,*place *Gemini* ; if *Albus,Cancer*;if *Via,Leo* ; if *Conjunctio* or the *Dragons Head,Virgo* ; if *Puella,Libra*;if *Amiſſio* or *Triſtitia,Scorpio*;if he *Dragons Tail,Sagittary*;if *Populus,Capricorn* ; if *Fortuna major,Aquary* ; if *Carcer,*then put *Piſces* for the Aſcendent. Afterwards in the ſecond Houſe, let that ſigne be placed which immediately ſucceeds the other. In the third Houſe the third Signe, and ſo place the reſt in order until you come unto the end of the Signes ; and make one ſquare figure divided into twelve equal parts, and therein place the Signes in order , as it is in Aſtrology , and as you may finde them in this figure : neither are we here to regard the * witneſſes, or * Judge, or any other thing which belongs to Geomancie; but onely the ſixteen Figures, that by them we may have the twelve Signes, to which they agree ; and obſerve the maner of the Figure as it is here placed.

Look how the twelve
Signes are placed in
the figure, and so may
any other Signe be aſ-
cending in his turn, as
Aries is here.

Afterwards it is requifite to make four Lines by courfe for every Planet, by points cafually pricked down; and likewife for the *Dragons Head*, as you have done for the Afcendent, and divide thofe points by twelve ; and that which remaineth above twelve, or the twelfth it felf, if a greater number doth not remain, retaine, and the Planet for which the projection was made, place in that Houfe of which the fuperabounding number fhall be ; that is , if there remain twelve , let the Planet be placed in the twelfth Houfe; if ten , in the tenth Houfe ; if one, in the firft Houfe ; if two, in the fecond Houfe; and fo of the reft. And you ought alwayes to begin from the *Sun*, and afterwards from the *Moon*, then from *Venus* and *Mercury*, and from *Saturn*, *Jupiter* and *Mars*, and the *Dragons Head* and *Dragons Tail* ; but you muft alwayes take heed, that you do not make a queftion in a rainy , cloudy , or a very windy feafon, or when thou art angry, or thy minde bufied with many affairs ; nor for tempters or deriders, neither that you may renew and reiterate the fame Queftion again under the fame figure or forme ; for that is error.

Queftions of the firft Houfe.

IF you are defirous to know concerning the life of any man whether it fhall be long or fhort, behold the Lord of the Afcendent, who if he be in ftrong Angles, it fignifies long life ; in fuccedents, a middle age ; and in cadent Houfes, a fhort life ; and if he be in ftrong Angles, he fignifies greater years ; if in Succedents, meaner years; if in Cadents, leffer years. The leffer years of *Saturn* are thirty, the meaner are forty four years, and the greater fifty eight. The leffer years of *Jupiter* are twelve , the meaner years forty, and the greater accordingly are forty feven. The leffer years of *Mars* are fifteen, his meane years forty , and the greater years forty feven. The leffer years of the *Sun* are are nineteen, his mean years forty five, and his greater years eighty two. The leffer years of *Venus* are eight, her mean years forty five, and her greater years eighty two. *Mercury's* leffer years are twenty , his

mean

mean years forty nine, and his greater years eighty. The leffer years of the *Moon* are fifteen, her mean years thirty nine, and her greater years a hundred and feven. And alfo look if *Mars* or *Saturn* fhall be in the firſt Houfe, and the Lord of the eighth with them; and if the *Sun* fhall be in the eighth, the Querent fhall not live: likewife if the Lord of the Afcendent fhall happen to be void of courfe, and *Mars* be in the eighth, the Querent fhall not live; but if the *Sun* and the *Moon* fhall be in conjunction in the feventh Houfe, and *Venus* in the fecond, he fhall live well.

The accidents of the nativity are likwife to be confidered. If you finde *Saturn* or *Mercury* in the firſt, · he is foolifh and talkative; if it be *Mars* and *Mercury*, he will not be fervile, but a wrangler and fcoffer; if the *Sun* and *Mercury*, he will be a fpeaker of truth; and if the *Sun* be in *Aries*, he will apply himfelf to learn whatfoever he fhall hear; if *Venus* be in the feventh, he will be luxurious; and if *Saturn*, *Mercury* and *Venus* be in their fall, he will be a Sodomite; if the *Sun* and *Venus* be in the tenth, and the *Moon* in the firſt, he will be very liberal; if *Venus*, *Mercury* and the *Dragons Head* be in the firſt, he will be covetous; if the *Moon* and *Mars* be in the firſt, he will be fubject to great bondage; and if *Mars* be Lord of the nativity, he will be rich, and an evil fpeaker, and litigious; and if the *Sun* be in the firſt, he will be envious, having a fair body, not very lean, nor very fat; and if *Venus* be in the firſt, he will be white and fair; if *Mercury* be in the firſt, he will not be ſtable, but alwayes in motion; but if the *Moon* be found there, it denotes him to have a graceful face, breſt and arms; if *Saturn* be there, the man will be black and filthy; if *Jupiter*, he will have a round face, a fair forehead, a ruddy complexion mixt with a little white. If you would know his office or art: if the *Moon* be in the feventh with *Saturn*, or in the fourth, or in the tenth, or in the firſt, it is not good for him to build any houfe in a City, nor to build a fhip, neither is it good for him to be a tiller of land, or to drefs vines, or plant trees; but to be imployed about fome office belonging to the water, or concerning mariages, or

to

to be a Post or a Messenger; neither let him apply himself much to his master, because he shall gain no repute from him: if the *Moon* be in the fifth or third, it will be good to him; in the second, eighth, sixth and twelfth, neither good nor evil.

Jupiter signifies Bishops, Prelates, Nobles, Potentates, Judges, Wise men, Merchants and Usurers.

Mars signifies Warriors, Incendiaries, Homicides, Physitians, Barbers, Hangmen, Gold-smiths, Cooks, furnaces, and all fireworks. And if *Mars* be in strong Signes, he will be poor and die in captivity, unless he put himself in arms with some souldier or vassal.

The *Sun* signifieth Emperors, Kings, Princes, Nobles, Lords and Judges.

Venus signifies Queens and Ladies, Marriages, Communications, Friendship, Apothecaries, Taylors, and such as make Ornaments for playes, sellers of Cloth, Jesters, Vintners, Players at dice, Whores and Robbers.

Mercury signifies Clerks, Philosophers, Astrologers, Geometricians, Arithmeticians, Latine writers, and Painters, and all subtil Artists, as well men as women, and their Arts.

Concerning the intention of the Querent, look unto the Signe ascending, and his Lord; and where you finde the Lord of the Ascendent, he comes to inquire about something pertaining to that House; and if the *Sun* be Lord of the Ascendent, his Question is concerning fear which he is in of some man; if *Venus*, he enquireth of Arts, that he may know some proper Arts, or he enquireth concerning things belonging to women. If *Mercury* be Lord of the Ascendent, he seek-after something that is lost, or enquireth concerning some infirmity. If the *Moon*, he seeketh also for something lost, or inquireth about sickness, or some disease in his eyes. If *Saturn* be Lord of the Ascendent, he enquireth about some sickness, or concerning a Prince; and keepeth silence, but hath some great grief or anguish in his heart. If *Jupiter* be Lord of the Ascendent, his Question is concerning some infirmity, or restitution, or for some office which he desireth to have. If *Mars*, he enquireth for some fear, or of an enemy, death, sickness, riches, or substance.

Questions

Questions of the second House.

IF you would be informed concerning the substance of any man whether he shall be rich or not, behold the Lord of the second, which if he shall be with a good Planet, & a good Planet likewise in the second, he shall be rich ; but if the Lord of the second be joined with evil Planets, and an evil Planet shall be in the second, he shall be poor.

If you would know whether you shall have again a thing lent, or not, look if there be an evil Planet in the second, and disagreeing with his Lord ; then he that detaineth the thing lent, will not willingly render back the same : But if there be a good Planet in the second, and agreeing with his Lord, it shall easily be recovered ; and if the Lord of the second be exalted and be evil , or if an evil Planet be with him in the second , or if the Lord of the second be exalted , be which keepeth the thing deposited , will not willingly restore the same, but he shall do it whether he will or not. And if an evil Planet be in the second, it's to be recovered : But if *Mercury* be in the second so that he be his Lord, and bringeth contrariety, then it shall be recovered ; and if a good Planet be in the second House, he signifies recovery, although he be the Lord thereof.

Mark therefore the concord and discord of the Planets: the *Moon* and *Jupiter* are friends , the *Moon* and *Mars* enemies ; *Mercury* and the *Sun* are friends, *Mercury* and *Venus* enemies ; *Venus* and *Jupiter* are friends, *Jupiter* and the *Moon* are enemies.

The Planets are said to be friends, when they agree in one nature and quality, as *Mars* and the *Sun*, because both their natures is hot and dry ; *Venus* and the *Moon* do agree in cold and moisture : or when Planets do agree in substance and nature, as *Jupiter* and *Venus* are friends : or when the House of one is the exaltation of another, or on the contrary.

Questi-

Questions of the third House.

IF that you defire to know, how many brethren a man hath, fee the Lord of the third, and it is to be held, that to fo many Planets as he is joyned, fo many brethren the Querent hath; and the Mafculine Planets fignifie brethren, and the female Planets fifters; and note, That *Saturn* and *Mars*, the *Sun*, *Jupiter*, & the *Dragons Head*, are mafculine; but the *Moon*, *Venus* and the *Dragons Tail* are fœminine: but *Mercury* is promifcuous, fometimes mafculine, and fometimes fœminine ; he is mafculine when he is joyned to mafculine Planets, or when he is in a mafculine quarter of the *Zodiacke*; and he is fœminine, when he is joyned to fœminine Planets, or when he is in a fœminine quarter of the *Zodiacke*.

Questions of the fourth House.

IF thou wouldſt know whether it be good for thee to ſtay in any Land, City, Village, Territory, or Houſe, or not, behold the Lord of the Afcendent of the fourth, and of the feventh ; and if the Lord of the fourth be in the feventh, and be good, and the Lords of the firſt and the tenth Houſe be good, and with good Planets, then it is good for thee to continue in that place wherein thou art. And if the Lord of the feventh be with a good Planet, and the Lord of the fourth with an evil Planet, then it is not good for thee to abide there, becaufe if thou doſt continue there, thou fhalt fuffer many loffes, & have evil reports raifed on thee in that Country.

But if thou wouldſt know when any one that is abfent will return, behold the Lord of the Afcendent ; and if you finde him in any one of the four Angles, he will return in that year ; and if he be not in an Angle, then fee how far he is diſtant from the firſt Angle : for fo long he will ſtay, and fo many years as there be Houſes.

If you would be informed of the dearth or plenty of things, behold the ſtrong Houſes, the Succedents and the Cadents ;

for

for the ſtrong Houſes ſignifie dearth and ſcarcity , the Succedents a moderate ſeaſon, neither too dear, nor too cheap, the
Cadents ſignifie plenty and profitableneſs of things.   Conſider alſo the Planet , and their places,   which if they be in
ſtrong Houſes ,   the things which are ſignified by thoſe Planets will be rare : and note, That *Saturn* doth ſignifie fields,
vines, and inſtruments to work in fields, and leather, and of
fruits, corn, acorns, oak-apples, and pomegranates.   *Jupiter*
hath oil, honey, ſilk-wormes, cloth, wine , and graſs , and
things that are odoriferous.   *Mars* ſignifies wine, andfleſh,
and eſpecially hogs , wars, and armour , and ſuch things
as belong thereunto, and red garments.   The *Sun* hath ſignification of wheat, and wine , purple colours , and cloth,
and all things that are aſſimulated unto gold , horſes and
birds, ſuch as hawks and falcons. *Venus* doth ſignifie fatneſs
and grapes, figs and dates, fiſh and paſtimes. *Mercury* hath
barley , millet, grain, money, and quickſilver. The *Moon*
ſignifies oats, milk, cheeſe, fire and ſalt,cows, rams, hens,and
ſilver, and accordingly plenty and ſcarcity of them.

Queſtions of the fifth Houſe.

IF you would know whether a woman be with Child , or
whether ſhe will have any children, or not, look if the
Lord of the Aſcendent be in the ſeventh, or the Lord of the
fifth in the firſt, or the Lord of the firſt in the fifth, or if the
Lord of the fifth be in the ſeventh , or if the Lord of the ſeventh be in the fifth, or the *Moon* with them ; or if good Planets be in the firſt, or the fifth, or with the Lord of the fifth,
or * R * in Angles , ſhe is with child, or may have children ;
but if you finde none of them , but evil Planets in
the ſame places,   ſhe neither is with childe, neither
will ſhe have any children : and if there be both good and
evil Planets in the ſaid places , then happily ſhe may have
children, but they will not live ; but if *Cancer* , *Scorpio* or
Piſces ſhall be in the firſt or fifth Houſe , ſhe may have children; but if *Leo* and *Virgo* be there, ſhe is not with child, neither

ther fhall fhe ever have any children; or if the Lord of the fifth fhall be in them Houfes.

And if, you would know, within how many years fhe fhall have children , look where you finde the Lord of the fifth ; for in that year fhe fhall have iffue ; if he be in the firft, in the firft year ; if in the fecond, in the fecond year ; and fo you may number unto the twelfth Houfe. And if mean Signes be in the Afcendent , fhe that is with child hath twins in her wombe, which will live, if a good Planet be in the firft ; and if an evil Planet, they will die; and if there be one good and another evil, one fhall live , and another die ; and if a mean Signe fhall be afcending, and *Mars* in that Signe, the mother fhall die, and not the childe ; if *Saturn*, both the mother and child fhall die ; and if the *Dragons Tail* be there, its poffible they will both die ; but the infant fhall not e-fcape ; and if the *Dragons Tail* be fo in the firft, and the tenth Houfe fallen: the mother fhall die; likewife if *Mars* and the *Moon*, or *Mars* and *Saturn* be in the firft, feventh or tenth, the mother fhall die.

Whether the party with child fhall mifcarry, or not. Con-fider if a moveable Signe be afcending, becaufe if it be fo, fhe will mifcarry.

If you would know whether a woman fhall bring forth a man-child, or a woman-child ; behold the Afcendent and his Lord, which if he be mafculine, and in a mafculine Signe, or in a mafculine quarter of the Figure , it is a male-childe ; but if the Lord of the Afcendent be feminine, and in a femi-nine Signe, or in a feminine quarter of the Circle, it will be a woman-child ; and fo you fhall confider alfo of the *Moon*. Confider alfo if more of the Planets be in mafculine Signes, then it will be a male-child ; and if many Planets be in feminine Signes, then it is a female-childe.

And if you would know whether the child be legitimate or adulterate ; fee if *Saturn*, *Mars* or the *Dragons Tail* be in the fifth, or with the Lord of the fifth ; becaufe if it be fo, it is adulterate ; but if a good Planet fhall be there , it is le-gitimate : and if the Lord of the firft , be in the fifth , or

X   with

with his Lord, it is legitimate ; and ſo likewiſe if the Lord of the fifth be found in the firſt, or with the Lord of the firſt.

If you deſire to know whether rumours be true or falſe, ſee if you finde *Saturn, Mars* or the *Dragons Tail*, in the Aſcendent ; becanſe if they be ſo, then the rumours are falſe ; but if you finde the *Sun, Jupiter* or the *Dragons Head* there, then they are true ; and if there be maſculine Planets in maſculine Signes, & feminine Planets in feminine Signes, then they are true; and if both good and evil Planets be there, then they are partly true and partly falſe ; and if there be a good Signe with the Planet, it teſtifies the truth ; and if the Planet fall with an evil Signe, then it is falſe ; likewiſe if *Mercury* be in the firſt , the news is falſe : but if the *Moon* be in the firſt in a feminine Signe , or joyned with the Lord of the Aſcendent in a feminine Signe, then the rumours are true ; alſo if good Planets be in the firſt, fifth or ninth, and feminine Signes, they are true ; but if otherwiſe, they are not.

If you would know whether any one that is abſent will return , and when ; ſee the Lord of the Aſcendent and the firſt , which if you finde them together , for certain he will come , and is now beginning his Journey. Likewiſe if the Lord of the fifth be in the firſt, or with the Lord of the firſt, and if he be in his fall, the meſſenger is ſick in his way ; but if the Lord of the fifth be exalted, then he cometh joyfully. And if he be in a cadent Signe, he ſhall be grievouſly afflicted with ſickneſs, or ſhall die.

If you would know if he bringeth that with him for which he went, or not, behold the Lord of the ſeventh; which if he be good, he bringeth that which he ſought for ; and if he be in his fall, or an evil Planet be there, he bringeth nothing with him.

Queſtions of the ſixth Houſe.

WHether the ſick ſhall recover his health, or die. If the Queſtion be concerning his ſickneſs , ſee if *Saturn,* or *Mars,* or the *Dragons Tail* be in the firſt, and whether his
Lord

Lord be joyued with an evil Planet , then he fhall die foon. And if the Lord of the firft be good , and evil Planets be in the firft with his Lord, or likewife in the firft or the eighth, for certain he will die : But if the Lord of the firft be in the eighth, or with the Lord of the eighth ; or the Lord of the eighth in the firft, or with the Lord of the firft, there is doubt of his death. And if evil Planets do poffefs the Angles, evil and deftruction is threatned to the fick. But if good Planets fhall be in the firft , fixth and eighth, and likewife in the Angles, and the Lord of the firft be from the eighth & his Lord, then the fick perfon fhall live and recover his health.

If you defire to know whether he will be cured by medicines , give the firft Houfe to the Phyfician, the tenth to the fick, the feventh to his difeafes , and the fourth to the medicines. If evill Planets be in the firft, the Phyfician fhall profit him nothing ; but they teftifie that this will be worfe for the difeafed : but the Fortunes do fignifie , that he fhall be profitable to him. And if evil Planets do occupy the tenth Houfe, the fick perfon is the caufe ; for they teftifie , that he himfelf is the caufe of his own difeafe : but the Fortunes being there, fignifie the contrary. But if evil Planets be in the tenth Houfe , they change the condition of the fick out of one difeafe into another ; but the Fortunes being there, do deliver him without the help of Phyfitians or medicines. Alfo evil Planets being in the fourth , do teftifie , that the medicines do augment his grief ; & the Fortunes being there, do mitigate and heal him.

If thou wouldft know if thou fhalt go unto the perfon and heal him ; confider the place then : for if he fhall be with *Saturn, Mars* , or the *Dragons Tail,* or * R * with the *Sun,* go not unto him ; but if *Jupiter, Venus* or the *Dragons Head* be in the firft or in the feventh, go, for it will be good : and if there be the *Moon* with a good Planet, go, and give him phyfick ; but if fhe fhall be with an evil Planet, and efpecially in the feventh Houfe, then thou fhalt not go ; becaufe thou fhalt profit him nothing : and if there be good Planets there, go and look diligently to him, where or in what mem-

bers

bers he ſuffers ; becauſe *Aries* hath the head, *Taurus* the neck, *Cancer* the breaſt and lungs, *Leo* the heart and ſtomack, *Virgo* the belly and inteſtines, *Libra* the reins and loyns, *Scorpio* the ſecret members, *Sagittary* the thighs, *Capricorn* the knees, *Aquary* the legs, and *Piſces* the feet.

Queſtions of the ſeventh Houſe.

FOr theft, look unto the Lord of the ſeventh : which if he be in the firſt, the theft ſhall be reſtored again ; but if the Lord of the firſt be in the ſeventh, it ſhall be a long time ſought after, and at length ſhall be found : but if the *Moon* be in the firſt, or with his Lord, it ſhall be found ; if the *Moon* be in the fifth, or with the Lord of the firſt, or * R * in the firſt, it may be found ; but if the *Sun* and the *Moon* be in the fifth, and if the Lord of the eighth be with the Lord of the firſt in the firſt, it ſhall be found ; but if the Lord of the ſecond be in the eighth, it ſhall not be found. And if *Saturn*, or *Mars*, or the *Dragons Tail* be in the ſecond, it ſhall not be found, nor be altogether loſt. And if the Lord of the ſecond be in the firſt, the thing that is loſt ſhall be found ; but it ſhall not be known from whence it came. If the Lord of the firſt be in the ſecond, it may be found after much labour. And if the Lord of the ſecond be in his fall, it will never be found ; but if he be exalted, it ſhall be found very well : but the ſeventh Houſe ſheweth the thief.

But if you would know what it is that is ſtollen , behold the Lord of the ſecond ; which if he be *Saturn*, it is lead, iron, a kettle, a trivet, a garment, or ſome black thing, or leather. If he be *Jupiter*, then it is ſome white thing, as tin, ſilver, or mixt with white & yellow veins. The *Sun* ſignifies gold and precious pearles. *Mars* ſignifies things belonging to the fire. *Venus* ſignifies things belonging to women , as gloves, rings, and fair ornaments. The *Moon*, beaſts, ſuch as horſes, mules, &c. perfumes and wars. *Mercury* ſignifies money, books, writings, pictures, or garments of divers colours.

If you would know how many thieves there were , ſee
the

the Lord of the fixth ; which if he be in the fecond, or with the Lord of the fecond, there were many thieves ; and if they be in the third, the brethren or kinfmen of the Querent have committed the theft.

If you would know whether the thief do yet remain in the Town : if they be in fuccedent Houfes, he is not gone far off ; but if they be in cadent Houfes, he is far remote.

If you defire to know towards what Country the thief is fled, fee in what Signe the Lord of the feventh is ; for if he be in *Aries*, he is in the middle of the Eaft part. If in *Taurus*, in the South towards the Eaft. If in *Gemini*, in the Weft towards the South. If in *Cancer*, full North. If in *Leo*, in the Eaft towards the North. If in *Virgo*, in the South towards the Weft. If in *Libra*, full Weft. If in *Scorpio*, in the North neer the Weft. If in *Sagittary*, in the Eaft nigh the North. If in *Capricorn*, full South. If in *Aquary*, in the Weft towards the North. And if in *Pifces*, in the North towards the Weft.

If you would know whether the thief hath carried all the things ftollen away with him, fee the Lord of the feventh and the eighth; and if the Lord of the feventh be in an Angle, he had a defire to carry away the fame with him, but could not. If the Lord of the eighth be in a mean Houfe, or in a cadent Houfe, and the Lord of the fecond in a ftrong Houfe, he hath carryed the theft wholly with him. And if the Lord of the feventh and the eighth be both in cadent Houfes, he neither carryed it away, nor hath it. See by the feventh who is his companion, and what is his gain.

If you would know the defcent or nobility of a man or woman, look unto the Lord of the feventh ; which if you finde him in Angles, and the Lord of the firft in Succedents or cadents, the woman is more noble then the man. But if the Lord of the Afcendent be in an Angle, & the Lord of the feventh in a fuccedent or cadent Houfe, the man is more noble then the woman. And after the fame manner thou maift judge of two companions, or of any other perfons whatfoever. And if the Lord of the feventh be in the ninth Houfe, he will take a wife out of a forreigne Country.   If

If you deſire to know whether an intended marriage ſhall take effect, or not, look to the Aſcendent and his Lord, and the *Moon*, for the Querent ; and the ſeventh Houſe, and his Lord, for the woman. And if the Lord of the Aſcendent or the *Moon* be joyned to the Lord of the ſeventh, or be in the ſeventh, the marriage will be effected ; or if the Lord of the ſeventh be in the firſt, or with the Lord of the firſt, it will eaſily be brought to paſs ; and the woman is more deſirous thereof, then the man.

If you would know whether thy wife or friend hath any o-ther lover or not, look if *Mars* be in the ſeventh, ſo that he be not in his own Houſe, for then ſhe hath not any other lover. And if *Saturn* be there, ſhe loveth another; but he lieth not with her. And if the *Dragons Tail* be in the ſeventh, he lieth with her. And if *Jupiter* be there, ſhe hardly con-taineth her ſelf chaſte. If *Venus*, ſhe is merry, and much given to play and laughter, by reaſon whereof, ſhe may be accounted a whore, and is not ſo. If *Mercury* be in the ſe-venth, ſhe had a lover, but now hath none. But if the *Moon* be in the ſeventh, ſhe hath had no lover as yet, but will have one, and will be common. But if the *Sun* or the *Dragons Head* be there, ſhe is chaſte. And after the ſame manner may you judge in the * ninth * concerning friends or lovers.

* ibidem
ſorte.
If you would know which of them ſhall live longeſt, ſee the Lord of the firſt and of the ſeventh, which of them ſhall be in the ſtronger and better place, or joyned to the ſtrongeſt Planets ; and that perſon who is moſt free and remote from the Lord of the eighth and his participation, to whom the Lord of his Houſe anſwereth, ſhall live longeſt.

If you deſire to make a ſociety or alliance, and would know whether it ſhall be brought to paſs or not, or what ſhall happen thereupon, ſee if there be good Planets in the ſe-venth and the firſt : and if ſo, the fellowſhip will be made, and good will come thereof ; and you may judge it to con-tinue ſo many years, months or dayes, as the Lord of the ſe-venth hath ſignification of.

If you would know when ſuch ſociety ſhall be, look
what

what Planet is in the ſeventh; for if he be good, it ſhall come to paſs that ſame year: or wedlock, * R * if the Queſtion be thereof.

If you would know whether they will well agree, ſee the firſt and his Lord, which is the ſignifier of the Querent; and the ſeventh Houſe and his Lord, which is the Houſe of companions, wives and concubines; which if they be concordant amongſt themſelves, there will be peace and union between them, and they ſhall profit; but if the Planets be in diſcord, there will be ſtrife between them, and the ſociety will not profit.

If you would know which of them ſhall gain moſt, ſee the firſt and his Lord, and the ſeventh and his Lord, and which of them ſtandeth beſt; or if they be evil, which of them falleth: and he that falleth ſhall loſe, and he that is exalted ſhall gain. Or otherwiſe, and which is better, ſee the ſecond and his Lord, and the eighth and his Lord; and in which Houſe is the better Planet, or his Lord that ſhall be found in the better place, or joyned with the better Planets he ſhall be the greater gainer. The ſecond Houſe and his Lord ſignifies the gain of the Querent: and the eighth Houſe and his Lord ſignifies the gain of his fellow, or his part: and if they be both good, they ſhall both gain; and if both evil, they ſhall both loſe: and if one be good and the other evil, he whoſe ſignificator is good, ſhall gain; and he whoſe is evil, ſhall loſe.

And if you would know if two fellows ſhall love one another, look if the Lords of the firſt and the ſeventh be friends and agreeing, then they will love one to another; but if they be enemies and diſagree, then they will not.

If you deſire to know who ſhall overcome in any cauſe, matter or controverſie, behold the Lords of the firſt and the ſeventh, which if they be in Angles, neither of them ſhall overcome; and ſee which of them is joyned with an evil Planet, becauſe he ſhall overcome; and if the Planet be evil from them both, the victor ſhall kill the conquered; if one of them be ſtrong, and the other weak, and the Planet

which

which is in the ſtrong Houſe do not fall, nor hath not an evil
Planet with him ; and if he which is weak be not in his own
Houſe, nor in his exaltation , nor with a good Planet , he
whoſe Planet is in the ſtrong Houſe, ſhall overcome ; likewiſe he whoſe ſignificator is in a mean Houſe, ſhall have great
fear and doubt in his heart, becauſe ſometimes he ſhall hope
to conquer, and otherwhiles fear to be overcome. And note,
that in a Queſtion concerning war and kingdom, it is ſaid that
there is more power and efficacie , or fortitude in the exaltation of a Planet, then in his Houſe ; but in all other Queſtions the contrary.

If you would be informed concerning any one being that
is gone to any fight, whether he ſhall return ſafe , ſee the
Lord of the Aſcendent ; if he be good , that is , with good
Planets, and a good Planet in the firſt , he will return ſafe;
but if the _Sun_ be with the Lord of the firſt, in any part of the
Queſtion, let him not go, becauſe the _Sun_ burneth him. And
if the Lord of the ſeventh be with a good Planet , and the
Lord of the firſt with a good Planet likewiſe, he ſhall have
ſome impediment in the way ; but he will not die. And
if an evil Planet be with the Lord of the firſt, and a good
Planet in the firſt , if he goeth he ſhall ſuffer great damage,
but not death ; neverthelefs he may be grievouſly wounded.
And if _Saturn_ be in the firſt, or with the Lord of the firſt , let
him not go ; becauſe ſome impediment will happen unto
him by ſome man that he will meet. And if there be an e-
vil Planet with the Lord of the firſt, or _Saturn_ be in the firſt,
or with the Lord of the firſt, he will be wounded with wood
or with a ſtone. If _Mars_ and the _Dragons Tail_ be in the firſt,
or with the Lord of the firſt ; or if there be evil Planets in
the firſt, or with the Lord of the firſt, he will ſuffer wounds
or death. See likewiſe if there be an evil Planet in the eighth,
becauſe then death is to be feared. And if the _Sun_ be with
the Lord of the ſeventh, or in the eighth , it ſignifies that it
is ill to go. The like judgement is of the ſeventh and the
tenth.

And if a Queſtion be propoſed concerning the event of
war

War, fee the feventh and the firft, and their Lords : for the firft Houfe and his Lord fignifies the Querent ; and the feventh Houfe and his Lord the adverfary. So that if there be good Planets in the firft, and evil in the feventh ; and if the Lord of the firft and feventh be evil, the Querent fhall overcome : but if there be an evil Planet with the Lord of the firft, and an evil Planet in the firft, and the Lord of the feventh good, or ✶ R. ✶ in the feventh, the Querent fhall be overcome, or taken, or flain. And if the Lords of them both be in the firft, and there be good Planets from the part of the firft Houfe, unto the end of the Houfe which is the middle of the Queftion ; and if evil Planets do poffefs the other half of the Queftion, that is to fay, from the feventh unto the end of the twelfth houfe, the adveffary fhall overcome. But if both the Lords fhall be in the Afcendent, and if they be good from the part of the firft, and evil from the part of the feventh, they fhall both fuffer great lofs ; but the Querent fhall have the better in the end. But if the Lord of the Afcendent be in the feventh, or in his Queftion, it fignifies fortitude of the adverfary : and if the Lord of the feventh be in the firft, or in his Queftion, it fignifies fortitude of the actor. And if the Lord of the Afcendent be in the eighth, or with the Lord of the eighth ; or the Lord of the eighth in the firft, or with the Lord of the firft, it fignifies the death of the Querent. And if the Lord of the feventh be in the fecond, or with his Lord ; or the Lord of the fecond in the feventh, or with the Lord of the feventh, it fignifies the death of the enemy.

If you would know whether War fhall continue long or not, if mean or meanly ; if the Lords of the firft and the feventh do agree, the parties fhall be pacified after the War.

If thou wouldeft depart from the place wherein thou art, and remove thy felf to fome other place ; and if thou wouldeft know whether it be better for thee to ftay or go : or concerning two bufineffes, if thou defireft to know which of them is moft expedient for thee to undertake, confider

Y   the

the Lords of the firſt and the ſecond, for thoſe places to which thou wouldeſt go, the place wherein thou art, and the gain which thou getteſt there ; and the ſeventh and the eighth, and their Lords, for the place to which thou wouldeſt go, and the gain which thou mayſt get there : and thoſe places chuſe, whoſe Lords are the better, or joyned to the better Planets. Or otherwiſe: behold the Lord of the Aſcendent, and the Moon ; which if they be ſeparated from evil Planets, and joyned to good and fortunate Planets, it is better for thee to go from the place where thou art, then to ſtay there, and to do what buſineſs ſoever thou haſt in thy minde. And if the Lord of the Aſcendent and the Moon be ſeparated from the Fortunes, and joyned to evil Planets, then it is not good for thee to remove thy ſelf, nor to do thy buſineſs. Or thus: See the Moon; and if the Planet from which ſhe is ſeparated be better then that to whom ſhe is joyned, do not remove : and if the Planet which ſhe is joyned to, be better then that from which ſhe is ſeparated, then go.

Queſtions of the eighth Houſe.

Concerning any man or woman, if you would know what kinde of death they ſhall die, ſee if *Leo, Scorpio,* or †R.† *Mars,* be in the eighth, the party ſhall die by a beaſt. And if *Saturn* be in the eighth, or with the Lord of the eighth in *Scorpio, Cancer,* or *Piſces,* he ſhall die in water. And if an evil Planet be in the eighth, or with the Lord of the eighth ; or if *Mars* or the *Dragons Tayl* be there, he ſhall die by fire, iron, or of a fever. And if there be a good Planet in the eighth, or with the Lord of the eighth, he ſhall die a good death.

Questions of the ninth House.

COncerning long journeys, fee if the Lord of the eighth have good Planets with him : and if *Saturn* be in the ninth, and exalted in the tenth, fo that he be not in his own Houfe, do not go : for thou wilt meet with many obftacles, and War. And if an evil Planet be in the ninth, or with the Lord of the ninth, and the Lord of the ninth in his fall, he fhall fuffer great damage in the way : for if he goeth by water, he fhall fuffer fhipwrack ; and if by Land, he fhall have misfortunes, be taken, or die. If *Saturn* be in the ninth, or with his Lord, go fecurely. And if a good Planet be in the ninth, or with the Lord of the ninth, the way is good and fecure. And if *Mars* be in the ninth, thou mayeft not go : for thou wilt meet with mortal enemies in the way. And if the Lord of the ninth be with an evil † Planet, or the Sun, it fignifies ill : but he fhall not be taken. And if the Lord of the ninth have a good Planet neer him, he fhall efcape : but if evil, he fhall be taken. If *Venus* be in the ninth, or with the Lord of the ninth, the way will be good, becaufe he fhall have comfort from women. And if *Mercury* be in the ninth, and the Lord of the ninth with good Planets, the way will be very good : and if he be with evil Planets, it will be evil. And the fame is faid of the Moon, as of *Mercury.* If the *Dragons Tayl* be in the ninth, he will meet with theeves, or fome evil people. And if the *Dragons Head* be in the ninth, the way will be good, becaufe he fhall be accompanied with Noble-men. And in this maner may you judge in the third Houfe concerning fhort journeys.

If you would know when the journey fhall be accomplifhed, fee the Lord of the ninth, and according to his fortitude or debility judge, becaufe according to the place wherein he is, is fignified yeers, months, or days : and fo you fhall judge concerning his ftay, about what time he will

come,

come , by turning the yeers of the Lord of the ninth into days; becauſe ſo many days he ſhall tarry, as the Planet ſignifies in the place where he is. Or otherwiſe : weak Angles ſignifie a ſpeedy journey, mean Angles a mean journey; and the Lord of the ninth likewiſe, according to the place wherein he is found.

And this I ſay concerning his return.

If you would know whether he ſhall return from his journey with an imperfect voyage or not , ſee if the Moon be joyned with the Lord of the firſt, the third, or the ninth, and the Planet thereof be in his fall ; becauſe if it be ſo, he ſhall return with an imperfect voyage. And if the Moon be in her exaltation , the journey ſhall ſpeedily be effected. And if there be two ſtrong Planets, and one cadent , the journey ſhall be made ; and if one be ſtrong, and another in his fall, he ſhall retire back.

Queſtions of the tenth Houſe.

IF thou wouldeſt know whether thou ſhalt have any honour or benefit from a King, Biſhop, or Lord, or not, look unto the firſt Houſe, and the ninth, and their Lords : and if the Lord of the firſt be in the ninth, or with the Lord of the ninth , or with any other good Planet ; or if the Lord of the ninth be in the firſt , or with the Lord of the firſt , or with any other good Planet , as *Venus, Jupiter,* or the *Dragons Head*; or if any of them be the Lord of the ninth, or ✴ R.✴ of the firſt, he ſhall receive honour and benefits from them.

And if you would know whether he ſhall have it in his own Country, or in a forraign Country, look if the Lord of the ninth be in angles, then it ſhall be in his own Country : and if in ſuccedents, it ſhall be neer ; but if in cadent Houſes, very far off.

Queſtions of the eleventh Houſe.

IF you would know when it is good to ſet forth a Ship to Sea, ſee the Aſcendent; which if it be ſtable, the Ship will be ponderous ; but if the Lord thereof be with a good Planet, ſhe will ſuſtain a great weight. And if the Aſcendent be inſtable, and with a good Planet, the Ship will be ſwift, and carry a good burden. And meanly, if the Aſcendent be mean. And after this maner may you judge concerning an Horſe, if a Queſtion be thereof.

And if any unſtable Signe be aſcending, and his Lord be in his exaltation, or otherwiſe fortunate, and the Moon behold him with a lowring Aſpect, or Sextile ; let the Ship be applied to the water, becauſe ſhe will be very ſwift. And if any evil be impoſed upon her, or that ſhe be like to be drawn into it ; then ſet her out when a ſtable Signe is aſcending, or when the Moon is in the third, fifth, eighth, ninth, or tenth houſe or manſion.

If you would know what winde ſhe ſhall have, behold the Aſcendent and his Lord, whether he be with good or evil Planets, and in what place, and accordingly judge.

And if you would have a ſtong winde, ſpread forth your Sayls at the riſing of *Aquary* : if a ſmall winde, ſpread your Canvas when *Libra* is aſcending : If a moderate winde, then direct your Sayls under *Gemini*.

Queſtions of the twelfth Houſe.

FOr Impriſonment, conſider the twelfth and the firſt ; and if the Lord of the twelfth be in the firſt, or with the Lord of the firſt, &c.

ארבע-

ארבעתאל

Of the MAGICK of the Ancients,
The greateſt Studie of Wiſdom.

In all things, ask counſel of the Lord; and do not thou think, ſpeak, or do any thing, wherein God is not thy counſellor.

Proverbs 11.

He that walketh fraudulently, revealeth ſecrets: but he that is of a faithful ſpirit, concealeth the matter.

ARBATEL of MAGICK:
OR,
The ſpiritual Wiſdom of the Ancients,
as well Wiſe-men of the people of God,
as *MAGI* of the Gentiles : for the illuſtration of the glory of God, and his love to Mankinde.

Now firſt of all produced out of darkneſs into the light, againſt all caco-Magicians, and contemners of the gifts of God ; for the profit and delectation of all thoſe, who do truely and piouſly love the creatures of God, and do uſe them with thankſgiving, to the honour of God, and profit of themſelves and their neighbours.

Con-

Containing nine Tomes , and feven Septenaries of
APHORISMS.

The firſt is called *Iſagoge* , or, A Book of the Inſtitutions
of Magick: or, *ἡ πνδυματκῆς ·* which in fourty and nine A-
phoriſms comprehendeth the moſt general Precepts of the
whole Art.

The ſecond is Microcoſmical Magick, what *Microcoſmus*
hath effected Magically , by his Spirit and Genius addicted
to him from his Nativity, that is, ſpiritual wiſdom : and how
the ſame is effected.

The third is Olympick Magick , in what maner a man may
do and ſuffer by the ſpirits of *Olympus.*

The fourth is Heſiodiacal, and Homerical Magick, which
teacheth the operations by the Spirits called *Cacodæmones,*
as it were not adverſaries to mankinde.

The fifth is Romane or Sibylline Magick , which acteth
and operates with Tutelar Spirits and Lords , to whom the
whole Orb of the earth is diſtributed. This is *valde inſignis
Magia.* To this alſo is the doctrine of the *Druids* referred.

The ſixth is Pythagorical Magick , which onely acteth
with Spirits to whom is given the doctrine of Arts, as Phy-
ſick, Medicines, Mathematicks, Alchymie , and ſuch kinde
of Arts.

The ſeventh is the Magick of *Apollonius,* and the like, and
agreeth with the Romane and Microcoſmical Magick: onely
it hath this thing peculiar, that it hath power over the hoſtile
ſpirits of mankinde.

The eighth is Hermetical, that is, Ægyptiacal Magick; and
differeth not much from Divine Magick.

The ninth is that wiſdom which dependeth ſolely upon
the Word of God; and this is called Prophetical Magick.

The

The firſt Tome of the Book of
Arbatel of Magick,
CALLED
I S A G O G E.

IN the Name of the Creator of all things both viſible and inviſible, who revealeth his Myſteries out of his Treaſures to them that call upon him ; and fatherly and mercifully beſtoweth thoſe his Secrets upon us without meaſure. May he grant unto us, through his onely-begotten Son Jeſus Chriſt our Lord, his miniſtring ſpirits, the revealers of his ſecrets, that we may write this Book of *Arbatel,* concerning the greateſt Secrets which are lawful for man to know, and to uſe them without offence unto God. *Amen.*

The firſt Septenary of Aphoriſms.

The firſt Aphoriſm.

Whoſoever would know Secrets, let him know how to keep ſecret things ſecretly ; and to reveal thoſe things that are to be revealed , and to ſeal thoſe things which are to be ſealed : and *not to give holy things to dogs, nor caſt pearls before*
Z

ſwine.

swine. Obferve this Law, and the eyes of thy Underftanding fhall be opened, to underftand fecret things ; and thou fhalt have whatfoever thy minde defireth to be divinely revealed unto thee. Thou fhalt have alfo the Angels and Spirits of God prompt and ready in their nature to minifter unto thee, as much as any humane minde can defire.

Aphor. 2.

In all things, call upon the Name of the Lord : and without prayer unto God through his onely-begotten Son, do not thou undertake to do or think any thing. And ufe the Spirits given and attributed unto thee, as Minifters, without rafhnefs and prefumption, as the meffengers of God ; having a due reverence towards the Lord of Spirits. And the remainder of thy life do thou accomplifh , demeaning thy felf peaceably , to the honour of God, and the profit of thy felf and thy neighbour.

Aphor. 3.

Live to thy felf, and the Mufes : avoid the friendfhip of the Multitude : be thou covetous of time, beneficial to all men. Ufe thy Gifts, be vigilant in thy Calling ; and let the Word of God never depart from thy mouth.

Aphor. 4.

Be obedient to good Admonitions : avoid all procraftination : accuftom thy felf to Conftancie and Gravity, both in thy words and deeds. Refift the temptations of the Tempter, by the Word of God. Flee from earthly things ; feek after heavenly things. Put no confidence in thy own wifdom ; but look unto God in all things, according to that fentence of the Scripture : *When we know not what we fhall do, unto thee, O God, do we lift up our eyes , and from thee we expect our help.* For where all humane refuges do forfake us , there
will

will the help of God shine forth, according to the saying of
Philo.

Aphor. 5.

Thou shalt love the Lord thy God with all thy heart, and with
all thy strength, and thy neighbour as thy self : And the Lord
will keep thee as the apple of his eye, and will deliver thee
from all evil, and will replenish thee with all good ; and
nothing shall thy soul desire, but thou shalt be fully endued
therewith, so that it be contingent to the salvation of thy
soul and body.

Aphor. 6.

Whatsoever thou hast learned, frequently repeat, and fix
the same in thy minde : and learn much,but not many things,
because a humane understanding cannot be alike capable in
all things,unless it be such a one that is divinely regenerated;
unto him nothing is so difficult or manifold, which he may
not be able equally to attain to.

Aphor. 7.

Call upon me in the day of trouble, and *I will hear thee,* and
thou shalt glorifie me, saith the Lord. For all Ignorance is tri-
bulation of the minde ; therefore call upon the Lord in thy
ignorance, and he will hear thee. And remember that thou
give honour unto God, and say with the Psalmist, *Not unto
us, Lord, not unto us, but unto thy Name give the glory.*

The second Septenary.

Aphor. 8.

Even as the Scripture testifies, that God appointeth names

to

to things or perfons, and alfo with them hath diftributed
certain powers and offices out of his treafures : fo the Characters and Names of Stars have not any power by reafon of
their figure or pronunciation, but by reafon of the vertue or
office which God hath ordained by nature either to fuch a
Name or Character. For there is no power either in heaven
or in earth, or hell, which doth not defcend from God ; and
without his permiffion, they can neither give or draw forth
into any action, any thing they have.

Aphor. 9.

That is the chiefeft wifdom, which is from God ; and
next, that which is in fpiritual creatures ; afterwards, in corporal creatures ; fourthly, in Nature, and natural things. The
Spirits that are apoftate, and referved to the laft judgement,
do follow thefe, after a long interval. Sixthly, the minifters
of punifhments in hell, and the obedient unto God. Seventhly, the Pigmies do not poffefs the loweft place, and they who
inhabit in elements, and elementary things. It is convenient therefore to know and difcern all differences of the
wifdom of the Creator and the Creatures , that it may be
certainly manifeft unto us, what we ought to affume to our
ufe of every thing, and that we may know in truth how and
in what maner that may be done. For truely every creature
is ordained for fome profitable end to humane nature , and
for the fervice thereof; as the holy Scriptures, Reafon, and
Experience, do teftifie.

Aphor. 10.

God the Father Almighty, Creator of heaven and earth,
and of all things vifible and invifible , in the holy Scriptures
propofeth himfelf to have an eye over us ; and as a tender
father which loveth his children, he teacheth us what is profitable, and what not ; what we are to avoid, and what we
are to embrace : then he allureth us to obedience with great
promifes

promifes of corporal and eternal benefits, and deterreth us
(with threatning of punifhments) from thofe things which
are not profitable for us. Turn over therefore with thy
hand, both night and day, thofe holy Writings, that thou
mayft be happie in things prefent, and bleffed to all eternity.
Do this, and thou fhalt live, which the holy Books have
taught thee.

Aphor. 11.

A number of Four is *Pythagorical*, and the firft Quadrate;
therefore here let us place the foundation of all wifdom, after the wifdom of God revealed in the holy Scriptures, and
to the Confiderations propofed in Nature.

Appoint therefore to him who folely dependeth upon
God, the wifdom of every creature to ferve and obey him,
nolens volens, willing or unwilling. And in this, the Omnipotency of God fhineth forth. It confifteth therefore in
this, that we will difcern the creatures which ferve us, from
thofe that are unwilling ; and that we may learn how to ac-
commodate the wifdom and offices of every creature unto
our felves. This Art is not delivered, but divinely. Unto
whom God will, he revealeth his fecrets ; but to whom he
will not beftow any thing out of his treafuries, that perfon
fhall attain to nothing without the will of God.

Therefore we ought truely to defire τὴν πνδμαικὴν ἐπιςμμὴν
from God alone, which will mercifully impart thefe things
unto us. For he who hath given us his Son, and commanded us to pray for his holy Spirit, How much more will he
fubject unto us the whole creature, and things vifible and
invifible ? *Whatfoever ye ask, ye fhall receive.* Beware that
ye do not abufe the gifts of God, and all things fhall work
together unto you for your falvation. And before all things,
be watchful in this, That your names be written in heaven :
this is more light, That the fpirits be obedient unto you, as
Chrift admonifheth.

Aphor-

Aphor. 12.

In the *Acts of the Apostles*, the Spirit faith unto *Peter* after the Vifion, *Go down, and doubt not but I have fent them*, when he was fent for from *Cornelius* the Centurion.   After this maner, in vocal words, are all difciplines delivered , by the holy Angels of God, as it appeareth out of the Monuments of the Ægyptians. And thefe things afterwards were vitiated and corrupted with humane opinions ; and by the inftigation of evil fpirits , who fow tares amongft the children of difobedience, as it is manifeft out of St. *Paul* , and *Hermes Trifmegiftus*.   There is no other maner of reftoring thefe Arts, then by the doctrine of the holy Spirits of God ; becaufe true *faith cometh by hearing*.   But becaufe thou mayft be certain of the truth , and mayft not doubt whether the fpirits that fpeak with thee, do declare things true or falfe , let it onely depend upon thy faith in God ; that thou mayft fay with *Paul* , *I know on whom I truft*.   If no fparrow can fall to the ground without the will of the Father which is in heaven, How much more will not God fuffer thee to be deceived, O thou of little faith, if thou dependeft wholly upon God, and adhereft onely to him ?

Aphor. 13.

The Lord liveth ; and all things which live , do live in him.   And he is truely יהוה, who hath given unto all things , that they be that which they are :   and by his word alone, through his Son, hath produced all things out of nothing, which are in being.   He calleth all the ftars, and all the hoft of heaven by their names.   He therefore knoweth the true ftrength and nature of things , the order and policie of every creature vifible and invifible , to whom God hath revealed the names of his creatures.   It remaineth alfo , that he receive power from God, to extract the vertues in nature, and hidden fecrets of the creature ; and to produce their
power

power into action, out of darknefs into light. Thy fcope therefore ought to be, that thou have the names of the Spirits, that is, their powers and offices, and how they are fubjected and appointed by God to minifter unto thee ; even as *Raphael* was fent to *Tobias*, that he fhould heal his father, and deliver his fon from dangers, and bring him to a wife. So *Michael*, the fortitude of God governeth the people of God : *Gabriel*, the meffenger of God, was fent to *Daniel*, *Mary*, and *Zachary* the father of *John Baptift*. And he fhall be given to thee that defireft him, who will teach thee whatfoever thy foul fhall defire, in the nature of things. His miniftery thou fhalt ufe with trembling and fear of thy Creator, Redeemer, and Sanctifier, that is to fay, the Father, Son, and holy Ghoft : and do not thou let flip any occafion of learning, and be vigilant in thy calling, and thou fhalt want nothing that is neceffary for thee.

Aphor. 14.

Thy foul liveth for ever, through him that hath created thee: call therefore upon the Lord thy God, and him onely fhalt thou ferve. This thon fhalt do, if thou wilt perform that end for which thou art ordained of God, and what thou oweft to God and to thy neighbour. God requireth of thee a minde, that thou fhouldeft honour his Son, and keep the words of his Son in thy heart : if thou honour him, thou haft done the will of thy Father which is in heaven. To thy neighbour thou oweft offices of humanity, and that thou draw all men that come to thee, to honour the Son. This is the Law and the Prophets. In temporal things, thou oughteft to call upon God as a father, that he would give unto thee all neceffaries of this life : and thou oughteft to help thy neighbour with the gifts which God beftoweth upon thee, whether they be fpiritual or corporal.

Aphor.

Therefore thou shalt pray thus :

O Lord *of heaven and earth, Creator and Maker of all things visible and invisible ; I, though unworthy, by thy assistance call upon thee, through thy onely-begotten Son Jesus Christ our Lord, that thou wilt give unto me thy holy Spirit, to direct me in thy truth unto all good.* Amen.

Because I earnestly desire perfectly to know the Arts of this life, and such things as are necessary for us, which are so over-whelmed in darkness, and polluted with infinite humane opinions, that I of my own power can attain to no knowledge in them, unless thou teach it me : Grant me therefore one of thy spirits, who may teach me those things which thou wouldest have me to know and learn, to thy praise and glory, and the profit of our neighbour. Give me also an apt and teachable heart, that I may easily under-stand those things which thou shalt teach me, and may hide them in my understanding, that I may bring them forth as out of thy inexhaustible treasures, to all necessary uses. And give me grace, that I may use such thy gifts humbly, with fear and trembling, through our Lord Jesus Christ, with thy holy Spirit. Amen.

The third Septenary.

Aphor. 15.

They are called *Olympick* spirits, which do inhabit in the firmament, and in the stars of the firmament: and the office of these spirits is to declare Destinies, and to administer fatal Charms, so far forth as God pleaseth to permit them : for nothing, neither evil spirit nor evil Destiny, shall be able to hurt him who hath the most High for his refuge. If there-fore any of the *Olympick* spirits shall teach or declare that which his star to which he is appointed portendeth, never-thelefs he can bring forth nothing into action, unless he be permitted by the Divine power. It is God alone who giveth them power to effect it. Unto God the maker of all things,

are

are obedient all things celestial, sublunary, and infernal. Therefore rest in this: Let God be thy guide in all things which thou undertakest, and all things shall attain to a happie and desired end ; even as the history of the whole world testifieth, and daily experience sheweth. There is peace to the godly : *there is no peace to the wicked, saith the Lord.*

Aphor. 16.

There are seven different governments of the Spirits of *Olympus,* by whom God hath appointed the whole frame and universe of this world to be governed : and their visible stars are ARATRON, BETHOR, PHALEG, OCH, HAGITH, OPHIEL, PHUL, after the *Olympick* speech. Every one of these hath under him a mighty *Militia* in the firmament.

ARATRON ruleth visible Provinces XLIX.
BETHOR, XXXII.
PHALEG, XXXV.
OCH, XXVIII.
HAGITH, XXI.
OPHIEL, XIIII.
PHUL, VII.

So that there are 186 *Olympick* Provinces in the whole Universe, wherein the seven Governours do exercise their power : all which are elegantly set forth in Astronomy. But in this place it is to be explained, in what maner these Princes and Powers may be drawn into communication. *Aratron* appeareth in the first hour of *Saturday,* and very truely giveth answers concerning his Provinces and Provincials. So likewise do the rest appear in order in their days and hours. Also every one of them ruleth 490 yeers. The beginning of their simple *Anomaly,* in the 60 yeer before the Nativity of Christ, was the beginning of the administration of *Bethor* ; and it lasted until the yeer of our Lord Christ 430. To whom succeeded *Phaleg,* until the 920 yeer. Then

A a   began

began *Och*, and continued untill the year **1410**. and thence-forth *Hagith* ruleth untill the year **1900**.

Aphor. **17**.

Magically the Princes of the feven Governors are called fimply, in that time, day, and hour wherein they rule vifibly or invifibly, by their Names and Offices which God hath given unto them ; and by propofing their Character which they have given or confirmed.

The Governour *Aratron* hath in his power thofe things which he doth naturally, that is, after the fame manner and fubject as thofe things which in Aftronomy are afcribed to the power of *Saturn*.

Thofe things which he doth of his own free will, are,

1. That he can convert any thing into a ftone in a moment, either animal or plant, retaining the fame object to the fight.

2. He converteth treafures into coles, and coles into treafure.

3. He giveth familiars with a definite power.

4. He teacheth *Alchymy*, Magick, and Phyfick.

5. He reconcileth the fubterranean fpirits to men ; maketh hairy men.

6. He caufeth one to bee invifible.

7. The barren he maketh fruitful, and giveth long life.

His character.

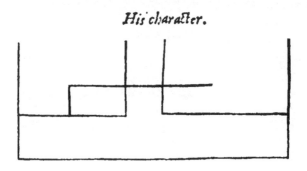

He hath under him 49 Kings, 42 Princes, 35 Prefidents, 28 Dukes, 21 Minifters, ftanding before him ; 14 familiars, feven meffengers : he commandeth 36000 legions of fpirits ; the numberof a legion is 490.

Bether governeth thofe things which are afcribed to *Jupiter :* he foon cometh being called. He that is dignified with his charaĉter ,he raifeth to very great dignities, to caft open treafures: he reconcileth the fpirits of the aire , that they give true anfwers :they tranfport precious ftones from place to place,and they make medicines to work miraculoufly in their effeĉts : he giveth alfo the familiars of the firmament , and prolongeth life to 700 yeares if God will

His charaĉter.

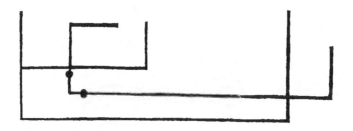

He hath under him 42 Kings, 35 Princes, 28 Dukes, 21 Counfellors,14 Minifters, 7 Meffengers, 29000 legions of Spirits.

Phalec ruleth thofe things which are attributed to *Mars,* the Prince of peace. He that hath his charaĉter, he raifeth to great honours in warlike affaires.

His character

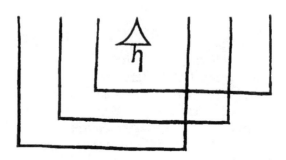

Och governeth folar things ; he giveth 600 yeares , with perfect health ; he beftoweth great wifdom, giveth the moft excellent Spirits, teacheth perfect Medicines : he converteth all things into moft pure gold and precious ftones : he giveth gold, and a purfe fpringing with gold. He that is dignified with his Character, he maketh him to be worfhipped as a Deity, by the Kings of the whole world.

The Character.

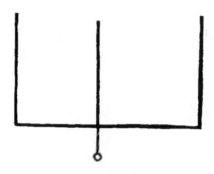

He hath under him 3 6 5 3 6 Legions : he adminiftreth all things alone : and all his fpirits ferve him by centuries.

Hagith

Hagith governeth *Venereous* things.   He that is dignified with his Character, he maketh very fair, and to be adorned with all beauty.   He converteth copper into gold, in a moment, and gold into copper: he giveth Spirits which do faithfully serve those to whom they are addicted.

His Character.

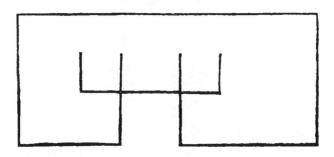

He hath 4000 Legions of Spirits, and over every thousand he ordaineth Kings for their appointed seasons.

Ophiel is the governour of such things as are attributed to *Mercury:* his Character is this.

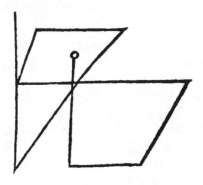

His

His Spirits are 1 oocoo Legions : he eafily giveth Familiar Spirits : he teacheth all Arts : and he that is dignified with
his Character, he maketh him to be able in a moment to convert Quickfilver into the Philofophers ftone.

Phul *hath this Character.*

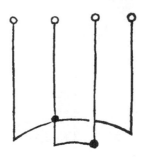

He changeth all metals into filver, in word and deed ; governeth Lunary things ; healeth the dropfie : he giveth fpirits
of the water, who do ferve men in a corporeal and vifible
form ; and maketh men to live 300 yeers.

The moft general Precepts of this Secret.

1. Every Governour acteth with all his Spirits, either naturally, to wit, always after the fame maner ; or otherwife of
their own free-will, if God hinder them not.

2. Every Governour is able to do all things which are
done naturally in a long time, out of matter before prepared ; and alfo to do them fuddenly, out of matter not before
prepared. As *Och,* the Prince of Solar things, prepareth
gold in the mountains in a long time ; in a lefs time, by the
Chymical Art ; and Magically, in a moment.

3. The true and divine Magician may ufe all the creatures
of God, and offices of the Governours of the world, at his
own will, for that the Governours of the world are obedient unto them, and come when they are called, and do execute

cute their commands : but God is the Author thereof : as *Joshua* caused the Sun to stand still in heaven.

They send some of their Spirits to the mean Magicians, which do obey them onely in some determinate businefs : but they hear not the false Magicians, but expose them to the deceits of the devils, and cast them into divers dangers, by the command of God ; as the Prophet *Jeremiah* testifieth, in his eighth Chapter, concerning the Jews.

4. In all the elements there are the seven Governours with their hosts, who do move with the equal motion of the firmament ; and the inferiours do always depend upon the superiours, as it is taught in Philofophy.

5. A man that is a true Magician, is brought forth a Magician from his mothers womb : others, who do give themfelves to this office, are unhappie. This is that which *John* the Baptift speaketh of: *No man can do any thing of himfelf, except it be given him from above.*

Every Character given from a Spirit, for what cause soever, hath his efficacie in this bufinefs, for which it is given, in the time prefixed : But it is to be ufed the same day and Planetary hour wherein it is given.

7. God liveth, and thy soul liveth : keep thy Covenant, and thou haft whatfoever the Spirit fhall reveal unto thee in God, becaufe all things fhall be done which the Spirit promifeth unto thee.

Aphor. 18.

There are other names of the *Olympick* spirits delivered by others ; but they onely are effectual, which are delivered to any one, by the Spirit the revealer, vifible or invifible : and they are delivered to every one as they are predeftinated: therefore they are called Conftellations ; and they feldome have any efficacie above 40 yeers. Therefore it is moft fafe for the young practifers of Art, that they work by the offices of the Spirits alone, without their names ; and if they are pre-ordained to attain the Art of Magick, the other parts of the Art will offer themfelves unto them of their own accord.

Pray

pray therefore for a conftant faith , and God will bring to pafs all things in due feafon.

*Aphor.*19.

Olympus and the inhabitants thereof, do of their own accord offer themfelves to men in the forms of Spirits ; and are ready to perform their Offices for them , whether they will or not : by how much the rather will they attend you, if they are defired ? But there do appear alfo evil Spirits, and deftroyers, which is caufed by the envy and malice of the devil ; and becaufe men do allure and draw them unto themfelves with their fins, as a punifhment due to finners. Whofoever therefore defireth familiarly to have a converfation with Spirits, let him keep himfelf from all enormious fins , and diligently pray to the moft High to be his keeper ; and he fhall break through all the fnares and impediments of the devil : and let him apply himfelf to the fervice of God, and he will give him an increafe in wifdom.

*Aphor.*20.

All things are poffible to them that believe them, and are willing to receive them ; but to the incredulous and unwilling, all things are unpoffible : there is no greater hinderance then a wavering minde , levity, unconftancy, foolifh babbling, drunkennefs, lufts, and difobedience to the word of God.   A Magitian therefore ought to be a man that is godly, honeft, conftant in his words and deeds , having a firm faith towards God, prudent, and covetous of nothing but of wifdom about divine things.

*Aphor.*21.

When you would call any of the *Olympick* Spirits , obfeve the rifing of the Sun that day , and of what nature the Spirit is which you defire ; and faying the prayer following, your defires fhall be perfected.   *Om-*

Omnipotent and eternal God, who haft ordained the whole creation for thy praife and glory, and for the falvation of man, I befeech thee that thou wouldft fend thy Spirit N. N. of the folar order, who fhall inform and teach me thofe things which I fhall ask of him; or, that he may bring me medicine againft the dropfie, &c. *Neverthelefs not my will be done, but thine, through Jefus Chrift thy onely begotten Son, our Lord.* Amen.

But thou fhalt not detain the Spirit above a full hour, unlefs he be familiarly addicted unto thee.

Forafmuch as thou cameft in peace, and quietly, and haft anfwered unto my petitions; I give thanks unto God, in whofe Name thou cameft: and now thou mayft depart in peace unto thy orders; and return to me again when when I fhall call thee by thy name, or by thy order, or by thy office, which is granted from the Creator, Amen.

Ecclefiaft. Chap. 5. *Be not rafh with thy mouth, neither let thy heart be hafty to utter any thing before God; for God is in Heaven, and thou in earth : Therefore let thy words be few; for a dream cometh through the multitude of bufinefs.*

The third Septenary.

Aphor. 22.

We call that a fecret, which no man can attain unto by humane induftry without revelation ; which Science lieth obfcured, hidden by God in the creature ; which neverthelefs he doth permit to be revealed by Spirits, to a due ufe of the thing it felf. And thefe fecrets are either concerning things divine, natural or humane. But thou mayft examine a few, and the moft felect, which thou wilt commend with many more.

B b   *Aphor.*

*Aphor.*23.

Make the beginning of the nature of the secret, either by a Spirit in the form of a person, or by vertues separate, either in humane Organs, or by what manner soever the same may be effected ; and this being known, require of a Spirit which knoweth that art, that he would briefly declare unto thee whatsoever that secret is : and pray unto God, that he would inspire thee with his grace, whereby thou maist bring the secret to the end thou desirest, for the praise and glory of God, and the profit of thy neigbour.

Aphor. 24.

The greatest secrets are in number seven.

1. The first is the curing of all diseases in the space of seven dayes, either by characters, or by natural things, or by the superior Spirits with the divine assistance.

2. The second is, to be able to prolong life to whatsoever age we please : I say, a corporal and natural life.

3. The third is, to have the obedience of the creatures in in the elements which are in the forms of personal Spirits ; * *Spirits of* also of Pigmies, * Sagani, Nymphes, Dryades, and Spirits of *the four ele-* the woods.
ments. Pa-
racelf. 4. The fourth is, to be able to discourse with knowledge and understanding of all things visible and invisible, and to understand the power of every thing, and to what it belongeth.

5. The fifth is, that a man be able to govern himself according to that end for which God hath appointed him.

6. The sixth is, to know God, and Christ, and his holy Spirit : this is the perfection of the *Microcosmus*.

7. The seventh, to be regenerate, as *Henochius* the King of the inferiour world.

These seven secrets a man of an honest and constant
minde

minde may learn of the Spirits, without any offence unto God.

The mean Secrets are likewise seven in number.

1. The first is, the transmutation of Metals, which is vulgarly called *Alchymy* ; which certainly is given to very few, and not but of special grace.

2. The second is, the curing of diseases with Metals, either by the magnetick vertues of precious stones, or by the use of the Philosophers stone, and the like.

3. The third is, to be able to perform Astronomical and Mathematical miracles, such as are *Hydraulick*-engines, to administer businefs by the influence of Heaven, and things which are of the like fort.

4. The fourth is, to perform the works of natural Magick, of what sort soever they be.

5. The fifth is, to know all Physical secrets.

6. The sixth is, to know the foundation of all Arts which are exercised with the hands and offices of the body.

7. The seventh is, to know the foundation of all Arts which are exercised by the angelical nature of man.

The lesser secrets are seven.

1. The first is, to do a thing diligently, and to gather together much money.

2. The second is, to ascend from a mean state to dignities and honours, and to establish a newer family, which may be illustrious and do great things.

3. The third is, to excel in military affairs, and happily to atchieve to great things , and to be an head of the head of Kings and Princes.

4. To be a good house-keeper both in the Country and City.

5. The fifth is, to be an industrious and fortunate Merchant.

6. To

6. To be a Philofopher, Mathematician, and Phyfitian, according to *Aristotle*, *Plato*, *Ptolomy*, *Euclides*, *Hippocrates* and *Galen*.

7. To be a Divine according to the Bible and Schooles, which all writers of divinity both old and new have taught.

Aphor. 25.

We have already declared what a fecret is, the kindes and fpecies thereof: it remaineth now to fhew how we may attain to know thofe things which we defire.

The true and onely way to all fecrets, is to have recourfe unto God the Author of all good ; and as Chrift teacheth, *In the firft place feek ye the kingdom of God and his righteoufnefs, and all thefe things fhall be added unto you.*

2. *Alfo fee that your hearts be not burthened with furfeting, and drunkennefs, and the cares of this life.*

3. *Alfo commit your cares unto the Lord, and he will do it.*

4. *Alfo I the Lord thy God do teach teach thee, what things are profitable for thee, and do guide thee in the way wherein thou walkeft.*

5. *And I will give thee underftanding, and will teach thee in the way wherein thou fhalt go, and I will guide thee with my eye.*

6. *Alfo if you which are evil, know how to give good things to your children, how much more fhall your Father which is in heaven give his holy Spirit to them that ask him?*

7. *If you will do the will of my Father which is in heaven, ye are truely my difciples, and we will come unto you, and make our abode with you.*

If you draw thefe feven places of Scripture from the letter unto the Spirit, or into action, thou canft not erre, but fhalt attain to the defired bound ; thou fhalt not erre from the mark, and God himfelf by his holy Spirit will teach thee true and profitable things : he will give alfo his miniftring Angels unto thee, to be thy companions, helpers, and teachers of all the fecrets of the world, and he will command every creature to be obedient unto thee, fo that cheerfully

re-

rejoycing thou maiſt ſay with the Apoſtles, That the Spirits are obedient unto thee ; ſo that at length thou ſhalt be certain of the greateſt thing of all, That thy name is written in Heaven.

Aphor. 26.

There is another way which is more common, that ſecrets may be revealed unto thee alſo, when thou art unwitting thereof, either by God, or by Spirits which have ſecrets in their power; or by dreams, or by ſtrong imaginations and impreſſions, or by the conſtellation of a nativity by celeſtial knowledge.   After this manner are made heroick men, ſuch as there are very many, and all learned men in the world, *Plato*, *Ariſtotle*, *Hippocrates*, *Galen*, *Euclides*, *Archimedes*, *Hermes Triſmegiſtus* the father of ſecrets, with *Theophraſtus*, *Paracelſus* ; all which men had in themſelves all the vertues of ſecrets.   Hitherto alſo are referred, *Homer*, *Heſiod*, *Orpheus*, *Pytagoras* ; but theſe had not ſuch gifts of ſecrets as the former.   To this are referred, the Nymphes, and ſons of *Meluſina*, and Gods of the Gentiles, *Achilles*, *Æneas*, *Hercules*: alſo, *Cyrus*, *Alexander* the great, *Julius Cæſar*, *Lucullus*, *Sylla*, *Marius*.

It is a canon, That every one know his own Angel, and that he obey him according to the Word of God ; and let him beware of the ſnares of the evil Angel, leſt he be involved in the calamities of *Brute* and *Marcus Antonius*.   To this refer the book of *Jovianus Pontanus* of Fortune, and his *Eutichus*.

The third way is, diligent and hard labor, without which no great thing can be obtained from the divine Deity worthy admiration, as it is ſaid,

*Tu nihil invita dices facieſve *Minerva*.*

Nothing canſt thou do or ſay againſt *Minerva*'s will.

We

We do deteſt all evil Magicians, who make themſelves aſ-
ſociates with the devils with their unlawful ſuperſtitions,
and do obtain and effect ſome things which God permitteth
to be done,inſtead of the puniſhment of the devils. So alſo
they do other evil acts,the devil being the author,as the Scriptures teſtifie of *Judas.* To theſe are referred all idolaters of
old, and of our age, and abuſers of Fortune, ſuch as the heathens are full of. And to theſe do appertain all Charontick
evocation of Spirits , as the work of *Saul* with the woman,
and *Lucanus* propheſie of the deceaſed ſouldier, concerning
the event of the Pharſalian war, and the like.

Aphor.2 7.

Make a Circle with a center A , which is B. C. D. E. At
the Eaſt let there be B. C. a ſquare. At the North,C. D. At
the Weſt,D. E. And at the South,E.D. Divide the ſeveral
quadrants into ſeven parts , that there may be in the whole
28 parts : and let them be again divided into four parts, that
there may be 1 1 2 parts of the Circle : and ſo many are the
true ſecrets to be revealed. And this Circle in this maner divided,is the ſeal of the ſecrets of the world, which they draw
from the onely center A, that is, from the inviſible God, unto the whole creature.   The Prince of the Oriental ſecrets
is reſident in the middle, and hath three Nobles on either
ſide, every one whereof hath four under him, and the Prince
himſelf hath four appertaining unto him.   And in this manner the other Princes and Nobles have their quadrants of
ſecrets, with their four ſecrets. But the Oriental ſecret is the
ſtudy of all wiſdom ; The Weſt, of ſtrength ; The South, of
tillage ; The North, of more rigid life. So that the Eaſtern
ſecrets are commended to be the beſt ; the Meridian to be
mean ; and the Eaſt and North to be leſſer. The uſe of
this ſeal of ſecrets is , that thereby thou maiſt know whence
the Spirits or Angels are produced, which may teach the
ſecrets delivered unto them from God. But they have
names taken from their offices and powers, according to the
gift

gift which God hath feverally diftributed to every one of
them. One hath the power of the fword ; another, of the
peftilence; and another, of inflicting famine upon the people,
as it is ordained by God. Some are deftroyers of Cities, as
thofe two were, who were fent to overthrow *Sodom* and
Gomorrha, and the places adjacent, examples whereof the
the holy Scripture witneffeth. Some are the watch-men
over Kingdoms; others, the keepers of private perfons; and
from thence, anyone may eafily form their names in his own
language : fo that he which will, may ask a phyfical Angel,
mathematical, or philofophical, or an Angel of civil wifdom,
or of furpernatural or natural wifdom, or for any thing whatfoever ; and let him ask ferioufly, with a great defire of his
minde, and with faith and conftancy ; and without doubt,
that which he asketh he fhall receive from the Father and
God of all Spirits. This faith furmounteth all feals, and
bringeth them into fubjection to the will of man. The Cha-
racteriftical maner of calling Angles fucceedeth this faith,
which dependeth onely on divine revelation ; But without
the faid faith preceding it, it lieth in obfcurity. Neverthelefs,
if any one will ufe them for a memorial, and no otherwife,
and as a thing fimply created by God to this purpofe, to
which fuch a fpiritual power or effence is bound ; he may ufe
them without any offence unto God. But let him beware,
left that he fall into idolatry, and the fnares of the devil,
who with his cunning forceries, eafily deceiveth the unwary.
And he is not taken but onely by the finger of God, and is
appointed to the fervice of man ; fo that they unwillingly
ferve the godly ; but not without temptations and tribula-
tions, becaufe the commandment hath it, That he fhall bruife
the heel of Chrift, the feed of the woman. We are therefore to exercife our felvs about fpiritual things, with fear and
trembling, and with great reverence towards God, and to
be converfant in fpiritual effences with gravity and juftice.
And he which medleth with fuch things, let him beware of
all levity, pride, covetoufnefs, vanity, envy and ungodlinefs,
unlefs he wil miferably perifh.

Aphor.

Aphor. 28.

Becaufe all good is from God, who is onely good, thofe things which we would obtain of him, we ought to feek them by prayer in Spirit and Truth, and a fimple hearr. The conclufion of the fecret of fecrets is, That every one exercife himfelf in prayer, for thofe things which he defires, and he fhall not fuffer a repulfe. Let not any one defpife prayer; for by whom God is prayed unto, to him he both can and will give. Now let us acknowledge him the Author, from whom let us humbly feek for our defires. A merciful & good Father, loveth the fons of defires, as *Daniel;* and fooner heareth us, then we are able to overcome the hardnefs of our hearts to pray. But he will not that we give holy things to dogs, nor defpife and contemn the gifts of his treafury. Therefore diligently and often read over and over the firft Septenary of fecrets, and guide and direct thy life and all thy thoughts according to thofe precepts; and all things fhall yield to the defires of thy minde in the Lord, to whom thou trufteft.

The fifth Septenary.

Aphor. 29.

As our ftudy of Magick proceedeth in order from general Rules premifed, let us now come to a particular explication thereof. Spirits either are divine minifters of the word, and of the Church, and the members thereof; or elfe they are fervient to the Creatures in corporal things, partly for the falvation of the foul and body, and partly for its deftruction. And there is nothing done, whether good or evil, without a certain and determinate order and government. He that feeketh after a good end, let him follow it; and he that defires an evil end, purfueth that alfo, and that earneftly, from divine punifhment, and turning away from the divine will.

There-

Therefore let every one compare his ends with the word of
God, and as a touchflone that will judge between good and
evil ; and let him propofe unto himfelf what is to be avoided,
and what is to be fought after ; and that which he confti-
tuteth and determineth unto himfelf, let him follow diligently, not procraftinating or delaying, until he attain to his
appointed bound.

*Aphor.*30.

They which defire riches, glory of this world, Magiftracy,
honours, dignities, tyrannies, (and that magically) if they endeavour diligently after them, they fhall obtain them, every
one according to his deftiny, induftry, and magical Sciences,
as the Hiftory of *Melefina* witneffeth , and the Magitians
thereof, who ordained, That none of the Italian nation fhould
for ever obtain the Rule or Kingdom of *Naples* ; and brought
it to pafs , that he who reigned in his age , to be thrown
down from his feat : fo great is the power of the guardian or
tutelar Angels of the Kingdoms of the world.

Aphor. 31.

Call the Prince of the Kingdom, and lay a command upon
him, and command what thou wilt, and it fhall be done, if that
Prince be not again abfolved from his obedience by a fucceed-
ing Magitian. Therefore the Kingdom of *Naples* may be again
reftored to the Italians, if any Magitian fhall call him who inftituted this order, and compel him to recal his deed ; he may
be compelled alfo, to reftore the fecret powers taken from the
treafury of Magick ; A Book , a Gemme, and magical Horn,
which being had, any one may eafily, if he will, make himfelf
the Monarch of the world. But *Judæus* chufed rather to live
among Gods, until the judgement, before the tranfitory good
of this world ; and his heart is fo blinde , that he under-
ftandeth nothing of the God of heaven and earth, or thinketh more , but enjoyeth the delights of things immortal, to

C c   his

his own eternal deſtruction.   And he may be eaſier called up, then the Angel of *Plotinus* in the Temple of *Iſis.*

Aphor. 32.

In like manner alſo, the Romans were taught by the Sibyls books ; and by that means made themſelves the Lords of the world, as Hiſtories witneſs. But the Lords of the Prince of a Kingdom do beſtow the leſſer Magiſtracies. He there-fore that deſireth to have a leſſer office, or dignity , let him magically call a Noble of the Prince , and his deſire ſhall be fulfilled.

Aphor. 33.

But he who coveteth contemptible dignities, as riches a-lone , let him call the Prince of riches, or one of his Lords, and he ſhall obtain his deſire in that kinde , whereby he would grow rich , either in earthly goods, or merchandize, or with the gifts of Princes, or by the ſtudy of Metals, or Chy-miſtry : as he produceth any preſident of growing rich by theſe means, he ſhall obtain his deſire therein.

Aphor. 34.

All manner of evocation is of the ſame kinde and form, and this way was familiar of old time to the Sibyls and chief Prieſts. This in our time, through ignorance and impiety, is totally loſt ; and that which remaineth, is depraved with in-finite lyes and ſuperſtitions.

Aphor. 35.

The humane underſtanding is the onely effecter of all wonderful works , ſo that it be joyned to any Spirit ; and being joyned, ſhe produceth what ſhe will. Therefore we are carefully to proceed in Magick, leſt that Syrens and other

mon-

monſters deceive us, which likewiſe do deſire the ſociety of the humane ſoul. Let the Magitian carefully hide himſelf alwaies under the wings of the moſt High, leſt he offer himſelf to be devoured of the roaring Lion ; for they who deſire earthly things, do very hardly eſcape the ſnares of the devil.

The ſixth Septenary.

Aphor. 36.

Care is to be taken, that experiments be not mixed with experiments; but that every one be onely ſimple and ſeveral: for God and Nature have ordained all things to a certain and appointed end: ſo that for examples ſake, they who perform cures with the moſt ſimple herbs and roots, do cure the moſt happily of all. And in this manner, in Conſtellations, Words and Characters, Stones, and ſuch like, do lie hid the greateſt influences or vertues in deed, which are in ſtead of a miracle.

So alſo are words, which being pronounced, do forthwith cauſe creatures both viſible and inviſible to yield obedience, aſwel creatures of this our world, as of the watry, aëry, ſubterranean, and Olympick, ſuperceleſtial and infernal, and alſo the divine.

Therefore ſimplicity is chiefly to be ſtudied, and the knowledge of ſuch ſimples is to be ſought for from God; otherwiſe by no other means or experience they can be found out.

Aphor. 37.

And let all lots have their place decently : Order, Reaſon and Means, are the three things which do eaſily render all learning aſwell of the viſible as inviſible creatures. This is the courſe of Order, That ſome creatures are creatures of the light ; others, of darknefs : thefe are fubject to vanity, becaufe they run headlong into darknefs , and inthral themfelves in eternal punifhments for their rebellion. Their Kingdom is partly very beautiful in tranfitory and corruptible things on the one part , becaufe it cannot confift without fome vertue and great gifts of God ; and partly moft filthy and horrid to be fpoken of, becaufe it aboundeth with all wickednefs and fin, idolatry, contempt of God , blafphemies againft the true God and his works , worfhipping of devils, difobedience towards Magiftrates, feditions , homicides , robberies , tyranny, adulteries, wicked lufts, rapes, thefts , lyes, perjuries, pride, and a covetous defire of rule ; in this mixture confifteth the kingdom of darknefs : but the creatures of the light, are filled with eternal truth, and with the grace of God , and are Lords of the whole world, and do reign over the Lords of darknefs , as the members of Chrift. Between thefe and the other , there is a continual war , until God fhall put an end to their ftrife , by his laft judgement.

Aphor. 38.

Therefore Magick is twofold in its firft divifion ; the one is of God, which he beftoweth on the creatures of light ; the other alfo is of God, but it is the gift which he giveth unto the creatures of darknefs : and this is alfo two-fold : the one is to a good end, as when the Princes of darknefs are compelled to do good unto the creatures , God enforcing them ; the other is for an evil end , when God permitteth fuch to punifh evil perfons , that magically they are deceived to deftruction ; or , alfo he commandeth fuch to be caft out into deftruction.

The fecond divifion of Magick is , that it bringeth to pafs fome works with vifible inftruments, through vifible things ; and it effecteth other works with invifible inftruments by invifible things ; and it acteth other things, afwel with mixed means, as inftruments and effects.

The

The third divſion is, There are ſome things which are brought to paſs by invocation of God alone : this is partly Prophetical, and Philoſophical ; and partly, as it were Theophraſtical.

Other things there are, which by reaſon of the ignorance of the true God, are done with the Princes of Spirits, that his deſires may be fulfilled ; ſuch is the work of the Mercurialiſts.

The fourth diviſion is, That ſome exerciſe their Magick with the good Angels in ſtead of God, as it were deſcending down from the moſt high God : ſuch was the Magick of *Baalim.*

Another Magick is, that which exerciſeth their actions with the chief of the evil Spirits ; ſuch were they who wrought by the minor Gods of the heathens.

The fifth diviſion is, That ſome do act with Spirits openly, and face to face ; which is given to few : others do work by dreams and other ſigns ; which the ancients took from their auguries and ſacrifices.

The ſixth diviſion is, That ſome work by immortal creatures, others by mortal creatures, as Nymphs, Satyrs, and ſuch-like inhabitants of other elements, Pigmies, &c.

The ſeventh diviſion is, That the Spirits do ſerve ſome of their own accord, without art ; others they will ſcarce attend, being called by art.

Among theſe ſpecies of Magick, that is the moſt excellent of all, which dependeth upon God alone. The ſecond, Them whom the Spirits do ſerve faithfully of their own accord. The third is, that which is the property of Chriſtians, which dependeth on the power of Chriſt which he hath in heaven and earth.

Aphor.

Aphor. 39.

There is a seven-fold preparation to learn the *Magick Art.*

The firſt is, to meditate day and night how to attain to the true knowledge of God, both by his word revealed from the foundation of the world ; as alſo by the ſeal of the creation, and of the creatures ; and by the wonderful effects which the viſible and inviſible creatures of God do ſhew forth.

Secondly, it is requiſite, that a man deſcend down into himſelf, and chiefly ſtudy to know himſelf ; what mortal part he hath in him, and what immortal ; and what part is proper to himſelf, and what diverſe.

Thirdly, That he learn by the immortal part of himſelf, to worſhip, love and fear the eternal God, and to adore him in Spirit and Truth ; and with his mortal part, to do thoſe things which he knoweth to be acceptable to God, and profitable to his neighbours.

Theſe are the three firſt and chiefeſt precepts of Magick, wherewith let every one prepare himſelf that covets to obtain true Magick or divine wiſdom, that he may be accounted worthy thereof, and one to whom the Angelical creatures willingly do ſervice, not occultly onely, but alſo manifeſtly, and as it were face to face.

Fourthly, Whereas every man is to be vigilant to ſee to what kinde life he ſhall be called from his mothers wombe, that every one may know whether he be born to Magick, and to what ſpecies thereof, which every one may perceive eaſily that readeth theſe things, and by experience may have ſucceſs therein ; for ſuch things and ſuch gifts are not given but onely to the low and humble.

In the fifth place we are to take care, that we underſtand when the Spirits are aſſiſting us, in undertaking the greateſt buſineſs ; and he that underſtands this, it is manifeſt,

feſt, that he ſhall be made a Magician of the ordination of God; that is, ſuch a perſon who uſeth the miniſtery of the Spirits to bring excellent things to paſs. Here, as for the moſt part, they ſin, either through negligence, ignorance, or contempt, or by too much ſuperſtition; they offend alſo by ingratitude towards God, whereby many famous men have afterwards drawn upon themſelves deſtruction: they ſin alſo by raſhneſs and obſtinacy; and alſo when they do not uſe their gifts for that honor of God which is required, and do prefer πἀριργα ἐργοις.

Sixthly, The Magitian hath need of faith and taciturnity, eſpecially, that he diſcloſe no ſecret which the Spirit hath forbid him, as he commanded *Daniel* to ſeal ſome things, that is, not to declare them in publick; ſo as it was not lawful for *Paul* to ſpeak openly of all things which he ſaw in a viſion. No man will believe how much is contained in this one precept.

Seventhly, In him that would be a Magician, there is required the greateſt juſtice, that he undertake nothing that is ungodly, wicked or unjuſt, nor to let it once come in his minde; and ſo he ſhall be divinely defended from all evil.

Aphor. 40.

When the Magician determineth with himſelf to do any incoporeal thing either with any exteriour or interiour ſenſe, then let him govern himſelf according to theſe ſeven ſubſequent laws, to accompliſh his Magical end.

The firſt Law is this, That he know that ſuch a Spirit is ordained unto him from God; and let him meditate that God is the beholder of all his thoughts and actions; therefore let him direct all the courſe of his life according to the rule preſcribed in the word of God.

Secondly, Alwaies pray with *David*, *Take not thy holy Spirit from me; and ſtrengthen me with thy free Spirit; and lead us not into temptation, but deliver us from evil: I beſeech thee, O heavenly Father, do not give power unto any lying Spirit, as thou*

didſt

didſt over Ahab *that he periſhed* ; *but keep me in thy truth.* A-men.

Thirdly, Let him accuſtome himſelf to try the Spirits, as the Scripture admoniſheth ; for grapes cannot be gatheted of thorns : let us try all things, and hold faſt that which is good and laudable, that we may avoid every thing that is re-pugnant to the divine power.

The fourth is, To be remote and cleer from all manner of ſuperſtition ; for this is ſuperſtition,to attribute divinity in this place to things, wherein there is nothing at all divine ; or to chuſe or frame to our ſelves, to worſhip God with ſome kinde of worſhip which he hath not commanded: ſuch are the Magical ceremonies of Satan,whereby he impudently offereth himſelf to be worſhipped as God.

The fifth thing to be eſchewed,is all worſhip of Idols,which bindeth any divine power to idols or other things of their own proper motion, where they are not placed by the Cre-ator, or by the order of Nature : which things many falſe and wicked Magitians faign.

Sixthly, All the deceitful imitations and affections of the devil are alſo to be avoided, whereby he imitateth the power of the creation, and of the Creator, that he may ſo produe things with a word, that they may not be what they are. Which belongeth onely to the Omnipotency of God, and is not communicable to the creature.

Seventhly, Let us cleave faſt to the gifts of God, and of his holy Spirit, that we may know them, and diligently embrace them with our whole heart, and all our ſtrength.

Aphor. 41.

We come now to the nine laſt Aphoriſmes of this whole Tome ; wherewith we will, the divine mercy aſſiſting us, conclude this whole Magical *Iſagoge.*

Therefore in the firſt place it is to be obſerved, what we underſtand by Magitian in this work.

Him then we count to be a Magitian, to whom by the grace

grace of God, the spiritual essences do serve to manifest the knowledge of the whole universe, & of the secrets of Nature contained therein, whether they are visible or invisible. This description of a Magitian plainly appeareth, and is universal.

An evil Magician is he, whom by the divine permission the evil Spirits do serve, to his temporal and eternal destruction and perdition, to deceive men, and draw them away from God; such was *Simon Magus*, of whom mention is made in the *Acts of the Apostles*, and in *Clemens*; whom Saint *Peter* commanded to be thrown down upon the earth, whenas he had commanded himself, as it were a God, to be raised up into the air by the unclean Spirits.

Unto this order are also to be referred all those who are noted in the two Tables of the Law; and are set forth with their evil deeds.

The subdivisions and species of both kindes of Magick, we will note in the Tomes following. In this place it shall suffice, that we distinguish the Sciences, which is good, and which is evil : Whereas man sought to obtain them both at first, to his own ruine and destruction, as *Moses* and *Hermes* do demonstrate.

Aphor. 42.

Secondly, we are to know, That a Magitian is a person predestinated to this work from his mothers wombe; neither let him assume any such great things to himself, unless he be called divinely by grace hereunto, for some good end; to a bad end is, that the Scripture might be fulfilled, *It must be that offences will come* ; *but wo be to that man through whom they come*. Therefore, as we have before oftentimes admonished, With fear and trembling we must live in this world.

Notwithstanding I will not deny, but that some men may with study and diligence obtain some species of both kindes of Magick, if it may be admitted. But he shall never aspire to the highest kindes thereof; yet if he covet to assail them, he shall doubtless offend both in soul

and

and body. Such are they, who by the operations of falfe Magitians, are fometimes carried to Mount *Horeb*, or in fome wildernefs, or defarts ; or they are maimed in fome member, or are fimply torn in pieces, or are deprived of their under-ftanding;even as many fuch things happen by the ufe thereof, where men are forfaken by God,and delivered to the power of Satan.

The feventh Septenary.

Aphor. 43.

The Lord liveth, and the works of God do live in him by his appointment,whereby he willeth them to be ; for he will have them to ufe their liberty in obedience to his commands, or difobedience thereof. To the obedient, he hath pro-pofed their rewards; to the difobedient he hath propounded their deferved punifhment. Therefore thefe Spirits of their freewil, through their pride and contempt of the Son of God,have revolted from God their Creator,and are referved unto the day of wrath ; and there is left in them a very great power in the creation ; but notwithftanding it is limited,and they are confined to their bounds with the bridle of God. Therefore the Magitian of God,which fignifies a wife man of God, or one informed of God, is led forth by the hand of God unto all everlafting good, both mean things, and alfo the chiefeft corporal things.

Great is the power of Satan, by reafon of the great fins of men. Therefore alfo the Magitians of Satan do perform great things, and greater then any man would believe : al-though they do fubfift in their own limits, neverthelefs they are above all humane apprehenfion, as to the corporal and tranfitory things of this life ; which many ancient Hiftories, and daily Examples do teftifie. Both kindes of Magick are different one from the other in their ends : the one leadeth to eternal good, and ufeth temporal things with thankfthankſgiving; the other is a little ſollicitous about eternal things; but wholly exerciſeth himſelf about corporal things, that he may freely enjoy all his luſts and delights in contempt of God and his anger.

Aphor. 44.

The paſſage from the common life of man unto a Magical life, is no other but aſleep, from that life; and an awaking to this life; for thoſe things which happen to ignorant and unwiſe men in their common life, the ſame things happen to the willing and knowing Magitian.

The Magitian underſtandeth when the minde doth meditate of himſelf; he deliberateth, reaſoneth, conſtituteth and determineth what is to be done; he obſerveth when his cogitations do proceed from a divine ſeparate eſſence, and he proveth of what order that divine ſeparate eſſence is.

But the man that is ignorant of Magick, is carried to and fro, as it were in war with his affections; he knoweth not when they iſſue out of his own minde, or are impreſſed by the aſſiſting eſſence; and he knoweth not how to overthrow the counſels of his enemies by the word of God, or to keep himſelf from the ſnares and deceits of the tempter.

Aphor. 45.

The greateſt precept of Magick is, to know what every man ought to receive for his uſe from the aſſiſting Spirit, and what to refuſe: which he may learn of the Pſalmiſt, ſaying, *Wherewith ſhall a yong man cleanſe his way? in keeping thy word,* *Oh Lord.* To keep the word of God, ſo that the evil one ſnatch it not out of the heart, is the chiefeſt precept of wiſdom. It is lawful to admit of, and exerciſe other ſuggeſtions which are not contrary to the glory of God, and charity towards our neighbours, nor inquiring from what Spirit ſuch ſuggeſtions proceed: But we ought to take heed, that we

D d 2 are

are not too much bufied about unneceffary things, according
to the admonition of Chrift ; *Martha, Martha, thou art*
troubled about many things ; but Mary hath chofen the better
part,which fhall not be taken from her. Therefore let us alwaies
have regard unto the faying of Chrift, *Seek ye firft the kingdom*
of God and his righteoufneß, and all thefe things fhall be added
unto you. All other things, that is, all things which are due
to the mortal Microcofme, as food, raiment, and the neceffary arts of this life.

Aphor.46.

There is nothing fo much becometh a man , as conftancy
in his words and deeds , and when the like rejoyceth in his
like ; there are none more happy then fuch, becaufe the holy
Angels are converfant about fuch, and poffefs the cuftody of
them : on the contrary, men that are unconftant are lighter
then nothing, and rotten leaves.   We chufe the 46 Apho-
rifme from thefe.   Even as every one governeth himfelf,
fo he allureth unto himfelf Spirits of his nature and condition ; but one very truely advifeth , that no man fhould
carry himfelf beyond his own calling, left that he draw unto himfelf fome malignant Spirit from the uttermoft parts of
the earth, by whom either he fhall be infatuated and deceived, or brought to final deftruction. This precept appeareth moft plainly : for *Midas,* when he would convert all
things into gold, drew up fuch a Spirit unto himfelf , which
was able to perform this ; and being deceived by him , he
had been brought to death by famine , if his foolifhnefs had
not been corrected by the mercy of God.   The fame thing
happened to a certain woman about *Fanckford* at *Odera* , in
our times, who would fcrape together & devour mony of any
thing. Would that men would diligently weigh this precept,
and not account the Hiftories of *Midas* , and the like, for fa-
bles ; they would be much more diligent in moderating their
thoughts and affections , neither would they be fo perpe-
tually vexed with the Spirits of the golden mountains of *U-*
topia.   Therefore we ought moft diligently to obferve , that
fuch

fuch prefumptions fhould be caft out of the minde, by the word, while they are new ; neither let them have any habit in the idle minde, that is empty of the divine word.

Aphor. 47.

He that is faithfully converfant in his vocation, fhall have alfo the Spirits conftant companions of his defires, who will fucceffively fupply him in all things.But if he have any knowledge in Magick, they will not be unwilling to fhew him, and familiarly to converfe with him,and to ferve him in thofe feveral minifteries, unto which they are addicted ; the good Spirits in good things,unto falvation ; the evil Spirits in every evil thing, to deftruction. Examples are not wanting in the Hiftories of the whole World ; and do daily happen in the world. *Theodofius* before the victory of *Arbogaftus*, is an example of the good ; *Brute* before he was flain , was an example of the evil Spirits, when he was perfecuted of the Spirit of *Cæfar*, and expofed to punifhment , that he flew himfelf, who had flain his own Father, and the Father of his Country.

Aphor. 48.

All Magick is a revelation of Spirits of that kinde , of which fort the Magick is ; fo that the nine Mufes are called, in *Hefiod*, the ninth Magick, as he manifeftly teftifies of himfelf in *Theogony*. In *Homer*,the genius of *Ulyffes* in *Pfigiogagia*. *Hermes*, the Spirits of the more fublime parts of the minde. God revealed himfelf to *Mofes* in the bufh. The three wife men who came to feek Chrift at *Jerufalem*, the Angel of the Lord was their leader. The Angels of the Lord directed *Daniel*. Therefore there is nothing whereof any one may glory ; *For it is not unto him that willeth, nor unto him that runneth ; but to whom God will have mercy*, or of fome other fpiritual fate. From hence fpringeth all Magick, and thither again it will revolve, whether it be good or evil. In
                                                                this

this manner *Tages* the firſt teacher of the Magick of the Ro-
manes, guſhed out of the earth. *Diana* of the Epheſians
ſhewed her worſhip, as if it had been ſent from heaven. So
alſo *Apollo*. And all the Religion of the Heathens is taken
from the ſame Spirits ; neither are the opinions of the Sad-
duces, humane inventions.

Aphor. 49.

The concluſion therefore of this *Iſagoge* is the ſame which
we have above already ſpoken of, That even as there is one
God, from whence is all good ; and one ſin, to wit, diſo-
bedience, againſt the will of the commanding God, from
whence comes all evil ; ſo that *the fear of God is the beginning
of all wiſdom*, and the profit of all Magick ; for obedience to
the will of God, followeth the fear of God ; and after this,
do follow the preſence of God and of the holy Spirit, and the
miniſtery of the holy Angels, and all good things out of the
inexhauſtible treaſures of God.

But unprofitable and damnable Magick ariſeth from this ;
where we loſe the fear of God out of our hearts, and ſuffer
ſin to reign in us, there the Prince of this world, the God of
this world beginneth, and ſetteth up his kingdom in ſtead of
holy things, in ſuch as he findeth proficable for his kingdom ;
there, even as the ſpider taketh the flye which falleth into his
web, ſo Satan ſpreadeth abroad his nets, and taketh men with
the ſnares of covetouſneſs, until he ſucketh him, and draweth him to eternal fire : theſe he cheriſheth and advanceth
on high, that their fall may be the greater.

Courteous Reader, apply thy eyes and minde to the ſacred
and profane Hiſtories, & to thoſe things which thou ſeeſt daily
to be done in the world, and thou ſhalt finde all things full of
Magick, according to a two-fold Science, good and evil, which
that they may be the better diſcerned, we will put he.. ..eir
diviſion and ſubdiviſion, for the concluſion of theſe *Iſagoges* ;
wherein every one may contemplate, what is to be followed,
and which to be avoided, and how far it is to be labored for
by every one, to a competent end of life and living.   Sci-

Sciences
- Good
  - Theoſophy
    - Knowledge of the Word of God, and ruling ones life according to the word of God.
    - Knowledge of the government of God by Angels, which the Scripture calleth watchmen; and to underſtand the myſtery of Angels.
  - Anthroſophy given to man
    - Knowledge of natural things.
    - Wiſdom in humane things.
- Evil
  - Cakoſophy
    - Contempt of the word of God, and to live after the will of the devil.
    - Ignorance of the government of God by Angels.
    - To contemne the cuſtody of the Angels, and that their companions are of the devil.
    - Idolatry.
    - Atheiſme.
  - Cacodæmony
    - The knowledge of poiſons in nature, and to uſe them.
    - Wiſdom in all evil arts, to the deſtruction of mankinde, and to uſe them in contempt of God, and for the loſs and deſtruction of men.

FINIS.

CPSIA information can be obtained
at www.ICGtesting.com
Printed in the USA
LVHW041216161222
735287LV00005BC/1698